INSIDE
THE ROOM

Dedicated to my wife, Carol Hanney, and to our three children, Gráinne, Oisín and Seán.

INSIDE THE ROOM

THE UNTOLD STORY OF IRELAND'S CRISIS GOVERNMENT

EAMON GILMORE

MERRION
PRESS

Published in 2016 by
Merrion Press
8 Chapel Lane
Sallins
Co. Kildare

© 2016 Eamon Gilmore

British Library Cataloguing in Publication Data
An entry can be found on request

978-1-78537-034-2 (paper)
978-1-78537-035-9 (cloth)
978-1-78537-036-6(PDF)
978-1-78537-045-8 (Epub)
978-1-78537-046-5 (Kindle)

Library of Congress Cataloging in Publication Data
An entry can be found on request

CONTENTS

ACKNOWLEDGEMENTS

After I had stepped down as Labour Party Leader and had been removed from government office, several friends suggested that I should write about my time in office, and especially about Ireland's recovery from the crisis. I want to thank them for their encouragement, without which I would not have started this task in the first place.

Getting the project to publication depended on the work of several people: my agent Peter O'Connell; Paul O'Connor who edited my first draft; Conor Graham, Lisa Hyde and all at Merrion Press who brought the book to fruition, and especially my staff Aideen Blackwood and Sharon Gibbons who laboured with it at every step.

This book is my story of Ireland's crisis government. It is inevitably subjective, but I have made every effort to ensure that it is factually accurate.

While it is my own personal recollection of the years from 2007 to 2014, it tells of a journey which I travelled with a dedicated, committed and loyal team.

My Chief of Staff Mark Garrett was a former Chairperson of Labour Youth, who had worked in public relations, and was a management consultant with McKinsey in New York, when I asked him to come home to head up my team, after I was elected Leader of the Labour Party in 2007.

Dr Colm O'Reardon, was employed by Ruairi Quinn in 2001,

when he was Leader, to be Economic Advisor to the Labour Party. He remained on with Pat Rabbitte and was Labour's Director of Policy during our years in opposition. I appointed him as my Principal Policy Advisor in Government, and he served with me on the Economic Management Council.

Jean O'Mahony had worked as a policy advisor for the Labour Party since 2006. She was an indispensable part of our team in Government, covering the broad range of policy issues coming before Cabinet.

Cathy Madden, who had worked as a radio journalist with Newstalk, came to work for Labour at the end of 2010. I appointed her as Deputy Government Press Secretary shortly after the formation of the new Government. When Cathy went on maternity leave in 2013, I brought in former Labour TD Derek McDowell, to fill this role.

Niamh Sweeney had worked as a journalist for RTE, the Irish Times and Bloomberg, and was based in New York when I asked her to return home to work for me in the Department of Foreign Affairs and Trade.

David Leach was a former Treasurer of the Labour Party who managed his own construction company. Mark Garrett brought him in to manage the Local and European Election campaign in 2009 and subsequently I appointed him as national organiser and as Political Director of the Party. My successor subsequently appointed him as the Party's General Secretary.

Karen Griffin had worked for the Irish Family Planning Association, and was head hunted by Mark Garrett to manage my campaign tours and to act as my liaison with the Labour Party organisation and members.

Kevin Eager provided transport services to the Labour Party and he and I travelled the country together during the years in opposition. Kevin did not believe in being late for anything "We were never late, but the schedule had changed," he used to re-assure those who were waiting!

Doreen Foley was Personal Assistant to the Party Leader, having been appointed to that position by my predecessor, Pat Rabbitte. She had for many years been PA to the Managing Director of the student travel company USIT, the late Gordon Colleary. Doreen had the unenviable task in Government of responding to complaints from the public about me, the Party and the Coalition.

Angela Loscher managed my constituency office from the early 1990s, with great efficiency and enormous compassion for the problems of constituents. She retired during the life of the Government.

She was replaced by Sharon Gibbons, who along with Aideen Blackwood make up the hard-working and committed team that remained working with me after I stepped down as Tánaiste and Labour Party Leader.

And over the years Anne Coleman, Stephen Fitzpatrick and Jeni Gartland also worked in my constituency office.

Tony Heffernan, whose reputation in Leinster House and among the press corp has never been rivalled, headed the press office until his retirement around the time of the General Election. His replacement Dermot O'Gara continues this fine service.

Ronan Farren had previously worked in the Press Office and I brought him back as Deputy Political Director and he also advised me on Northern Ireland matters.

Shauneen Armstrong did a great job in charge of photography and the Party's online presence.

I want to pay tribute to the staff of the Labour Head Office, headed then by General Secretary Ita McAuliffe, and I want to thank her predecessor, Mike Allen, for his help in my early days as

Leader.

It was a privilege to work with my colleagues in the Parliamentary Labour Party, especially the Chairperson Jack Wall TD and Party Whip Emmet Stagg TD.

I thank all the Labour Councillors, none of whom were ever found to have done wrong by any tribunal. It is a great tribute to their personal integrity, and to the strong public service ethic of the Party itself.

A special thanks to all the Labour Party members throughout the country. They give their time and energy voluntarily to our common cause. In Dun Laoghaire I have been particularly fortunate to have the support and friendship of hundreds of members, among them Senator Aideen Hayden and the Labour Councillors with whom I've served: Carrie Smyth, her late father Frank Smyth, Niamh Bhreathnach, Jane Dillon Byrne, Denis O'Callaghan, Lettie McCarthy, Richard Humphreys, Stephen Fitzpatrick, Donna Pierce, Paddy Fitzgerald, Sean Misteail and Deirdre Kingston.

Finally, a special word of appreciation for former Labour TD Barry Desmond and his wife Stella who supported me and gave me good advice during difficult times.

Above all I want to thank my family Carol, Gráinne, Oisín and Seán for their love and incalculable strength over the years.

PROLOGUE

The Sycamore Room

"How long will it take to get the Punt back into circulation?" I ask.

"Notes and coins could be produced within a week, maybe two," replies the Governor of the Central Bank, Dr Patrick Honohan. "But it will take a lot longer to re-establish a national currency."

It is a Friday afternoon in the summer of 2012. The euro is in crisis. The Irish Government's Economic Management Council (EMC) is meeting to consider what to do if the euro suddenly collapses.

Ireland has no intention of leaving the euro. But what would happen if our shared European currency were to suddenly fall apart? If, for example, a big Eurozone state were to pull out unexpectedly? Big events have happened quickly before in this economic crisis. The crash had come unannounced four years ago in 2008. Lehman Brothers collapsed overnight. The Irish Bank Guarantee was put together in a few hours of panic.

Here, in the Sycamore Room, the Economic Management Council is managing the worst economic crisis since Ireland's independence. We cannot afford to be caught unawares. We must be ready for every eventuality. That is our job. We function like a War Cabinet. Now we must prepare a Plan B, lest the euro fail.

The Sycamore Room is probably the best known and most used meeting room in government. Television viewers know it from shots of large delegations meeting the Irish Government; from social partnership negotiations; and from the State visit of Queen Elizabeth, who, in 2011, was introduced to the members of the Cabinet between its wood-panelled walls.

The room is named for the impressive oval table, made from polished sycamore, which dominates the space. The table itself can seat meetings with over twenty participants, while another thirty or so can attend seated on chairs around the walls. At either end of the room are two electric clocks. One is permanently stopped. The other always fast! In one corner is a podium, occasionally used for technical presentations. And in another corner, a small table with cups, coffee, tea dispenser, and a small supply of sweetened oatmeal biscuits.

This was the room from which Ireland's economic recovery was steered and secured. Around the oval sycamore table, Ireland's exit from the bailout was mapped and managed; battles over budgets were fought between Fine Gael and Labour ministers; and strategies were devised to help create jobs and grow businesses.

This summer day, as always, the Taoiseach sits in the middle on one side, with his back to the windows. As at Cabinet meetings, I sit directly opposite him. To his right is Michael Noonan and his officials from the Department of Finance, including his Secretary General John Moran, and Second Secretary General Ann Nolan. To my left is Brendan Howlin, his Secretary General Robert Watt and advisor, Ronan O'Brien. To my right is Dr Colm O'Reardon, my economic advisor and David Cooney, the Secretary General of the Department of Foreign Affairs and Trade. To the Taoiseach's left sits Martin Fraser, Secretary General to the Government, Geraldine Byrne Nason, the Second Secretary General who managed the EMC and Andrew McDowell, the Taoiseach's economic advisor.

Initially, our meetings were set for every Wednesday after lunch. Every meeting was held in the heat of crisis. Would the banks collapse? Would unemployment reach half a million or more? Would investment dry up? Would the ECB really insist on us paying over €3 billion a year to a dead bank? Time and time again we peered into the financial abyss, at the possibility that the State would become bankrupt.

Today's meeting is no less urgent. No agenda has been circulated and the attendance is limited to ministers along with a few officials and advisors on a 'need-to-know' basis. The Governor of the Central Bank, Dr Patrick Honohan, has been invited to attend, and he sits to my right just beyond Secretary General David Cooney. What would we do if the euro collapsed?

How exactly would the Government manage such an eventuality? What exactly would happen on the morning after? We would have to close the banks, but for how long? For how long would ATMs continue to dispense euros?

How long would it take to re-establish the punt? How many days would it take to print notes and mint coins? How quickly would they get into circulation? And what would they be worth?

What would shops do in the meantime? How would workers be paid? And people on social welfare? What if the value of the currency changed over days or weeks? Who would be at the loss in the commercial transactions that occurred in the interval?

This is no idle academic discussion. We have to make practical plans for the chaos of a currency collapse and the uncertainty of launching a new national currency in a crisis.

I have the feeling that this is not the first time that Finance officials and the Central Bank have teased out the practical issues, but there are also wider social and political considerations – including the possibility of public panic and disorder – that we, as the Government, need to prepare for.

Legislation will have to be prepared and contingency plans put in place. And we have to be very careful to keep all of this confidential. One leak and we could be fuelling panic, and ourselves contributing to a monetary catastrophe.

Already, journalists are asking the awkward questions about the stability of the euro. Doorstepped at the EU Foreign Affairs Council in Brussels last Monday, I was asked if Ireland had a Plan B in the event of the euro failing. I dismissed the notion, because even to entertain the question was to give credence to the possibility that it might happen and risk making the situation worse.

But how do we describe the legislation we are drafting, so as not to cause panic? We can hardly have drafts of a 'Bill to Relaunch the Punt' floating around government offices! We agree, instead, to say we were working on emergency legislation to deal with the unlikely possibility of a flu pandemic!

1 THE CALM AND THE STORM

The 2007 General Election resulted in a three-in-a-row victory for Bertie Ahern's Fianna Fáil. Though he failed to get overall majorities in both 1997 and 2002, Ahern had put together coalitions with the Progressive Democrats and Fianna Fáil-leaning Independents, stable enough to see him through ten years as leader of the Government. The 2007 campaign began badly for Ahern, with his snubbing of the Dáil in a Sunday morning 'dawn rush to the Áras,' to call the election. Nonetheless, by polling day, there were enough 'devil-you-know' voters to enable him to cling to power, this time in coalition with the Greens.

Labour won twenty seats, one less than in 2002, and secured 10 per cent of the vote – roughly the same as in 2002 and 1997. My predecessor, Pat Rabbitte, was very disappointed with the results, and after the summer holidays decided to resign as leader. Mid-morning on 23 August, he stood at the door of my fifth-floor office in Leinster House and told me that he had just called a press conference and would be announcing his resignation at 3 p.m. I tried to talk him out of it, arguing that he was doing a good job, but it was too late; he had made up his mind while walking the beach in Kerry a few weeks previously.

I then went for a walk myself around Merrion Square to get some perspective and try to decide what to do. Five years earlier in 2002, when Ruairí Quinn had resigned the leadership after an equally disappointing general election, I had delayed my decision to contest the Labour Party leadership and ended up being the last of the candidates to declare. My campaign never recovered from that procrastination. Pat Rabbitte convincingly defeated Brendan Howlin, Róisín Shortall, and me. I finished a poor third. Walking through Merrion Square on this occasion, and consulting with family by phone, I decided to throw my hat into the ring again and, this time, early on. My enthusiasm for it was tempered by my preference for Pat to stay on, but I was not going to repeat my error of 2002. I anticipated that Brendan Howlin would be the front runner, having finished second to Pat in 2002 and having previously lost out to Ruairí Quinn in 1997. During the afternoon, I rang Brendan, mainly because I had requests for TV interviews which I presumed were also issued to him. I felt it was too soon for us to engage in a media debate about the leadership, and we agreed to meet to discuss things the following morning in my office.

Whether we wanted it or not, though, the race was already on. Throughout the afternoon, I got several pledges of support from members of the parliamentary party, councillors and influential members. The most significant was the statement on RTÉ from Michael D. Higgins – who had nominated me in 2002 – that I should be the next leader of the Party.

When I met Brendan the following morning, he was still unsure. He had recently been elected Leas Ceann Comhairle of the Dáil, and was keen to serve the full term. I had known Brendan since we were student union presidents in the early 1970s – he in St Patrick's, Drumcondra, and me in University College Galway. His late father, John Howlin, who was Branch Secretary of the Irish Transport and

General Workers' Union in Wexford, was always very kind and helpful to me during my early years as a trade union official. Despite being in different parties in those days, Brendan and I remained friendly throughout the years, and we eventually worked together to merge the Democratic Left and the Labour Party in 1998. Our conversation that August morning was, as always, very honest and open. Brendan was still thinking of contesting, but leaning away from it. He said he would decide over the weekend and call me on Monday. It sounded familiar: in 2002, Brendan had at one stage considered backing me, but ended up running himself. I still expected a leadership election between the two of us.

By Monday morning, I had secured pledges from most of the parliamentary party. Ruairí Quinn rang me on Sunday evening on his way back from a holiday in Connemara. I had difficulty hearing him as I was at the Festival of World Cultures on Dun Laoghaire seafront and his voice had to compete with the beat of a great African band on Sandycove Green, but I got the drift: he was going to support my candidacy.

Meanwhile, I had also assembled a campaign team, headed by Senator Dominic Hannigan, and as I approached Buswell's Hotel to meet them for breakfast on Monday, I got the call from Brendan to say that he would not be standing, and that he would support me. He had suggestions and requests that I was happy to entertain, including that I should express no preference for Deputy Leader, and that Wexford should be the venue for the next Labour Party conference!

Later that morning I met Joan Burton. I knew she had been canvassing support to contest the leadership, and some members told me of their conversations with her. However, she told me that she had decided not to contest the leadership on this occasion and would be a candidate for Deputy Leader instead. She asked me to remain neutral in that election and I readily agreed to this.

So, within days, I was nominated formally by Willie Penrose and Michael D. Higgins, and elected unopposed as the tenth Leader of the Labour Party on 6 September 2007. It was unexpectedly sudden. I felt honoured and humbled to join the pantheon of Labour leaders including Connolly, Corish, Cluskey and Spring. But there was little fanfare. Press comment on the Labour Party itself was that it had 'flatlined' at 10 per cent, and that it was ageing. I was generally wished well, but there were few compliments. Some commentators thought me strong on policy and substance but lacking in charisma. For others I was 'Rabbitte-lite' and even 'the greyest of grey men'. A radio vox pop revealed no surge of popular enthusiasm, but did feature some people who had never heard of me.

Bertie Ahern welcomed me as the fourth Labour leader whom he would have to put through his hands, after having seen off the other three. As it turned out, I would soon be seeing him off. He was gone in just over six months, and I would go on to put three Fianna Fáil Leaders through mine instead.

Every leader has a vision and ambitions for their party. At the heart of mine was my sense that Labour itself had always lacked ambition. Only when Dick Spring lifted its sights in the late eighties and early nineties did Labour achieve significant electoral success with the election of Mary Robinson as President in 1990, and the so-called Spring Tide in 1992. The merger of Democratic Left and Labour in 1998 was intended to create a critical mass and a strengthened centre-left party capable of greater electoral success, but it had not yet achieved its potential. From the outset, I stated that my objective was to win close to thirty seats at the next general election. Both inside and outside the Party this was considered an unrealistic target, and some colleagues cautioned that I was making myself a hostage to fortune. But I was determined to set the Party's sights beyond the usual twenty seats and 10 per cent of the vote.

To achieve this, I knew the Party would have to change dramatically, and there was not much time for it to do so, since the local and European elections were set for mid-2009. I had little more than eighteen months to find new and younger candidates, and to lay the foundations for a successful general election. Before that, my first Party Conference as Leader was set for mid-November, leaving me just two months to prepare for it. Unusually, it would not be televised: the Party had already held a one-day conference before the general election and this had taken up our broadcast entitlement for the year 2007.

Three days before the start of the conference, my mother, Celia, died. She had developed Alzheimer's disease and her health had been in decline for the previous five or six years. During this time, I had the primary responsibility for her care, as my only brother, John, lives in the United States, and our step-father, Tommy Keane, had died in 2004. Though it meant I was constantly on the road between my own home in Shankill and hers in Caltra between 2002 and 2006, I managed, with help from wonderful neighbours and carers, especially Margaret Carney, to enable my mother to stay living in her own home for a long time: something I know she wanted. Caring for her over those years was probably the most personally rewarding work I have ever done, and it allowed me, in some sense, to repay her for the sacrifices she had made to give me the opportunities I've had in life.

I went from the funeral in Co. Galway to Wexford to deliver my first Leader's speech, on Saturday, 17 November. With little time to prepare or rehearse, I was going straight onto the stage without even a chance to judge the mood of the Conference. I was emotionally very raw, and as I waited backstage I worried that I might not get through my opening words of thanks and appreciation to delegates for their sympathy and to all those who had travelled to Caltra.

Somehow I managed it, and went on to deal with some of the key matters facing us as a Party. I told delegates that Labour, which had 'led so much change in the country, must now have the courage to change itself. At every level of our organisation we need to do better,' I declared, and the Conference accepted my motion to establish a '21st Century Commission' to bring about the transformation that I felt was so urgently needed for the Party.

Over the following year, to my satisfaction, the Commission, chaired by accountant Greg Sparks, came forward with a wide range of proposals for a major overhaul of the structures and governance of the Party. Most importantly, we dealt with the out-moded way candidates were selected.

I remember before the 2004 local elections going to a mid-sized town to chair the Labour Party selection convention. There were just six members in the room. At the start of the meeting, the oldest man present stood up and declared, 'I am the Labour man in this town!' In effect, he was nominating himself. He had contested every local election unsuccessfully for nearly three decades, leaving Labour without a councillor to represent the people or the Party all those years. Despite my efforts at cajoling, no other candidate came forward, so 'the Labour man' was selected. And of course, to form, he went on to lose once again. In the course of discussions later in the meeting, I identified among the members an articulate young woman who I thought would have made a great candidate. When I asked her afterwards why she wouldn't go forward, she confirmed my suspicions, saying that she was interested but, as she put it, 'Sure, I couldn't do that to him.'

Her attitude reflects the culture of decency among Labour members: reluctant to be ruthless, and respectful of service, experience and age. And while I admired it, I realised that traditional selection conventions in many constituencies were just not fit for purpose. They were not capable of bringing forward new candidates, or a candidate with some prospect of being elected! Good candidates are critical to electoral success, because in the Irish electoral system voters often express preferences for individual candidates, irrespective of party affiliation. The Commission recommended a new method, whereby the Party would interview prospective candidates; put a short-list before the selection convention, and let the local members then make the ultimate choice. This was a critical step in enabling us to bring on a new generation of candidates for the 2011 General Election.

All the Commission's reforms would have to be approved by the Party Conference, which was planned for the end of November in Kilkenny. But after I got back from attending the US Democratic Party Convention in Denver, it became clear that the deadline would not be met. We decided to put the reforms to a subsequent Conference in Mullingar in early 2009, and to turn Kilkenny into a Conference concentrating on the economy, which by then had started to nosedive.

Ireland had become, in July 2008, the first Eurozone country to go into recession. Unemployment had increased by 80,000 in just one year. The Fianna Fáil/Green Government had brought forward the Budget to October and had introduced many unpopular cuts, including to the medical cards for over-70s. The latter had brought tens of thousands of pensioners onto the streets in protest and prefaced the difficult times that lay ahead for the country.

The Kilkenny Conference was my first televised Leader's speech. It was very important that I do it well. I had been Leader for a year, and had, it was widely agreed, made good progress. I was making an impact in the Dáil, and the Party organisation was responding well to my reforms. However, there was still no major improvement in Party support. In fact, on the Saturday morning of my conference speech, my advisors, Mark Garrett and Colm O'Reardon, called to my hotel room to tell me there was bad news: a poll in a Sunday newspaper the next day was going to show a drop in Labour support.

We had to plough on regardless. Colm and my policy advisor, Jean O'Mahony, had worked with me to draft the speech. We decided it should be hopeful and optimistic, outlining solutions to the country's growing problems, rather than just slamming the Government for everything. Barack Obama had just been elected President of the United States, so it was almost inevitable that some echoes of his rhetoric would find their way into the speech. I liked his now-iconic slogan, 'Yes, we can', which had been translated from Caesar Chavez's '*Sí, se puede*' among Obama's Hispanic-American supporters. I thought about an Irish version: '*Is féidir linn*'. As in, '*Is féidir linn daoine a chur ar ais ag obair. Is féidir linn gnóanna a mhéadú agus séirbhísí a leasú. Is féidir linn an tír a chur ar ais ar a cosa. Sea, is féidir linne freisin.*' Obama himself would later use the Irish version when he spoke in College Green during his visit in May 2011!

'*Is féidir linn*' was not the only slogan to make its debut in Kilkenny. Just before I went into the hall, my team told me that the members of Labour Youth intended to hold up posters declaring 'Gilmore for Taoiseach'. And indeed they did.

The speech was a success. Mark Hennessy described it in the *Irish Times* as 'a masterclass; the best that he has ever given and, probably, one of the finest orations given by any political leader at a party conference of any hue in Ireland for many a long year.' It also attracted favourable comment from the public. I noticed that after Kilkenny there was a broadening in the range of people contacting my office, many of them from parts of the country that had no Labour representative. That was a good result for me, and things were starting to look better for the party.

There are times, though, when party perspectives have to be put aside. One such time had now come. It would blow all other considerations away. It was a calamity that would define Irish people's lives for many years to follow; it would impact on the country's viability and international standing more than any trauma since the Civil War; and determine Labour's distinct place in Irish politics for my entire time as leader: the collapse of the banks.

At about 7 a.m. on Tuesday 30 September 2008, my phone rang and woke me from my sleep. A conversation something along these lines followed:

'Good morning, is that you, Eamon?'
'Yes. Hello.'
'Brian Lenihan here. I hope I haven't woken you too early.'
'No, I was getting up now, anyhow.'
'We've been working right through the night here with the Taoiseach and officials. We have a crisis in the banking system and the Government has made some decisions which I want to tell you about. I am also briefing Enda Kenny. We need to put legislation through the Dáil and Seanad today and we will need the co-operation of the main opposition parties, and I hope we will also have your support, as the measures are in the national interest.'

Brian went on to tell me that the Government had become aware the previous evening that there was an imminent risk to the Irish banks and immediate action was required. With the necessary legislative changes, there would be a State guarantee for all the major Irish banks and building societies.

I told him that the Labour Party would, as always, be cooperative in re-arranging the business of the Dáil to enable urgent legislation to be debated, but that I could give no commitment with regard to our support for it. The Labour Party would need to see the detail of what was being proposed and consider it. He offered to have officials brief us later in the day.

After the call, I alerted the Labour Party press office spokesperson, Tony Heffernan, readied myself for a busy day, and set out for Leinster House to meet staff and parliamentary colleagues. It was immediately clear that we first needed to know more about this guarantee. What banks would be covered? What amounts? What was the exposure for the taxpayer? Would any protection be built in for the public? Would there be changes in the banks? What would happen to non-performing loans, particularly those related to property? None of this was clear from the Government statement that was issued.

From the outset, I was sceptical about the guarantee. I think I surprised Pat Rabbitte early that morning when I told him I wanted to oppose the guarantee. Even before consulting with colleagues, I issued a statement early that morning that said as much. I said the Government was effectively writing the biggest blank cheque in history, exposing the Irish taxpayer to enormous liabilities. While the USA's rescue package for its banking system amounted to around 6 per cent of its GNP, estimates of the potential exposure for Ireland varied between two and three times its GNP, perhaps as much as €500 billion. Aside from this, there was also a worrying lack of detail being provided as to the terms and conditions attached to such a massive guarantee. Finally, it wasn't clear what authority the Government had to even make such an offer to the banks.

Throughout the day, my colleagues and I tried to unearth more information. Joan Burton and I went to the Department of Finance, where we were briefed by its head of banking, Kevin Cardiff. He was understandably exhausted, having been up all night, and he left us none the wiser. Indeed, he seemed unsure of what he could or could not say to us. He left the room at one stage, presumably to get instructions on such matters. He also objected to the presence of Colm O'Reardon at the briefing, which he said was confidential and intended for members of the Oireachtas only. But Colm stayed for the full meeting, and as we walked back across the car park, I said that Labour would have to oppose the bank guarantee.

By 4 p.m., we still had no details about the proposed scheme and no sight of the legislation. Meanwhile, I pressed the Taoiseach, Brian Cowen, for information at Leaders' Questions. 'I can see what is in this guarantee for the banks and their shareholders, some of whom have already made gains today on the strength of it,' I said in the Dáil. 'I can see what is in it for the six bank chief executives who between them earn €13 million a year. However, I cannot see what is in it for the people or the taxpayers who may yet have to foot the bill. If the Taoiseach is proposing to hand over the deeds of the country to bail out the banks, what are we getting in return?'

As the day wore on, through several informal meetings of TDs and staff in my Leinster House office, my colleagues and I increasingly felt that such a broad guarantee was not the right course of action and that the Party should oppose it.

The Bill was supposed to appear at 4 p.m., then at 5.45 p.m., then at 6.30 p.m.. The actual printed document was eventually circulated at around 9 p.m., with the debate to start at 10 p.m. and presumably to go on all night. By this stage, I was concerned not only about the contents of the Bill, but also about how a possibly heated, late-night Dáil debate could do further damage to the country's reputation. I wondered about the international reaction if the debate was still going on when markets re-opened in the morning. I suggested that, therefore, only the second stage of the Bill, that is, its overall content, should be debated that night, and that the other stages be left for the following day. This, of course, would have the added advantage of allowing Labour more time to deal with our concerns and to focus public attention, for a second day, on what we now considered a very bad deal for the taxpayer. The Taoiseach and the leader of Fine Gael, Enda Kenny, agreed to the suggestion.

No vote was called at the end of the debate at about 2 a.m., so I decided to make the Labour position crystal clear the following morning at Leaders' Questions. I told the Tánaiste, Mary Coughlan, that if the fundamental objections raised by Labour were not dealt with to our satisfaction, we would not support the Bill. 'That would be most unfortunate,' she replied, 'but it is a matter for the Labour Party.'

Throughout that next day, Joan Burton, Pat Rabbitte, Michael D. Higgins and Emmett Stagg battled the Labour case, but the necessary assurances were not forthcoming. It would be some days later before we learned that so-called 'dated unsubordinated debt' was covered by the guarantee, amounting to a windfall for those who had been speculating in this form of bonds in the months before the guarantee.

When the vote was eventually called, there were 124 TDs in favour of the guarantee and just 18 against, all Labour. Fine Gael, Sinn Féin and Independents, including Michael Lowry and Finian McGrath, all voted with the Government. An inviolable guarantee, effectively underwriting all kinds of private debt originating in our banks, was now in place – with almost total support from the country's two Houses of Parliament.

Sinn Féin were enthusiastic supporters of the legislation. Arthur Morgan suggested that it would 'prove to be a move that other states will seek to emulate', and the voluble Senator Pearse Doherty announced that his party welcomed 'this decisive move … in the national interest'. Even as more problematic details emerged in the immediate weeks after, Arthur Morgan elaborated on Sinn Féin's reasons for supporting the scheme: 'We did so because we believed it was necessary to stabilise the State's banking system. Our judgement has been proved correct. Since its implementation, Ireland has not lost a bank or been forced to bail out a bank with cash.'

How wrong Sinn Féin and the other parties were! They all focused blindly on the fact that a blanket guarantee from the State would save the banks. But what about the State itself? Labour's analysis of this was proven correct: the guarantee seriously damaged the country's credit-worthiness, to the extent that the saved banks almost sank our entire economy. As a direct result of the guarantee, Ireland ended up committing up to €64 billion for bank recapitalisation, we were locked out of the financial markets, and we wound up in a bailout programme that deprived us of our hard-won fiscal sovereignty for three long years.

The bank guarantee did not by itself cause Ireland's recession, but it certainly added to it. It led directly to the worst economic crisis Ireland had ever faced. The country was now stuck with it.

2 IRELAND IN RECEIVERSHIP

At the time of the bank guarantee, Ireland was already in recession. By September 2008, the Irish economy had shrunk for two successive quarters and 80,000 jobs had been lost in the previous twelve months. The economy was collapsing. The complex international financial crisis, which had already taken down the Northern Rock bank in the UK and Lehman Brothers in the United States, played its part. But the main domestic cause of the collapse of Ireland's 'Celtic Tiger' economy was more concrete – literally.

The 'Rainbow' Government of Fine Gael, Labour and Democratic Left was in power from 1994 to 1997, led respectively by John Bruton, Dick Spring and Proinsias de Rossa. I served as Minister of State for the Marine in that Government. With Ruairí Quinn as Minister for Finance, the public finances were back in surplus for the first time in decades; new jobs were being created at a rate of 1,000 per week and an era of economic prosperity was about to take off, led by export growth.

For most of the 1997 campaign, it was widely expected that the Rainbow Coalition would be re-elected. The three parties had agreed to run on prudent, steady policies. Opinion polls were in our favour, approval ratings were strong and the mood on the canvass was positive. Then, in the final week, in a desperate bid for support and power at any cost, Fianna Fáil promised tax reductions. The Independent Media Group weighed in to support Fianna Fáil, with an *Irish Independent* editorial proclaiming 'It's Pay Back Time.'

The Rainbow lost, and though no one would have predicted it at the time, Fianna Fáil went on to hold power for fourteen years, winning the next two general elections with further promises of tax breaks and increased spending. House prices had already begun to rise in 1997, but instead of managing an increased supply of new homes, Fianna Fáil drove a decade of frenzied speculative construction, which created the property bubble and, in turn, caused the economic crash in 2008. Developers were incentivised to build through a range of tax breaks. Local planning authorities, who were normally cautious and careful about their responsibility to the built environment and to communities, were incentivised to re-zone more land for building and to grant more planning permissions. Under a new Planning Act, both city and county councils could now generate additional income through new development levies attached to planning permissions.

To stimulate demand, elaborate tax incentive schemes for investment in apartments, nursing homes, holiday homes, car parks, student accommodation and office buildings were concocted. A landlord, who bought a single investment property in say, Carrick-on-Shannon, could get tax relief on his or her entire rental portfolio in Dublin. At the peak, the State was committing about €8 billion per annum in tax subsidies to construction. To drive it even further, Finance Minister Charlie McCreevy announced a plan to 'de-centralise' the public service, which would deliver reliable State tenants for office developers throughout the country.

To entice more buyers into the property market, cheap finance was needed, so the traditionally cautious banks were introduced to the concept of 'light touch regulation', and soon began competing aggressively with each other for new speculative business. Some stockbrokers and commentators cheered it on demanding that the other banks deliver the same kind of profits as Anglo Irish Bank. And the newspaper industry itself had a vested interest in the frenzy. They were doing very well from property advertising.

In my own constituency of Dun Laoghaire, the Council was required (under the new Planning Act) to draw up a housing strategy to meet house building targets set by the Department of the Environment. The strategy resulted in a stated need to increase housing units by 50 per cent in a county which was already well stocked. This necessitated additional re-zoning of land – including, for example, the lands of Dun Laoghaire Golf Club on Glenageary Road, which then moved to a new course at Ballyman on the Wicklow border. When a majority of the elected Council sought to challenge this particular instance of over development, they were met with an 'instruction' from the Fianna Fáil Environment Minister, Martin Cullen, and the re-zoning went ahead.

The Labour Party was consistently critical of the way Fianna Fáil pursued inflationary policies in the property market in those years. Following the merger of Democratic Left and Labour in 1998, the then leader Ruairí Quinn appointed me as Party Spokesperson on Environment and Local Government, with a specific mandate to address the problem of rising house prices and affordability. In early 1999, I established a Housing Commission, chaired by Dr P.J. Drudy, Professor of Economics at Trinity College, Dublin. This Commission produced a report that acknowledged the need to increase housing supply to serve a growing economy and population, but warned against incentivising property speculation and excessive lending. It included a comprehensive set of recommendations to address the housing problem. These were dismissed as 'communistic' by the Progressive Democrat Housing Minister, Robert Molloy. Charlie McCreevy's answer to critics of his Government's economic policy was to encourage people to 'party on'. In a similar vein, as late as 2007, Taoiseach Bertie Ahern wondered aloud why those who were negative about the economy did not just go and 'commit suicide'.

It was generally accepted that housing output needed to be around 50,000 units per annum, but at the peak in 2006/7, over 90,000 units were being completed. This was clearly unsustainable, as were average prices of €350,000 for a second-hand home – almost ten times the average industrial wage. And despite the wishful thinking that there might be a 'soft-landing', the property crash came forcefully and suddenly in early 2008. House prices dropped rapidly. By the end of 2010, they had fallen 40 per cent from peak. Many young families found themselves with mortgage debt considerably greater than the value of their properties. Builders were stranded on sites which would not now realise their costs, and with assets no longer covering their borrowings from banks.

The construction sector, which, at its peak in 2006, represented 23 per cent of GDP, was now in free fall and the wider economy was being dragged down with it. Sites were closing; construction workers were being laid off; builders' providers, architects and conveyancing solicitors were among the first to be hit. House completions declined by 80 per cent between 2007 and 2010, taking 7.5 per cent off the country's GDP. Real GDP fell by 3.5 per cent in 2008 and 7.6 per cent in 2009. By the end of 2010, GDP had fallen 15 per cent in just three years. As the economy shrank, purse strings tightened. Domestic spending dropped, such that the Central Statistics Office reported in 2009 the largest annual fall in retail sales since 1975. New car sales fell by two thirds in 2009.

As job losses mounted and unemployment soared, our Spokesperson on Enterprise, Willie Penrose, highlighted the unprecedented nature of the crisis numerically. The year-on-year increase in the live register was 146,000 in February 2009; 36,500 in the month of January alone. By April there were 200,000 more on the register than at the time of the 2007 General Election. Soon job losses were experienced in sectors unrelated to construction. In the first few months of 2009, redundancies were announced in Ericsson (300), SR Technics (1,200), Ryanair (200), LR Donnelly in Limerick (470) as well as Bulmers in Clonmel, Waterford Crystal, Elan, Dell, Schering Plough and Acuman. By the end of 2010, the live register had climbed to 13.4 per cent and was heading for half a million. We could see small and medium businesses closing in unprecedented numbers all around the country. This was very clearly the worst economic crisis in the ninety-year history of our State. No job was secure and no business safe.

Next, the State's finances felt the impact. The exchequer had become overly reliant on taxes from the property sector, and this source of revenue disappeared almost overnight. People were spending less too, so VAT receipts were down, and every additional unemployed person cost the State €20,000 a year between lost taxes and increased social welfare payments.

The exchequer returns for January 2009 showed tax revenues down by €857 million (19 per cent) on the same month in the previous year. There had been a surplus of €630 million in January 2008. Now, a year later, there was a deficit of €744 million: a year-on-year reversal of €1.4 billion in the monthly figures. By December 2010, the State was taking in only €7 for every €10 it was spending. This could not continue for ever. The State would have to reduce its spending, try to increase income from new sources over time and, in the meantime, it would have to borrow the difference.

But therein lay a massive new problem. The State had guaranteed the banks and it turned out they were in a much worse state than Brian Cowen and Brian Lenihan had imagined. And it seemed no one knew to what extent. Estimates of the billions involved grew every month. International lenders began to doubt Ireland's ability to keep control and to repay its debts. The interest on our borrowings began to rise exponentially. The ten-year bonds' yield went from 4 per cent in 2006 to 14.55 per cent in July 2011. Eventually the ratings agencies – on whose somewhat arbitrary opinions international lenders partly base their decisions – consigned Irish bonds to 'junk' status. By the end of 2010, with a perfect storm of mounting debt and a deteriorating economy, Ireland was unable to pay its way and unable to borrow. The country was hurtling to bankruptcy or to bailout.

The Fianna Fáil-led Government was slow to see all this coming. Summer 2007 was a time for celebrating their three-in-a-row election win and for bonding with their new coalition partners, the Green Party. From September 2007 until April 2008, they seemed mostly preoccupied with their Leader's difficulties at the Mahon Tribunal.

The Mahon Tribunal (originally the Flood Tribunal) was set up in 1997 to examine allegations of corruption in the planning process in Dublin, including the activities of Minister Ray Burke, who resigned from politics when the Tribunal was established. The Tribunal continued for over ten years, despite court challenges and considerable political hostility, eventually producing a set of reports which detailed and documented extensive corruption and malpractice in the rezoning of lands in County Dublin.

As I had served as a member of Dublin County Council during the period under investigation, I was very familiar with the subject matter. I was called to give evidence and I was 'commended' by the Tribunal in their final report. It was not so for others. In September 2007, the Tribunal began to publicly examine payments which had been made to Bertie Ahern at various times. These payments included a 'whip-round' among some of his friends during a difficult time in his personal life. The collection had taken place after a dinner in a Manchester hotel, and a suitcase full of cash was brought to him in Dublin, by a UK-based Irish businessman. All the money amounted to tens of thousands of euros. But there was difficulty in tracing it because the former Minister for Finance did not have a personal bank account for about five years. There was enormous uncertainty and confusion about who lodged what monies and when to a particular account.

Ahern's answers were less than clear. In a Dáil exchange on the issue, I suggested to him that his explanations amounted to a cock and bull story. Eventually those close to him were called to give evidence, including his staff, and when public sympathy mobilised around one of his personal assistants, Gráinne Carruth, Bertie's days were numbered.

In my office in Leinster House a few days after Ms. Carruth's appearance at the Tribunal, I watched with my staff, the live coverage of Ahern emerging onto the steps of his department, surrounded by ministers, and announcing his resignation. I thought of all his successes, all the elections he had won, his insatiable appetite for constituency work, his reputation as a mediator, and above all, his indispensable role in negotiating the Good Friday Agreement in Northern Ireland with Tony Blair. His popularity, too, was epitomised for me by a night in St Joseph's Boys Football Club in Sallynoggin when he officially opened the new club-house. When the formalities were over, I made my way towards the stage to welcome him to my constituency, only to find myself being pushed aside by a group of female constituents eager to get up close and personal with him. 'Get out of our way, Eamon,' they said with a smile, 'we want to give Bertie a kiss.'

And now, it was all coming to a sad end for him.

Leadership of Fianna Fáil and the office of An Taoiseach was handed over to the only candidate offering to succeed, Brian Cowen. It was a long transition, with Cowen taking time away from the capital to celebrate in his Offaly constituency. The Government had yet to wake up to the recession, it seemed.

Brian Cowen's first test was the referendum on the Lisbon Treaty now only a few weeks away. Very quickly it became painfully clear that the Government had not prepared for this. The Irish EU Commissioner, Charlie McCreevy, proudly proclaimed he had not even read it. In a radio interview, the new Tánaiste Mary Coughlan, seemed to have only the most rudimentary knowledge of it. It was a fiasco. Among citizens, there appeared to be resistance to this Treaty, even from among those who usually supported the EU. A new and credible opposition to Lisbon appeared in the form of Declan Ganley and his mysterious Libertas organisation.

My own first public meeting on the referendum was in Liberty Hall. To my surprise, the place was full when I got there, and when I started to speak, I sensed the mood was quite hostile. All of a sudden, I heard a voice asking gruffly from the audience: 'What about the Passerelle?' – a reference to an obscure detail in the Treaty. I knew I was in for a rough ride. When the meeting was over, one of my co-speakers, Proinsias de Rossa, who was an MEP at the time, was knocked to the ground and assaulted by a menacing group waving a video camera. What about the Passerelle, indeed.

Ruairí Quinn reported to the parliamentary party that on current trends the Treaty would be lost. It was decided that I should liaise with Brian Cowen and Enda Kenny, offer them our grim assessment and try to work out a joined-up campaign with them. This led to the plan that the Taoiseach and I would canvass together on a particular day in Dundrum Shopping Centre. When Tony Heffernan went out to reconnoitre the location for the photo shoot he discovered that the backdrop to the intended photo shoot was a Next shop front. I was repeatedly rejecting the notion of a Fianna Fáil-Labour coalition after the next election, and a picture of Cowen and me under a Next headline could not be allowed. But he couldn't control everything: Cowen and I ended up –to the delight of the photographers and to the horror of my team – scoffing tea and scones together in a nearby café. We were joined on the canvass by local Fine Gael TD, Olivia Mitchell and by Seamus Brennan TD, then in the final stages of his illness. It was the last time I saw Seamus alive.

The Lisbon Treaty was defeated. In a poor TV interview afterwards, I came out with the words 'Lisbon is Dead'. My intention was to say that the Treaty in its current form could not be put to the people again, but it was interpreted that I would oppose the holding of any second referendum. WikiLeaks later released a report by the American Ambassador of a conversation which he claimed that I had with him and which suggested that while I was publicly opposing a second referendum, I was privately indicating Labour support for one if held. I never met that particular US Ambassador at all!

We were halfway through 2008 and the Government had still not woken up to the fact that the country was in a critical condition, haemorrhaging businesses, jobs and reputation. It seemed that Fianna Fáil ministers who had become accustomed to government by auto-pilot could not mentally adjust to the new realities that economic circumstances had changed.

At first, nationalisation of the banks, as called for by Labour, was rejected by the Fianna Fáil-led Government. Eventually they were forced into it, first nationalising Anglo and later AIB. On the public finances, they were equally undecided. They began in July 2008 with a mini-budget which reduced expenditure by €1 billion. Reacting to the worsening circumstances, they brought forward the date of the 2009 Budget to October 2008. In a panicked attempt to compensate for some of their traditional overspending, they attempted to remove the automatic medical card to which citizens over 70 years old had been entitled. It brought thousands of angry pensioners onto the streets in an impressive show of strength.

The sudden economic implosion left people shocked at first, then frightened, and eventually angry. An entire generation of people with little or no experience of hard times were suddenly faced with the personal financial consequences of a recession. The past decade and a half had been one of optimism, growth, rising living standards, and unfortunately, massive borrowing. The payback would be different from anything Ireland had ever experienced. But it would not be the first time that some had lived through hard times, including myself.

I had grown up in rural Ireland in the 1960s when emigration was the norm, and I graduated from university in the mid-70s to see many of my contemporaries forced to leave the country to get work. I worked as a trade union official through the 1980s and recall the trauma of regular job losses. On many occasions I had to bring news of redundancy to meetings of union members, and I spent many hours in factory canteens talking through crises with men and women in their 40s and 50s who thought they would never work again.

I therefore had some understanding of the apprehension that now swept through homes across the country and I was determined that, in critiquing the Government's performance, the Labour Party should always offer hope, clear solutions and a way out of the crisis. The situation and outlook were indescribably bad, but I felt things would get worse if the public mood turned to despair.

I travelled the country, addressing Party meetings, visiting workplaces, community centres, and accompanying candidates in walkabouts through towns and villages. We listened and gathered as much detail as possible on what people were going through, what they could be facing ahead and what solutions might help. These tours had an election focus; first, the local and European elections, in the first half of 2009; then the second Lisbon Referendum, in the autumn of 2009; and from then on, the general election.

Labour's rise in the opinion polls came in phases. Through the summer of 2008, the Red C polls were showing Labour around its traditional 10 per cent. By the end of the year, it had nudged up to 13/14 per cent. The big breakthrough came in a series of polls in 2009.

I spent Thursday 12 February campaigning with Councillor Aodhán Ó Ríordáin in his new electoral area in Dublin North Central, visiting a school in Clontarf, meeting a community group campaigning for better bus services in Marino, a GAA club in Donnycarney, and eventually attending a meeting above a pub in Fairview to officially launch Aodhán's campaign for re-election to the City Council. Broadcaster Eamon Dunphy had agreed to perform the launch, and as we gathered around before making our speeches, I was called out to a phone call from Tony Heffernan. He informed me that the IPSOS/MRBI poll in the next day's *Irish Times* would show Labour on 22 per cent, only four points behind Fianna Fáil, who had fallen to 26 per cent. I knew it was just one poll, but couldn't help feeling that the tectonic plates of Irish politics were beginning to shift. Fianna Fáil had never been this low, nor Labour so high.

Two weeks later the good news continued. A Red C poll in the *Sunday Business Post* showed Labour on 22 per cent and Fianna Fáil down to 23 per cent. We were now facing into the local and European elections with the wind behind us. The question was, could we convert favourable opinion polls into votes and seats in the elections on 5 June.

Our biggest challenge related to candidates and organisation. Outside the big urban centres, Labour was not organised at all or only minimally in many constituencies. In many Local Electoral Areas we had no candidate and no prospect of a candidate. Something drastic had to be done about this. I recruited David Leach to co-ordinate the campaign and Mags Murphy, who had worked in local radio, and had a good knowledge of the Party and local media, to trawl the country, especially the northern half, head hunting possible candidates. She, together with regional organisers George Cummins in Munster and Brian McDowell in Leinster, came up with several new faces for the Party to consider.

We had just one Member in the European Parliament: Proinsias de Rossa in Dublin. I persuaded Proinsias to stand one last time and he reluctantly agreed. The previous summer I had consulted the members of the parliamentary party in the Munster constituency. None of the TDs wished to stand for Europe, so the choice came down to the senators.

Senator Alan Kelly appeared to me to be the best prospect. He was from Tipperary and looked like he would be the only candidate from that county. He also possessed a great campaigning energy. Even if he didn't win, a run in the European elections would at least assist him in the general election. I floated the idea to him in a conversation in my office in Leinster House. He, shortly after, arranged a breakfast meeting in the Westbury Hotel between himself, his brother Declan who flew in that morning from New York, Mark Garrett and I. We talked through the pros and cons of his candidacy, and he eventually agreed to run, provided we held the selection convention before the summer break, which would give him most of the year to campaign. I agreed and the convention was arranged for Saturday 25 July in the Silver Springs Hotel, Cork.

Then, unexpectedly, another candidate stepped forward. Arthur Spring, a young businessman in Tralee and nephew of Dick, had been expected to stand in the local elections for Tralee Town Council and Kerry County Council but now announced that he wished to stand for Europe. Within the Party I was put under considerable pressure to drop Kelly in favour of Spring. The argument was that the Spring name would harvest more votes than an unknown Senator from Tipperary, whose name had never appeared on a ballot before. I was repeatedly pressed to postpone the convention until the autumn. I refused. I thought a selection contest would be a good start to the campaign. It was intensely fought. At one point I felt it was getting a bit too rough and I asked the Chairman of the Parliamentary Party, Jack Wall, to travel to Newcastle West to meet both men and to cool things down a bit. Jack reported back that I should stop worrying; the future of the Party was secure with such fine young candidates available, and to let them at it.

Saturday 25 July was sunny and warm in Cork, as the buses from Tralee, Killarney, Nenagh, and Thurles pulled up in front of the Silver Springs Hotel. I had travelled there earlier to meet privately with Arthur and Alan and seek agreement on what each would say after the convention so that Party unity in Munster would be assured. As Jack Wall had indicated, there was no cause for worry: the two had already met that morning and worked out everything themselves.

Kelly won the nomination, and ran one of the most thorough and energetic campaigns I have ever seen. It included a rap song and endorsements from many well-known figures, such as rugby legend Peter Clohessy.

I had great difficulty finding a European candidate for the Leinster constituency. None of the parliamentary party would stand. I pressed Willie Penrose, Dominic Hannigan, and Liz McManus in particular, but they would not agree. I also spoke, unsuccessfully, to a number of suitable high-profile figures. I was getting desperate when out of the blue I was approached at a business dinner in Dublin by somebody whom I had known since my student days. He wondered if I had considered running two candidates in Dublin, and mentioned that Nessa Childers, daughter of the late President Erskine Childers, and at the time a Green Party councillor, might be interested. I had already agreed a one-candidate strategy with Proinsias de Rossa and I was not going to go back on that. I wondered, though, if Nessa might fit the bill for Leinster.

The Childers family was from Wicklow. Nessa's grandfather, Erskine Childers, whose yacht *The Asgard* had smuggled guns into Howth harbour in 1914, had later been arrested in Wicklow during the Civil War and was held in Wicklow Gaol before his execution in 1922. Nessa had been a member of the Labour Party up to 2004, when she had sought a nomination for the local elections in the Clonskeagh Local Electoral Area where she then lived. She was unexpectedly defeated for the nomination at the selection convention, and she took it badly. I was the Party's National Director of Elections at the time and I offered to have her added as a candidate in some other electoral area, but she declined and left the Party to stand successfully as a Green Party candidate in Blackrock. She was still a Green Party councillor when, as arranged, she called to my home in Shankill to discuss the possibility of standing as a Labour candidate for Europe in the Leinster constituency. She agreed to stand and we discussed the choreography for her to leave the Green Party and announce her candidacy. I advised her to avoid bitterness in her resignation from the Greens.

Liz McManus undertook to manage Nessa's campaign, which was often rocky. Nessa had difficulties during some local radio debates. I recall offering words of encouragement to her during canvasses in Kilkenny and in Kells. Fine Gael's Avril Doyle tore into her, an approach which, in the end, backfired to Nessa's benefit. A colour piece by Lise Hand in the *Irish Independent* gave a flavour of the campaign:

> ... while Nessa is obviously sincere, it's hard to get to grips with which issues she really feels passionately about. Ask her what her Big Issue is, and she simply sticks to the party line. 'The' answer that all the Labour Party candidates will give is jobs, and going out to Europe and representing people with integrity and competence'.
>
> In Hennessey's sports shop, Eamon and Nessa pose for photographs brandishing a pair of hurleys. Eamon gently pokes the candidate in the side with the stick. 'A' dig in the ribs -- this is how to do it, Avril, sorry, Nessa,' he grins.

Outside of Galway City and Sligo, Labour had only a patchy organisation in Connaught/Ulster or the Ireland North-West constituency. There was no obvious candidate, and those who had stood in the previous two European elections had fared badly.

Former Labour Senator Kathleen O'Meara mentioned Susan O'Keeffe to me. Susan was the Grenada TV journalist who, in 1991, had made a documentary about the Irish beef industry which led to the establishment of the Beef Tribunal. Susan herself was the only one to be subsequently brought to court in connection with the broadcast. She was still working as a journalist and living in Sligo. She is a woman of great personal courage, and displayed it once again in standing for Labour in the North-West constituency, in effect risking her professional career.

She was a determined candidate, and raised many issues including the inadequacy of cancer services in the North-West. She debated effectively in the media with Declan Ganley, who, despite his high profile in European referenda, ran unsuccessfully as a Libertas candidate. Though she didn't get elected, Susan polled a very respectable 28,708 votes, which set her up as a possible Dáil candidate for the future. Happily, Ganley called a recount and while it didn't help him, an extra 2,000 votes were found for O'Keeffe. This brought her over the threshold for a State refund of election expenses. Ganley's recount ended up benefitting the Labour Party by €38,000.

Proinsias de Rossa was comfortably elected in Dublin, as was Nessa Childers in Leinster. Alan Kelly's result was a closer call, the count going to the very end before he became the third Labour MEP elected. I travelled to Cork to celebrate Labour's best European Election since 1979, and indeed Labour's best ever local elections. We won 132 city and county council seats, resulting in the highest numbers of Labour councillors since the foundation of the State.

I was the toast of the Party of European Socialists leaders' meeting the following week in Brussels. Overall, it had not been a particularly good election for Europe's social democratic parties, and in the post-election analysis, the party leaders felt that in the election the PES should have put forward a name for President of the European Commission. José Manuel Barroso was about to be re-appointed by default. The idea was born, that in future EU Parliament elections, the European parties should nominate candidates for the office of Commission President.

Europe continued to dominate the Irish political agenda through the summer and early autumn. The Government had negotiated some important changes to the original Lisbon Treaty to address the principal concerns of Irish voters in the referendum the previous summer. Each country would have the right to nominate a commissioner. Binding protocols would be added to the European treaties to guarantee Ireland's neutrality and to underpin Ireland's constitutional position on abortion.

A second referendum on Lisbon was set for 2 October. The campaign was difficult, and Labour's pro-European position was attacked by Sinn Féin and the ultra-left, who had always opposed the European Union and who had campaigned for a no vote in every referendum to date. The Treaty was comfortably passed. I got a congratulatory telephone call from Commission President José Manuel Barroso.

Later the same day, at the Dublin count centre in the RDS, a journalist from the *Sunday Tribune* asked me for my reaction to documents the Ceann Comhairle, John O'Donoghue, had just released about his expenses. As I hadn't seen the material, I gave only a vague comment, and undertook to examine the matter.

Earlier in the summer, O'Donoghue had come under pressure when the *Sunday Tribune* published details of expenses he had claimed for while he had served as Minister for Arts, Sport and Tourism. They included the hire of a limousine to transfer him between terminals at Heathrow Airport at a cost of €472, and the hiring of a car at the State's expense for the duration of the Cheltenham Races. As the recession and cutbacks were impacting hard on the public, there was, understandably, considerable anger at such waste of taxpayer's money. We heard complaints about the issue repeatedly during our canvass on the Lisbon Treaty. But O'Donoghue stuck to the line that as Ceann Comhairle he could not become involved in a controversy over a matter which arose while he was a minister. He left it to the Department to respond.

The Labour Party had issued a number of statements on the controversy, calling on O'Donoghue to explain his actions. I considered him to be a fair and very competent Ceann Comhairle, and I respected his office and the idea that it ought to be kept out of public controversy if at all possible. However, the latest information related to expenses he had incurred since he was appointed Ceann Comhairle and appeared to me to suggest an entirely unacceptable, sustained pattern of extravagance. I believed that the new revelations would bring the office of Ceann Comhairle, the Dáil, and the body politic into disrepute, and that firm and decisive political action needed to be taken to deal with the controversy. I felt this should be done on an all-party basis, and so I wrote to the leaders of Fianna Fáil, Fine Gael, Sinn Féin and the Green Party, suggesting a meeting of Party Leaders to consider the matter. I asked for a response in advance of the resumption of the Dáil at 2.30 p.m. on Tuesday 6 October.

Caoimhghín Ó Caoláin replied, agreeing to meet; Enda Kenny said he had 'no objection to such a meeting, but for it to be worthwhile it must be attended by all leaders including the Taoiseach. I am prepared to participate on that basis.' Brian Cowen replied on the day of the meeting, saying he did not agree to it: 'In view of the Ceann Comhairle's stated intention to make proposals to the meeting of the Oireachtas Commission to be held tomorrow, I believe that is the most appropriate forum in which to pursue these issues.' The Oireachtas Commission is the body which oversees the Houses of the Oireachtas and is chaired by the Ceann Comhairle himself. It meets in private. Five of the eleven members represent the Seanad. In a statement responding to the Taoiseach's proposal, I pointed out that 'the Oireachtas Commission is primarily an administrative body. This is a political problem, which must be dealt with through the political process.'

I was disappointed with Cowen's refusal to have a meeting of Party Leaders. It meant the O'Donoghue issue, already dominating the airwaves, would now have to be raised on the floor of the Dáil. There was growing public anger about it, and it was being made very clear to the Labour Party that people expected the opposition to do its duty and to confront the problem head on.

I travelled to Tralee to address the SIPTU Conference on Monday 7 October and discussed the matter at length with Mark Garrett over dinner in a restaurant in Adare, County Limerick. After my speech on Tuesday morning, members of the press asked me if I intended to raise the O'Donoghue issue at Leaders' Questions later that afternoon. I confirmed that I did.

On the drive back to Dublin, I got a call from O'Donoghue himself, enquiring as to my intentions. I told him that in the absence of a meeting of Party Leaders, I intended to raise the issue during Leaders' Questions. He pleaded with me not to, arguing that the Oireachtas Commission was where it should be addressed. I told him I considered it to be too serious at this stage to be passed on to a private committee meeting. It would be unthinkable, I told him, for the opposition not to raise it. He rang a second time pleading with me not to proceed, but again I refused, saying I believed the matter would not go away even if it was referred to the Commission.

In the Dáil, I asked the Taoiseach if he and the parties in government still had confidence in the Ceann Comhairle. The Taoiseach was visibly uncomfortable in his response, and said he regretted that I had raised the issue on the floor of the House, and that it should go to the Oireachtas Commission. He said nothing about the issue of confidence. It was hardly a ringing endorsement for O'Donoghue.

In response, I faced the Ceann Comhairle and said, 'I regret to say this, but I consider that your position is no longer tenable. I think you will either have to resign or be removed from office. Following the order of business today, it is my intention to meet with my colleagues in the Labour parliamentary party and to recommend to them the tabling of a confidence motion.' The die was cast. Later that evening O'Donoghue announced his intention to step down. I felt no sense of achievement or satisfaction. It was a necessary outcome, but travelling home that night I felt bad about what I had had to do.

Meanwhile, the economy continued to worsen. The Government was concentrating on the establishment of the National Asset Management Agency (NAMA). Shortly after the budget in December, Brian Lenihan was hospitalised. On 21 December he rang me from his hospital bed to consult with me about the membership of the NAMA Board of Directors, which he was shortly to appoint. He sounded in great form and joked with me about some of the contents of a book about the Workers' Party, *The Lost Revolution*, which had just been published. After Christmas, I saw him at Justin Keating's funeral on a snowy morning at Keating's farm in Ballymore Eustace. He struggled bravely with his illness and I was truly saddened to hear of his death while I was on an Irish Aid mission to Tanzania in June 2011 and I attended his funeral on my return.

The endgame for the economy came quickly. Ireland's bond spreads over Germany's began to widen, as Ireland found it more expensive to borrow on international markets. Greece's entry into a bailout programme gave rise to speculation that the International Monetary Fund (IMF) might step in and assume control here. But whoever heard of the IMF being called into such a prosperous, developed European state? Few took the prospect seriously, including some Fianna Fáil ministers who appeared on television saying they had heard nothing about Ireland making an application for a bailout. Within the week, however, the Governor of the Central Bank, Dr Patrick Honohan, was on RTÉ's *Morning Ireland* telling a shocked nation that the Government intended to apply for a 'programme of assistance'.

My first meeting with the Troika was on Thursday 25 November 2010 in the Labour Party parliamentary party room in Leinster House. A.J. Chopra of the IMF was accompanied by the other two members of the Troika (IMF, EU and ECB), Istvan Szekely from the European Commission and Klaus Masuch of the European Central Bank (ECB). With me were Joan Burton, Ruairí Quinn, Brendan Howlin, Pat Rabbitte, Colm O'Reardon, Mark Garrett and Jean O'Mahony. The meeting had been requested by the Troika. They wanted to brief the Labour Party on the contents of the bailout programme and how it would work. A.J. Chopra had a kindly bedside manner. The Irish economy was ill, was his line, and while a certain adjustment (11.9 per cent) had already been made, more was required. The financial sector needed to be 're-organised' and 'de-leveraged' over a period of time. The public finances needed correction and it all needed to be done and done thoroughly.

We were conscious that within months we might be in government having to work with the Troika, so we were keen to explore what scope there might be for flexibility and for re-negotiation of the programme. We emphasised the need for jobs and growth. They seemed positive about this and expressed confidence in the future of the economy, provided, of course, that the required corrective measures were taken.

We met them again on Tuesday 30 November, when they set out for us the deal which they had agreed with the Government, as defined in a series of official documents: a letter to be co-signed by the Minister for Finance and the Governor of the Central Bank, and a Memorandum of Understanding with all three institutions (IMF, EU and ECB), detailing the conditions for the loan finance being provided. The latter would indicate how much the State could spend on different programmes, what savings had to be made, what new taxes were to be raised, and what structural reforms were to be implemented. The programme would be supervised by Troika officials in Dublin, and the senior executives would visit every quarter for a review. Meanwhile, there would be a requirement for Ireland to report (sometimes weekly) on the measures being taken.

There, in the Labour parliamentary meeting room, between a mural based on the French Revolution and the 1916 Rising on one wall, and portraits of Labour Leaders back to James Connolly and Jim Larkin on the other wall, we were being shown how Ireland was in the process of losing its economic sovereignty. Being told so by the representatives of the economic institutions who were, in effect, taking charge of our affairs. As Ruairí Quinn put it, 'the country is now in receivership'.

The documents now being agreed by the Fianna Fáil/Green Government would constrain the State, and of course the next

Government, until the end of 2013. With Ireland no longer able to pay its way, and turning to the 'lenders of last resort', the conditions were bound to be onerous. To my mind, the worst was the interest rate. The institutions would borrow on the open markets for 22 per cent less than the rate at which they were lending it to us. I felt strongly that this mark-up or profit amounted to exploitation, and even a humiliation. I was determined to play my part in having these terms re-negotiated.

We used the two meetings to sound out where there might be flexibility, and we detected marginal differences in the attitudes between the Troika representatives. The IMF seemed the most reasonable. The European Commission, representing the Union, seemed to view us as errants in need of correcting. (Over time, the relationship with the Commission did improve.) The ECB was a bank, and behaved like a bank: Ireland was in debt; they were giving us credit based on terms; and we would have to stick to those terms.

One issue on which the Troika was insistent at these meetings (presumably because they were talking to the Labour Party) was privatisation. 'We are keen to move on this,' they told us. And when we pushed back, they countered by stating that Europe was putting up the money to keep us going. 'Ireland is one of the richest countries in the EU. How much are you putting up yourselves?' Such thinking was unacceptable to us. It was clear that our priority in government would be to re-negotiate the deal and to maximise flexibility.

As Christmas 2010 approached, there was a sombre and worried mood throughout the country. Uncertainty prevailed. What would the future hold? For jobs? For businesses? For families?

In the run up to Christmas every year, the Labour Party Leader hosts a drinks reception for staff, press and active members of the Party. It is normally held in the members' restaurant in Leinster

House a couple of days before the Christmas recess. This year there was no mood for celebration, and the public would hardly tolerate the idea of politicians celebrating while the people were suffering and the country was losing its economic freedom. We cancelled the Christmas party.

3 ELECTION CAMPAIGN

On Monday mornings, I held my constituency clinic at Park House, a small community centre on Library Road in the centre of Dun Laoghaire. Since becoming Party Leader, my conversations there with constituents about their housing, social welfare or other concerns were sometimes interrupted by phone calls from our press office or head office. On Monday 22 November, 2010 one such call came in from Tony Heffernan to tell me that the Leader of the Green Party, John Gormley, had just said that a general election should be held early in the New Year. Apparently, the Green Party intended to stay in government until then to see through the December budget and the Finance and Social Welfare Bills that would follow, but after that, they were out.

In effect, this was the start of the general election campaign. Gormley's declaration, coinciding with the arrival of the Troika, meant that the countdown to political change had started. There was no date set, but there was now no doubt there would be a general election sometime early in 2011. This was the moment I had been preparing for since I had become Leader of the Labour Party a little more than three years previously. Back then, my ambition to take Labour up to near thirty seats at the next election was considered to be overly ambitious, but not anymore. Opinion polls were now predicting that Labour would get twice, maybe even three times the level of support we got in the previous three general elections.

For most of its 100 year history, Labour had been a 10 per cent party. It got 10 per cent of the vote in the 1997 General Election under Dick Spring, the same in 2002 under Ruairí Quinn, and again in 2007 under Pat Rabbitte. Slightly better results were achieved in the Local and European Elections in 2004 (14.2 per cent) and 2009 (14.2 per cent). It was no wonder Ireland was often described as having a two-and-a-half party system, with the Fianna Fáil-Fine Gael civil war divide being defining. Since the 1920s, Labour was considered to be the 'half party' As Leader I was determined to lift Labour's sights and to make Irish politics a three way contest. As Dick Spring had shown in 1992, when he spoke about the idea of a 'rotating Taoiseach', many people wanted a credible government alternative to Fianna Fáil and Fine Gael. And it wasn't going to be easy, however, or happen overnight. Politics is a sluggish beast; it can take many laps before any significant change in positioning is noticed.

During my first two years as Leader, there was little sign of a lift. The Red C series of opinion polls had us consistently around 10 per cent. In fact, their poll in September 2008, just a year after I became Leader, put us on just 9 per cent. IPSOS/MRBI had us on 11-13 per cent until February 2009, when we shot up to 22 per cent and Fianna Fáil fell back to 26 per cent. In June 2010 it jumped again to 29 per cent, and to 33 per cent in their September 2010 poll.

I was canvassing in the Markets area of Belfast with my good friend Alasdair McDonnell of the SDLP in the Westminster Election in April 2010, when news came through that Labour had reached 24 per cent in the Red C poll. The news cheered everybody, including Alasdair, who was fighting a difficult battle for re-election in Belfast South. A Millward/Brown poll for TV3 News on 23 September 2010 put Labour on 35 per cent, Fine Gael on 30 per cent and Fianna Fail on 22 per cent. It concluded:

> A Labour Taoiseach is now a possibility. Our national poll reveals an electorate looking to break the two and a half party system. Who leads the next government looks to be the biggest question now facing the Irish people. With 35 per cent of first preference votes, the Labour Party have emerged as the strongest party in what is an extremely competitive scenario. It can now credibly assert its potential to lead the next government. Eamon Gilmore is also the most popular party leader for Taoiseach, underlining Labour's surge. 35 per cent opt for him, compared to 19 per cent for Enda Kenny and just 11 per cent for Brian Cowen.

Other polls were confirming this pattern. On June 27 2010, the Red C poll gave the choices for Taoiseach as Gilmore (40%); Kenny (28%) and Cowen (18%). In their poll on September 29 2010, IPSOS/MRBI asked the question: 'If the next General Election were to result in a Fine Gael and Labour coalition, who would you prefer to see as Taoiseach?' 48% replied Gilmore and 26% said Kenny. The lead was consistent over all regional, age, gender and social categories, including among farmers where the result was Gilmore 42% and Kenny 33%. The only exception was Connaught/Ulster where it broke even at 37% each.

'Gilmore for Taoiseach' was no longer an aspirational slogan on a Labour Youth poster. The idea was now being taken seriously right across the country.

For a political leader, opinion polls are a form of political continuous assessment. There is a poll almost every week. Whether you are up or down in them, for at least two days afterwards you are answering media questions about your performance. And then things move on. They can be misleading, though. Labour's local and European Election results in 2009, although they were our best ever, still fell short of the poll ratings both before and after the election. Short of my ambitions, as well. I wasn't about to get complacent over the general election because of surveys.

To convert opinion poll ratings into election results, a party needs good electable candidates; good organisation in the constituency; money to pay for a campaign; and then an effective election campaign. In 1992, Dick Spring did not have enough candidates to turn votes into seats. The Labour Party in 2010 still had little or no organisation in many parts of the country. We had far less money than Fianna Fáil, Fine Gael or Sinn Féin, and in previous elections our campaign had faltered in the last 10 days.

I knew the Party needed considerable modernising and looked to Mark Garrett to address these shortcomings. Mark was a former Chairperson of Labour Youth. He had supported my unsuccessful bid for the leadership in 2002, and subsequently we worked together on the Spring Commission that Pat Rabbitte set up to examine the constituencies. He was working with McKinsey Management Consultants in New York when I took over leadership and I asked him to come home to head up my team. Fortunately, Mark was up for the challenge. Brendan Halligan, who had performed a similar role in the 60s and 70s for Brendan Corish, suggested that this would be my most important appointment, and advised me to leave party business to Mark so that I could concentrate on national matters.

With a brief to open up the Party's communication to as wide an audience as possible, Mark set about updating and professionalising Labour's operations. Image and design were improved and standardised. All the Party's new promotional videos were professionally produced and we started to make more use of social media to get our message out. Constituency events were transformed from traditional-style meetings in dreary union halls to receptions in local hotels to which a broader range of people was invited. Party conferences were enhanced through the use of design, presentation and floor management. The 2010 Party Conference in Galway was the first time all these new strands came together.

Party conferences are invariably stressful for political leaders. As well as the routine of work that has to be done – motions to be addressed, reports passed, officers and supportive executives elected, the Leader is under an intense spotlight and suddenly very directly accountable to everyone face to face. And then there's the live television broadcast of the leader's speech – the keynote event of the year for every political party.

I would generally, with Colm O'Reardon and Jean O'Mahony, begin to prepare for my speech about two weeks in advance of the conference. The content had to be carefully researched, politically sharp, engaging, inspiring and fresh. The delivery had to be a full-scale performance that satisfied all expectations. To satisfy the television producer, the length had to be spot on – with allowances made for audience reaction and possible off-the-cuff remarks, or you could find yourself being cut just at the key moment.

On Friday afternoon, 16 April 2010, I arrived at the magnificent Bailey/Allen Hall on the NUI Galway campus for the usual full run-through of the speech with the RTÉ crew. The podium and autocue were situated right in the middle of the hall and, unusually, there was a tiered bank of seating to the rear of the speaking position. Mark intended to position a crowd of mostly young members here to give a sense of the audience for the viewers at home. Directly facing me on the opposite wall was a large screen on which I could see myself as I delivered the speech. Speaking in such an unconventional setting and having a large crowd behind me was unsettling enough, but I was just not ready for the screen. 'That screen has got to go, Mark,' I declared. 'It will distract me completely during the speech. I can't watch myself on television and deliver a convincing message at the same time.'

'Sorry, Eamon, no. The screen stays. It's not meant for you. It's there to give the people behind you something to look at during your speech so that they won't be moving their heads about and distracting the people watching at home.' I was too impressed with the thoroughness of how every angle had been considered to object further. I'd just have to put up with the mirror effect of the screen and play my part as best I could. Happily, the event was a success.

The selection of candidates for the 2011 General Election would prove a bit more challenging for our team and was controversial for us in many locations. I had made it clear from early on that I wanted to contest every constituency, and to have more than one candidate in some. Unlike the situation with the local and European elections, there was no shortage of prospective candidates for the general election. Labour's fortunes were on the rise and it was, in some respects, the jersey to wear at the time. I was approached by some high profile figures that were very keen to get on board. However, it soon became apparent that most had little interest in being TDs. They wanted to be ministers right away. One offered to run on condition that I assured him he would be Minister for Finance.

In constituencies where Labour was weak we did have to look

outside the Party for candidates. In Roscommon-South Leitrim we selected Independent Councillor, John Kelly, from Ballaghadereen, and to support his candidacy we held the 2010 annual parliamentary party meeting in the Abbey Hotel in Roscommon town. Independent Councillor, Jimmy Harte, whose father Paddy had been a long-time Fine Gael TD for Donegal, came on board. The Harte family are greatly respected in Donegal, and I recall Pat Rabbitte returning from a constituency visit there enthused that the local media thought Jimmy would take a seat.

A young Independent candidate, barrister and farmer Michael McNamara, caught our eye during the 2009 European Elections. I met him in Ennis during the second Lisbon Referendum, and with the generous support of Councillor Pascal Fitzgerald, he overcame some local resistance to become our successful candidate in Clare. In Mayo, the local media speculated that Councillor Michael Kilcoyne, a trade union official and former member of the Labour Party, might re-join, and that if he did, he would win a seat for Labour. He probably would have, but it never happened, and I therefore asked former Independent TD, Dr Gerry Cowley, to stand for Labour. He joined us at the 2010 Conference in Galway.

Encouraged by Willie Penrose, we asked the former Progressive Democrat TD, Mae Sexton, whose family has deep roots in the local trade union movement, to stand in Longford. John Whelan, the former editor of the *Leinster Leader*, was recommended to us by some of his friends in the media. After some strong resistance in the local organisation, he was selected as our candidate for the five-seater Laois-Offaly constituency, resulting in unpleasant scenes at the selection convention in Portlaoise and several resignations from the Party.

The new candidate selection system gave the Party's organisation committee the right to shortlist candidates, but ultimately the choice was made by the individual members at a constituency selection convention. Many of these conventions were very keenly contested.

In Wicklow, Liz McManus was retiring from the Dáil and she had hoped that her son Ronan, a councillor in Bray, would replace her. Instead, the convention selected Anne Ferris (Liz's Dáil assistant) who went on to win a seat. She was joined on the Labour ticket by Councillor Conal Kavanagh (son of former Labour minister Liam), and with the Mayor of County Wicklow, Councillor Tom Fortune.

In Dublin South Central, Councillors Eric Byrne and Michael Conaghan (both of whom were elected) were selected along with Councillor Henry Upton (son of the late Deputy Pat Upton, and nephew of Deputy Mary Upton). I received several communications of protest from members who complained that three men had been selected over the very able Councillor Rebecca Moynihan. But that was the outcome of the vote at the selection convention. (I have no doubt that Rebecca will make it to the Dáil and be an outstanding TD).

The selection of Deputy Tommy Broughan and former Deputy Seán Kenny by the members in Dublin North Central caused disquiet among younger members of the Party, who had supported the cause of the young Councillor Cian O'Callaghan. In Dublin North West, Róisín Shortall resisted the candidacy of Councillor Andrew Montague (the man who was responsible for the Dublin Bike Scheme), and John Lyons was chosen. As it turned out, both Shortall and Lyons were elected in this three-seater. When Senator Ivana Bacik failed to win a nomination in her own constituency of Dublin South East (where Ruairí Quinn and Kevin Humphreys went on to win two seats), I invited her to stand as my running mate in Dun Laoghaire.

In Sligo-Leitrim, the contest for the nomination between European election candidate Susan O'Keeffe and Councillor Veronica Cawley ended in a draw. After hearing from both candidates, the National Executive called it in O'Keeffe's favour. Cawley subsequently left the Party and stood as an Independent, as did two other former Labour representatives. The multiplicity of Labour and former Labour names on the ballot divided the vote and resulted in Sinn Féin taking the seat.

A number of strategic decisions were taken to add candidates who had not been through the selection conventions. Councillor Colm Keaveney from Tuam accepted that a second candidate, from the south of the county, would be needed if he were to have a realistic chance of winning in Galway East. He raised no objections to the addition of a young barrister, Lorraine Higgins from Athenry, who had been an Independent candidate in the 2009 Local Elections. Geography also dictated the necessity of adding a North Louth candidate to boost the chances of Drogheda-based Ged Nash. We nominated a well-known music teacher, Mary Moran from Dundalk. Deputy Brian O'Shea, who had been Chairperson of the Party, had decided not to seek re-election in Waterford. Local opinion polls suggested that Councillor Seamus Ryan was having difficulty picking up votes in the west of the county. We added a new young councillor from Dungarvan, Ciara Conway, who, remarkably, went on to outpoll Seamus and to take the seat.

Eventually, after careful preparations, Labour was set to contest the 2011 General Election in every constituency, with over seventy candidates in total, the highest number since 1969, and enough to become the largest party in the Dáil. We were offering the Irish people the choice of electing a Labour-led government for the first time ever. The 'Gilmore for Taoiseach' posters were intended to make that choice explicit; and in any event – according to the opinion polls – that was the people's preference at that stage.

Meanwhile, we had been preparing our campaign. I had appointed Ruairí Quinn as the National Director of Elections to head a special committee composed of senior politicians and senior Party staff. The committee would run the campaign on a day-to-day basis. We rented an open-plan floor in a modern office building in Golden Lane (now the home of TheJournal.ie) as our election headquarters. Based on the policy preparation work undertaken by Colm O'Reardon and Jean O'Mahony, posters, pamphlets and policy documents were produced to a standard design under the banner slogan of 'One Ireland: Jobs, Reform, Fairness', which became the title of the election manifesto.

The manifesto, which ran to 90 pages, was drawn up at a time of turmoil in Ireland. I believed that it had to offer hope to people who were by now traumatised by the economic collapse, and who were fast losing confidence in politics.

I had lived through the economic crisis of the 1980s and had seen, at first hand, the devastating effect of losing a job on the individual worker, on his or her family, and on their community. What the new Government would have to face was worse than the 1980s. Recovery would not happen just by cutting budgets. It would have to be built on job creation. Our manifesto would spell out how that would be done by growing new jobs in tourism, in the food industry, in the green economy and through innovation. It would spell out how Ireland could increase its exports and support small businesses. Our priority would be creating jobs. But I also felt that re-building the broken economy was not enough. We also had to repair public life and politics. I asked Brendan Howlin to draw up a blueprint for reform and he produced 140 proposals for the reform of politics and the public service.

I also knew that budgets would have to be cut, but I believed that this needed to be done fairly. No cut would be painless and every cut would have consequences for somebody. But we needed to maintain a threshold of decency, a floor below which people could not be allowed to fall. That's why we concentrated on ways to enable people to continue living in their homes, to maintain basic social welfare rates, and to restore the minimum wage.

Just after Christmas, I began my 'Leader's Tour' of the constituencies. It began on Wednesday January 5 at the Glen of the Downs, a short distance from my Shankill home. In the Glenview Hotel, with our three candidates and a large crowd of Labour supporters, I kicked off the general election campaign in Wicklow. Then on to Enniscorthy and Wexford to hook up with Brendan Howlin and the late Pat Cody, and from there to Clonmel to campaign with Phil Prendergast the following morning. After that it was back to Dublin for a press conference on Thursday afternoon. On Friday, it was Louth and Meath, and then back to campaign in the Dublin constituencies over the weekend. And it continued like that, every day, until polling day. We travelled in a fleet of estate cars decorated in the red Labour livery. We felt the cars would be more nimble than a campaign bus in urban traffic. I was in the first car, driven by Kevin Eager, accompanied by my Communications Manager, Karen Griffin. In the second car was a team of young election workers whom we labelled 'the red jackets'. They created a splash of Labour colour at each stop, handing out literature and leading the way for the candidates. Behind that came the press corps, made up of RTÉ and TV3 crews, news and feature journalists from the national newspapers, and a number of photographers.

The visits followed a consistent pattern. On arrival, there was a photographed welcome for us from the candidate and his/her supporters; a doorstep interview for the media's benefit; a walk-about with the candidate canvassing votes on the streets of the town; a visit to some venue of local significance, perhaps a shopping centre, a hospital, a factory or a community centre; a visit to the local radio station for an interview; a session with the local press on local issues and to highlight the credentials and prospects of the local candidate; a cup of tea in the local hotel or coffee-shop to give me a chance to have a 'word in the ear' with local people; and finally a short motivational speech for the local election team. Then, back into the cars and move onto the next town to do much the same thing all over again … and again and again.

The journey between visits was for my briefing. Karen Griffin had put together an information pack for every visit. It included a summary of the local issues, and the position being taken on them by the Labour Party. The new by-pass road; the controversial traveller housing scheme; the speculation about the future of the local hospital; the Council's plan for a waste/recycling centre at the edge of the town etc. On these short journeys, I read the cuttings from the local newspapers, absorbed their analysis of the election contest in that particular constituency, including any local polling, and familiarised myself with the strengths and weaknesses of the other parties and candidates. I also had to ensure that I caused no offence to our own candidates and supporters. Where there was more than one candidate, I had to prepare phrases which gave each equal emphasis; I needed to know the names of their spouses and to mention anything significant which may have recently happened in their lives, like a birth or a funeral. On these journeys, Karen also ran by me, the names and photographs of our local councillors, lest I forget a name during the canvass.

I had to be word perfect all the time. Modern media, in all its forms, now records everything. Political life is now permanently public.

I developed a good working relationship with the press corps covering my tour. They were, of course, suitably challenging and probing in their questioning. I was well prepared on the main news items and issues of the day, but they were also keen to test me with requests to respond to what other party leaders had said on any number of topics or to charges somebody (sometimes one of our own!) had made against the Labour Party just a few minutes previously. Accordingly, a portion of each journey was spent on the phone to our election headquarters, getting updated on the campaign, briefed on evolving issues and sometimes making final decisions on campaign tactics.

I have always loved canvassing – talking one-to-one with a voter about a public issue or a personal worry. But for the very same reason, I hated the canvass walkabouts: there was no chance to have normal interactions with people as the peloton of candidates, red jackets, election workers and media hustled down the street or through the busy shopping centres. They were largely for show, for photographers who often jostled to get their picture of the day, for our press people who fretted about getting positive coverage, for the six o'clock news. However, they did act as magnets for the concerns of the voting public and that made them important.

The messages that came our way were consistent: workers were worried about their jobs; parents were concerned about the future for their children; pensioners were worried that the State could discontinue paying their pensions. What was most surprising was that, unlike any previous election campaign I had been on, there was little talk now of local issues. Voters were worried about the future of the country.

On most streets the shops were empty. In the entire canvass, I rarely saw a customer actually buying anything in a clothes boutique, a sports shop, or in a furniture or hardware store. The only purchase appeared to be essentials in supermarkets and pharmacies.

It was a winter campaign and I picked up a heavy cold. My family doctor looked hopelessly at me, saying 'I suppose there's no point in suggesting you take a couple of days to rest.' Armed with a prescription, my Lemsip and a cough bottle, I struggled on.

I carried the cold into my first TV debate with Micheál Martin, the new leader of Fianna Fáil. For many decades, RTÉ had hosted television debates between the leaders of Fianna Fáil and Fine Gael. But the Labour Party had never been allowed into a 3-way Leaders Debate. Their rationale for the exclusion of Labour was that it was proper order to put head to head the potential candidates for Taoiseach. The tussle between Charlie Haughey and Garret FitzGerald was legendary. Bertie Ahern had debated with John Bruton, Michael Noonan and Enda Kenny in successive general elections. These big television debates had considerable influence on the outcomes of the elections, yet the Labour Party was not included. In more recent elections, RTÉ hosted a separate debate for the leaders of the smaller parties – the Progressive Democrats (PDs), Greens, Sinn Féin and Labour. The verbal tussle between Pat Rabbitte and Michael McDowell, the Leader of the PDs, in the 2007 General Election was especially memorable. But given how the polls were going, we were pushing for RTÉ to include me in the main Leader's debate.

As late as the Labour Party Conference in Galway in mid-April 2010, just nine months before the election was called, RTÉ was still maintaining the status quo. I used my opening speech at the conference to make the case for Labour to be included, and in an analysis piece the following Monday in the *Irish Times*, headed 'Savvy performer Gilmore would gain in three-way debate', Deaglán de Bréadún wrote: 'The fact that our nearest neighbours have now adopted this practice greatly increases the pressure to include the Labour Leader. It's not a prospect calculated to delight Fianna Fáil or Fine Gael, whatever public protestations they might make to the contrary.'

A highlight of the British General Election, then underway, was their series of debates between Gordon Brown, David Cameron and Nick Clegg. Shortly after his election as the new Fianna Fáil leader, Micheál Martin wrote to Enda Kenny and me proposing a three-way debate. TV3 offered to host it, but Enda refused to participate. TV3 decided to run a head-to-head between Micheál Martin and me, to be moderated by Vincent Browne. It was set for Tuesday night 8 February. Among commentators the feeling was that I would win such a debate. I was not quite so confident myself. I had been performing well in the Dáil, I was a competent public speaker, I had a good command of policy, and I could generally handle myself well in an interview. However, I had had my fair share of bad days in the studio, and these haunted me a little. In a radio interview with Marian Finucane in September, I came across, I realised afterwards, as unnecessarily evasive about my political past. A technical fault on the headphones had given rise to a poor lunchtime interview with Seán O'Rourke just before Christmas. And although I did fine on the *Late Late Show* in late November (despite the friendly forewarning from Ryan Tubridy: 'Eamon, we are not bringing you in for a hug'), I was subsequently criticised for saying that Labour in government would not be able to reverse Fianna Fáil's cuts.

I felt I needed to prepare thoroughly for the TV debates. I got some help from our English-speaking sister parties abroad. Kevin Rudd, who had led the Australian Labor Party back to government after eleven years, but who had since been toppled by his Deputy Leader, Julia Gillard, rang to wish me well and to offer support. I mentioned to him that the journalist Will Hutton had once said that I reminded him of Kevin Rudd, to which Rudd now replied, self-deprecatingly: 'Oh you poor man. I sincerely hope not.' Rudd's policy advisor, John O'Mahony, came over from Australia and worked with a unit in our election headquarters, compiling and updating the message book throughout the campaign. He also helped prepare me for the debates.

Ed Miliband, too, offered the support of the British Labour Party and among those who came over from Britain to help was David Muir, who had worked with Gordon Brown. David, with whom I remained in contact afterwards, organised rehearsals for me before each of the early TV debates.

On the night, I was quite nervous driving into the TV3 studios in Ballymount. No matter how much preparation I had done, I knew this would come down to being able to cope with an hour of intense scrutiny in front of the cameras. The preliminaries, including the press scrum on the way in: 'How do you feel, Eamon? Are you going to win?' 'What do you have to say about Enda Kenny's refusal to take part?' etc. was unnerving. Inside the studio building tension mixed with excitement. The debate was very important for both Micheál Martin and me, but it was arguably even more significant, certainly historic, for TV3, being their first leaders' debate. Everybody was on edge. Make-up, the pre-debate photographs and the on-set promo seemed to go on forever. I just wanted it to start.

To my surprise, Vincent Browne attacked neither of us. He was on his best behaviour and moderated the debate very fairly, concentrating on the questions, which he had prepared well. It was a robust debate. Micheál Martin is an experienced politician and a polished media performer. He tore into me in a kind of rear guard action. Even though Fianna Fáil had been in government for fourteen years, it was as if Labour were already in power and Martin in opposition. I was put on the defensive. Coming off the set at the end, I felt I had not won and would have settled for a draw. The immediate reactions from Mark Garrett and Tony Heffernan seemed to confirm that, but some of the 'après-match' commentators gave it to Martin. We moved on.

The second debate included the five party leaders, with Enda Kenny, Micheál Martin, John Gormley and Gerry Adams on RTÉ, moderated by Pat Kenny, and with a studio audience. There were too many of us, and there was no clear winner.

The third debate was another historic first, this time for TG4. There had never before been a leaders' debate *as Gaeilge*, and the first was to be an hour-long one between Micheál Martin, Enda Kenny and myself. It was expertly moderated by Eimear Ní Chonaola. It had 600,000 viewers and was considered by many to have been the best of all the debates. The preparation for this debate was very simple. I had dinner the previous evening, in the Radisson Hotel, Galway, with Kathleen Lough and Fidelma Mullane, both members of the Labour Party and both fluent Irish speakers. We talked, *as Gaeilge*, of course, about the issues likely to come up. We fashioned some phrases I could use and talked through the answers I would give. I reinforced all that the following morning when Fidelma accompanied me to the TG4 studio in Baile na hAmhann. In the end, I was proud to have taken part; and throughout the country, Irish speakers and those who love the language were encouraged by it. The mood was best captured by the message I received from the President of Conradh na Gaeilge, Pádraig Mac Fheargusa: *'Tá talamh nua briste agaibh. Ócáid stairiúil a bhí ann, agus mar a luaigh an tOllamh Gearóid Ó Tuathaigh sa chur is cúiteamh tar éis, b'iad pobal na Gaeilge na buateoirí móra. Pobal na hÉireann a déarfainn féin; b'ábhar misnigh agus comhaontais dúinn ar fad é.'* (We have broken new ground. This was a historic occasion and as Professor Gearóid Ó Tuathaigh remarked in the commentary afterwards, the Irish speaking community were the big winners. I would say the people of Ireland were the winners, it was a source of courage and unity for us all.)

The final debate, between Kenny, Martin and Gilmore that I had been seeking, was moderated on RTÉ by Miriam O'Callaghan on 22 February. I did no formal preparation for this one. My brother John had come home from the United States to help with the campaign and gave me some good advice. He had worked for over a quarter of a century with CNN, and, for the past decade, as the senior producer on *Larry King Live*. He had covered several American elections, and knew a thing or two about televised debates. He had been quietly observing my preparations so far and had come to the conclusion that I was being over-coached. He advised me to dispense with rehearsals for this one, to rest on the afternoon of the debate, to go for a walk and clear my head beforehand, and to 'just be yourself' in the studio. It worked. I was more relaxed, and although I'm probably the worst possible judge, I think it was my best television performance.

The new TV debates were not the only pioneering feature of the 2011 election. It was clear from the start that Fianna Fáil were finally going to be ousted from power, but what was not immediately apparent was who would lead the new government – the traditional struggle between Fianna Fáil and Fine Gael was now one between Fine Gael and Labour. With a new target in its sights, Fine Gael decided to launch a broadside against the Labour Party. Michael Noonan led the attack, claiming that Labour was a 'high tax party'. We had proposed a 48 per cent tax band on single incomes over €100,000 and on couples earning over €200,000. Yet we found it difficult to shake off Noonan's attacks among some voters. It seemed, too, that Fine Gael's 'Five Point Plan' (though its details were quite forgettable) was having more of an impact than Labour's 'Jobs, Reform, Fairness'.

We began our formal campaign in the Gravity Bar at the Guinness Storehouse with our intention to renegotiate the terms of the Troika bailout. We repeated the 'renegotiate' message over several days, at press conferences, interviews and speeches, but it was having no impact. It seemed as if nobody (the press, especially) believed that the terms of the bailout could be renegotiated. Fianna Fáil accused us of misleading the public about the possibility of renegotiating, with Micheál Martin stating that 'Labour was attempting to deliberately mislead voters about what changes to the IMF-EU bailout deal can be achieved.'

I met with my team on the morning of 3 February to run through things shortly before a scheduled press conference. Mark Garrett made it clear that our message on renegotiating the deal was not cutting through. Our finer points of reducing the interest rate, limiting privatisation and creating a space for jobs and growth were not being heard in the noisy electoral market place. It was clear we needed to simplify our message if it was to make an impact.

I summed up the situation for myself: the European Central Bank (ECB) was insisting that the bailout deal could not be renegotiated. But Labour would insist on renegotiation. A phrase came to me: Frankfurt's way or Labour's way. I used it for the first time at that press conference and repeated it a number of times for effect. It cut through alright. Just not quite in the way I had intended.

Often in politics, it is not what is said that matters, but what is heard. For instance, in 1969 Jack Lynch did not say, 'We will not stand idly by', but that's what people thought they heard, meaning that he intended to send Irish troops over the border to protect nationalists in Belfast and Derry. So too with 'Frankfurt's Way or Labour's Way'. It was heard not as the pledge to renegotiate that it was, but as an outright, Syriza-style rejection of the bailout, which it never was. Though in government, we succeeded in getting much of Labour's way and renegotiating the interest rate, and limiting privatisation, and restoring the minimum wage, and extending the time frame for reducing the deficit, and stopping paying the Anglo promissory note, and much more besides, some were determined to cast it as falling short of this promise.

The high point of Labour's poll ratings came in the summer of 2010 (33 per cent in September 2010 IPSOS/MRBI). I was on holiday in early August when I heard of one particularly good outcome for us and all I could think was, 'How long will it last?' I knew that when the electoral contest was at its peak, we would find it hard to compete with the financial resources of Fianna Fáil, Fine Gael and Sinn Féin, and that unlike Fianna Fáil and Fine Gael, we would not have the organisation and members on the ground to realise our vote potential.

And indeed, as predicted, by December, Labour's rating had dropped to 25 per cent (IPSOS/MRBI), and falling further to 19 per cent a week before the election. The pattern was the same in the Red C series, though not as dramatic. This decline was despite Fianna Fáil's drop from 24 per cent in September to 16 per cent in February (IPSOS/MRBI). The gains went to Fine Gael, Sinn Féin and Independents. Support for Independents rose from 11 per cent and 9 per cent in September to 17 per cent and 15 per cent in February in the respective IPSOS/MRBI and Red C surveys. Both of these polling organisations found that support for Sinn Féin shot up from 8 per cent and 10 per cent to 15 per cent and 16 per cent between September and December 2010, probably due to the Donegal South West by-election. Over all this time, Fine Gael continued to rise steadily and solidly from 24 per cent in the IPSOS/MRBI series in September to 37 per cent by 18 February.

What was causing this pattern? It seemed that, as long as it was theoretical, many people were happy to express support for Labour, but once the election was on the horizon (from December 2010) – coinciding, in this case, with the arrival of the Troika and the sense that solutions must be found immediately – voters began to reconsider their positions.

The arrival of the Troika was followed by a massive 6 billion euro budget adjustment. After Christmas, the Universal Social Charge began to hit pay packets. Anger gave way to fear in the public mood. Fine Gael played on the fear, and frightened many potential voters from supporting Labour, by hammering away at us on tax.

Furthermore, following our very high polls, the media, understandably and quite rightly, began to interrogate Labour more closely on policy issues, and to become more critical when it appeared to them that our responses were less than clear. Opponents made the most of this and (wrongly) began to allege that Labour had no policies. Some sections of the media, in my opinion, took editorial decisions that were aimed at stopping Labour's gallop. The *Irish Daily Mail*, which in the early years of my leadership had regularly invited me to contribute to their paper, published an editorial headed, 'Danger in the rise of Eamon Gilmore', which warned of Labour's record in government with that old chestnut that the Party was 'in thrall to the trade unions', and concluded that 'Mr Gilmore has done his country some considerable service in opposition – and will continue to do so.

Having him and his colleagues at the Cabinet table would be a different matter altogether.' The *Sunday Independent* continued its traditional hostility to the Labour Party and, on the Sunday before polling day, its front page cried out 'Poll: Give us Enda without Gilmore'.

There were powerful forces in Irish society, some of them in the media, who simply did not want Labour in government, and most certainly not leading it. And unfortunately there were some too in the Labour Party who felt the office of the Taoiseach was a step above our station! Another reason for the shifting preferences was that Fine Gael's job in the election was probably easier than ours. Voters who just wanted Fianna Fáil out of office and a change of government had to just make a one-step change to Fine Gael. Voting Labour required, in a sense, two steps.

Sitting across the aisle from me during Dáil votes was Mary Harney, who hails from the same County Galway parish as I do; she offered some insights of her own to me. She thought the Donegal South-West by-election did a lot of damage to Labour. It was certainly not the constituency we would have chosen for a by-election if we'd had a choice.

Pat 'The Cope' Gallagher was elected to the European Parliament in June 2009, and his Dáil seat had been vacant for almost a year and a half. The Government, having already lost two by-elections, to George Lee (Fine Gael) in Dublin South and Maureen O'Sullivan (Independent) in Dublin Central, did not want to risk another loss in what had always been a Fianna Fáil heartland. Sinn Féin saw their opportunity, and their young candidate Senator Pearse Doherty took a High Court case which forced the holding of the election. Armed with a high profile from the court case, Doherty always held the advantage. Labour had not had an elected public representative in the constituency since the highly respected Seamus Rodgers lost his county council seat in 1999. In the 2009 local elections, Joe Costello came to me with an idea for the Stranorlar electoral area, where Labour had no candidate (or party organisation). Would I consider Frank McBrearty Jr. in the local election?

The Morris Tribunal had found that Frank had been framed for a murder by certain Gardaí in Donegal. The State ended up settling Frank's case and paid him very considerable compensation. The shocking and unfair treatment to which Frank and his family were subjected by some had been taken up some years earlier by Brendan Howlin, then the justice spokesperson for the Labour Party. Brendan ended up being hauled through the courts because he refused to divulge the source of information which, at the time, he gave, in confidence to the then Minister for Justice, John O'Donoghue.

I agreed to have Frank as the Labour Party candidate for Donegal County Council. He was elected, and was therefore the only elected Labour representative in Donegal South-West at the time of the by-election. He quickly asserted his claim to be our candidate. There was considerable resistance to his candidacy, but I stuck by him. He was a colourful and sometimes controversial candidate. I enjoyed his company during the campaign, and I warmed to his family. As expected, though, Doherty easily won for Sinn Féin. Frank polled 8 per cent, far better than Labour had secured in this constituency for a very long time, but it was well below our national poll rating. The result on 26 November punctured a big hole in Labour's claim to become the largest party in the country and to lead the next government.

One of the factors in elections that is rarely captured by the pollsters is the 'retail politics' that take place 'on the ground'. How much direct selling a party can do depends on the size and strength of the local organisations. Even in our stronger constituencies, we found it hard to compete with the Fianna Fáil and Fine Gael machines. They had branches in every parish since the foundation of the State.

For example, even though we won two out of the four seats in Dublin Mid-West, we were stretched organisationally throughout. About a fortnight before polling day, I got an email from a woman in Adamstown, who said she had considered voting Labour but was now reconsidering because 'we have not had a single Labour person canvassing in our area'. I passed on the correspondence to Joanna Tuffy TD who was based in Lucan and Joanna wrote to the woman as follows:

> This campaign is being run in Lucan by me and Labour volunteers who are made up mainly of people from Lucan, including one member from Adamstown, who work during the day in their jobs, and come out at the evening to knock on doors, poster and drop leaflets. It has been a very difficult campaign because we are having to do a lot of this in the pouring rain and strong winds. Twice today I had to come home to change my clothes and shoes and dry my hair. I also have a young child at home to try and look after. My mother babysits for me and my partner while we both go out canvassing or to other activities to do with the campaign. There are 35,000 houses in the constituency, including yours. There are about ten of us out campaigning in Lucan on any one night.

This reply incensed the woman voter. She described it as 'a disgrace' and accused Joanna of 'making excuses'. She wrote: 'I as a voter have absolutely zero interest in the challenges you have personally or otherwise when it comes to getting out and canvassing for votes.' As the great American politician, the late Tip O'Neill, described in his memoir: on election day, his next door neighbour, Mrs O'Brien, whom he had not canvassed, said to him, 'Tom … let me tell you something: people like to be asked.'

Joanna Tuffy is one of Labour's very best public representatives. Indeed, prior to this she had taken some very courageous stands on the planning and development of Adamstown, where the complainant now lived. But it appeared that no matter what the track record, unless the latter was canvassed by the candidate, her vote was probably lost. In the context of our limited resources, I wondered how many other votes were slipping away because we simply didn't have the personnel to call to every door.

Midway through the election campaign, it was clear the contest for the leadership of the new government was effectively over. Fine Gael was now at twice Labour's standing in the polls, and heading for an overall majority. Our own private polling was telling us that the picture was possibly even worse than the published polls suggested. Transposed onto constituencies, it looked like Fine Gael would take most of the marginal seats, and would have a seat bonus over and above their vote share.

In previous general elections Labour's support had also ebbed away during the campaign. In our pre-election planning, we considered that this might happen again. As every election has its own momentum, the direction might need to change mid-way, and that we should, therefore, be prepared to change tack, if necessary, during the campaign. We thought of how in 1997 Fianna Fáil had come from behind in the last week with tax promises, and how in 2007, voters, who at the beginning of the campaign wanted to boot Bertie from office had, however reluctantly, decided to stay with the devil they knew and put Fianna Fáil back into power. We therefore decided to hold back €150,000 of our election budget for a late campaign push or advertising campaign in the final week. The time had now come to use it.

With ten days to go, the question was no longer who would lead the next government, but whether it would be a single party Fine Gael government or a coalition. We needed to re-define the choice facing voters on polling day and to give those who were reluctant a compelling reason to switch to Labour. Fine Gael had hammered us in the media on taxation policy. Labour's argument for a 50/50 split between tax and expenditure cuts in future budgets supplied the evidence that Labour, if not exactly the 'high tax party' that Fine Gael was painting us as, certainly leaned more in the tax direction. Fine Gael, on the other hand, were arguing for a 3:1 ratio between expenditure cuts and tax. (Leo Varadkar at one stage suggested it should be 4:1.) Therefore, there was no public debate about what a single party Fine Gael government might do, and no examination of their preference for expenditure cuts. We decided, therefore, to target Fine Gael's preference for cuts and to change our main campaign pitch summary to 'For a Fair and Balanced Government'.

A game-changing communications intervention at this stage of the campaign would need to be catchy and controversial. Mark Garrett and the team went to work on ideas. I was in the car, being briefed by Karen Griffin between stops, when Mark got back to me with a progress report. The team had an idea for a series of newspaper ads based on the Tesco catchphrase 'Every Little Helps'. It was proposed we would run a campaign based on the phrase 'Every Little Cut Hurts'.

Over the course of the day, the idea was developed further and applied to different formats. I eventually saw the final design proposals on my tablet computer that evening. The concept was good, and I felt the ads would get attention and could help change the outcome of the election. (They were certainly controversial, as evidenced by Tesco objecting strongly to them.) Unfortunately, I paid little attention to the detailed cuts which the ads mentioned and this was a mistake for which I would pay a very high price later. That mistake was then compounded further when those specific cuts were not weeded out in our negotiations on the Programme for Government.

I returned home to my constituency of Dun Laoghaire the day before polling, having travelled the country and given the campaign every ounce of effort and energy. 'I can do no more,' I told myself, and tried to relax. But without success. I found my anxiety suddenly coming to focus on my own seat in Dun Laoghaire. I felt I had spent too little time campaigning for myself locally and had effectively given my running mate, Ivana Bacik, a clear run. In the constituency I hoped that the national and media profile of a leader would compensate for my own absence from the doorsteps. As the broadcast moratorium came down on the evening of Thursday, 24 February, like the 565 other candidates, all I could do was resign my fate to that remarkable democratic phenomenon: the next morning at 7 a.m. the quiet procession of citizens to their polling stations would begin, and, in the privacy of the ballot box, they would make free choices about who would represent them in the next national parliament. Surely there is no greater honour in a democracy than to be selected for that role by our fellow citizens.

As always, I voted at around 10 a.m. in Scoil Mhuire, Rathsallagh. I was met by a bank of cameras and journalists looking for that shot and description of me dropping my voting paper into the ballot box. I returned home and spent the day with my team, planning as best we could for whatever the next days of 'the count' would bring.

4 FORMING A NATIONAL GOVERNMENT

The day of the count is nervous and tense for election candidates. We wait, like a student waiting for exam results, or a litigant counting down the hours while the jury deliberates. The adrenaline has abated after the intensity of a three- or four-week campaign. Now, the truth tumbles unstoppably from the count centre ballot boxes. There is nothing to do but wait.

Between local and general elections, I have been through ten of these mornings. Candidates have different coping mechanisms. Mine is to busy myself with domestic chores: cleaning out my car, tidying the house, visiting the recycling centre with the detritus of the campaign and shopping for the makings of a post-count get-together with my team later that night or in the early hours of the following morning.

Meanwhile, at the count in the Loughlinstown Leisure Centre, party activists are leaning over the barriers to record the destination of each vote as it is opened by the counter. This tally of votes will continue until a fairly accurate estimate is made of the total first preference votes for each candidate. Long before that insight, candidates are desperate to know how they are doing and it can be difficult to tell since the particular order in which ballot boxes are opened may well differ between strong and weak areas for a candidate. That is why it is essential to have experienced tally-masters at the count centre who can quickly analyse the piles and predict the results, from early indications.

Over the years, this role was fulfilled in our team by my wife, Carol Hanney, who had managed my election campaigns in the early part of my career. By 9.45 am or 10 am at the latest, she could predict whether I was safe or struggling, and make quite an accurate prediction of the election outcome in the constituency.

The count of Saturday 26 February 2011 started like none I had ever previously experienced. Our tally master on the day, Frank O'Connor, rang me at around 10 a.m. with the good news that I was likely to top the poll (which would have been a first for me in a general election). It was unclear whether or not Ivana Bacik would take a second seat.

Earlier that morning, RTÉ had broadcast the results of an exit poll which put Fine Gael on 36.1 per cent, Labour on 20.5 per cent, Fianna Fáil on 15.1 per cent, Sinn Féin on 10.1 per cent, Independents on 15.5 per cent and Greens on 2.5 per cent. As expected, the political map was being redrawn. If confirmed in the real count, I would be leading Labour to its best ever general election result, with twice the share of the vote we had received at each of the three previous general elections. Labour, for the first time ever, would be the second largest party in the State.

Barry Desmond rang me early that morning to congratulate me on both my own re-election and on the Party's performance. Barry had been the Labour TD for Dun Laoghaire from 1969 until his election to the European Parliament in 1989. Although we had been constituency rivals for a time, Barry and his wife Stella became fond friends and strong supporters of mine in the constituency. I was always glad of his experience and wise counsel, and that morning I especially welcomed his warm call.

But the overall result was still uncertain. If the Fine Gael tally was understated, they could yet form a single-party government or pick up enough support from Fine Gael-leaning Independents to form a minority government. We would not know that for definite until the final votes had been counted, well into Sunday. In the end, Fine Gael got seventy-six seats, just seven short of an overall majority of 83. Fianna Fáil with twenty seats were down to a quarter of their normal size. The Greens were wiped out. Sinn Féin had made a significant breakthrough with fourteen seats and there were nineteen Independents, including the ultra-left parties. Labour won thirty-seven seats with almost 432,000 (19.4 per cent) first preference votes. I had just led Labour to its greatest ever electoral success.

At home I watched the count on television with my principal advisors and my family as the final picture emerged. My happiest moment was the election of Colm Keaveney as the first ever Labour TD in my homeland of East Galway. Some results were stunningly good, like winning two seats in several Dublin constituencies. Others vindicated our candidate selection strategy; for instance, Waterford, Carlow-Kilkenny, Louth and East Galway showed that adding a second candidate had clearly given the geographic balance required to produce a seat.

There were, of course, some disappointments. I was disappointed that Ivana Bacik did not come through to take a second seat for us in Dun Laoghaire, and partly blamed myself for how little time I got to spend campaigning there. In Sligo-South Leitrim there were four unsuccessful candidates who had previously contested elections for Labour. The divided vote gave Sinn Féin the opportunity to take a seat. In Laois-Offaly we had lost members when we imposed John Whelan as the candidate, and Sinn Féin overtook him in this winnable five seater. And in South Tipperary, Senator Phil Prendergast finished sixth in a field of eight, with just 10 per cent of the vote.

I spent most of my waking hours that weekend on the phone congratulating successful Labour TDs, thanking and commiserating with those who had lost out, and hearing the thoughts and opinions of colleagues on what lay ahead: the formation of a new government.

Fine Gael had not won their overall majority. In the next Dail, there would be 90 TDs to their 76. A non-Fine Gael government was numerically feasible, and now, as Leader of the second largest party, I had to give some consideration to that possibility. But I didn't think about it for long! It would have had to include Fianna Fáil (which had just been emphatically rejected by the electorate), Sinn Féin (which was unacceptable) and a mixture of Independents, many of whose national politics were either a mystery, or in marked contradiction to each other. And the country was in crisis, and needed a stable government, and fast!

I should have been ecstatic about Labour's historic win, but as the hours wore on, the awesome responsibility dawned on me and dampened my spirits. I felt almost detached from the celebrations all around me, as I thought of the huge task facing the new Government, to rescue the country from near bankruptcy, to restore our economic sovereignty and to take the difficult decisions which would be necessary to make that happen.

Normally, the Dáil does not reconvene for two or three weeks after the completion of a count, but because of the economic urgency on this occasion, there were just nine days left until the thirty-first Dáil was due to meet on 9 March. Previously, if political parties had not agreed a coalition and a Programme for

Government by the time the Dáil reconvened, the Dáil adjourned while negotiations continued and the outcome was then put to the Dáil for approval. In 1992/93, when Dick Spring entered coalition with Fianna Fáil under Albert Reynolds, the entire process took six weeks. More recently, in Germany, Angela Merkel took two months to negotiate her party's coalition with Sigmar Gabriel's Social Democratic Party (SPD).

In these situations, the outgoing government usually remains in office on a 'caretaker' basis, but in the 2011 election in Ireland, there was no outgoing government to act in such a capacity. The outgoing Taoiseach had not stood for re-election; only two ministers from the outgoing Cabinet (Brian Lenihan and Éamon Ó Cúiv) had been re-elected to the Dáil. The country found itself in unchartered territory and in something of a constitutional vacuum. Not just that, but the State was running out of cash; deposits were flowing out of the banks; investment was drying up; and a series of critical European Council meetings were imminent. The ship of State was truly floundering in a storm with no captain or crew. Going beyond 9 March was to risk running aground, and was not an option. A government had to be agreed within days. There were only two realistic options. A Fine Gael/Labour coalition or a minority Fine Gael government. And Fine Gael would have to make the call.

But my phone didn't ring! All through Sunday, the media wondered if Eamon had received the call from Enda yet. No, was the answer. Meanwhile, to our annoyance, Fine Gael appeared to be spinning a story that Eamon wasn't returning Enda's call. They claimed that Enda was in fact ringing, but on my old number. In the run up to the election I had got a second mobile phone, and Enda didn't have the number. But this was a lame excuse. My home number was in the telephone directory. Finally, through our respective chief advisors, arrangements were made for us to meet on Tuesday morning in Leinster House.

Before I could meet him or negotiate at all, I had to obtain the approval of the Labour Party's Central Council, and that was not foregone. Labour has good reason to be wary of coalition. All its experiences up to that point suggested that participation in government inevitably results in a significant loss of votes and seats at the subsequent election. During Dick Spring's tenure as Leader, new rules were put in place, which required the Party Leader to obtain the approval of the Party's national governing body before even entering into coalition negotiation, and then to put the outcome of the negotiations to a Special Delegate Conference.

The meeting of the Central Council was called for Monday evening in the Radisson Blu Hotel on Golden Lane. Gathered together were representatives of the Labour Party members in each Dáil constituency; the representatives of the various sections of the Party – Labour Women, Labour Equality, Labour Trade Unionists, Labour Councillors, Labour Youth and Labour LGBT, the Party officers and the members of the Executive Board who had been elected by the Party Conference, representatives of the Party staff and the Party leadership; in all about sixty people.

An outsider might have been surprised that this was the first meeting of a party after it had just produced its best ever election result. There were, of course, words of congratulations and acknowledgements of our historic achievement, but there was little joy and no show of celebration. The faces were serious, the mood was sombre, and discussions were focussed on the important matters that lay before us. We all knew we were facing, in the short term, a difficult week of negotiations with Fine Gael to form a government, in the medium term (assuming the negotiations were successful), the toughest times of our political careers to date as we attempted to get the crisis under control, and, in the longer term, the most challenging five years imaginable in government as we attempted to get the country back on its feet.

There was an easier option. We could simply say to ourselves that Fine Gael had won the election (though they had not secured an overall majority); Labour had not succeeded in its attempt to lead the next government, so we should take up our role across the floor as the main party of opposition. On several long walks before the meeting, I had thought seriously about taking that course. It could actually be the safest and best course for the Labour Party. We would probably be swept into power at the next election if Fine Gael performed badly. But where would it leave the country, which was in such desperate need of a stable government, in the meantime? And how would Fine Gael manage the crisis on their own? Their manifesto called for expenditure cuts far in excess of those eventually implemented. They would have privatised more and would, I believe, have badly damaged the public service. Would a minority Fine Gael Government be stable? The people who voted Labour on 25 February had done so, I believed, for us to get stuck into finding solutions to the problems, not to dodge the responsibility. The country needed Labour in Government now, not in the relative comfort of opposition. I presented my report on the election, my analysis of the political situation and my recommendation that the Central Council should authorise me to commence negotiation with Fine Gael on the formation of a new government. The vast majority of my colleagues felt the same and so negotiating was given the green light.

The first meeting with Enda Kenny took place on Tuesday morning at 11 a.m. in Government Buildings. Mark Garrett walked to the meeting with me and waited outside with Mark Mortell of Fine Gael, while Enda and I sat at corners of the table inside to begin our discussions. The meeting did not go well.

At Christmas, a couple of months previously, Brendan Halligan, who had been General Secretary of the Labour Party under Brendan Corish at the time of the 1973-77 Fine Gael/Labour coalition, had called to my office. He handed me Stephen Collins' excellent book, *The Cosgrave Legacy*, recommending that I read the book over the break, as he believed that Kenny was an admirer of Cosgrave and would be aware of how Cosgrave had negotiated with Corish in 1973. After that election, Halligan and Corish prepared thoroughly for detailed negotiations. Corish set off for his first meeting with Cosgrave and, to Halligan's alarm, was back after a mere half-hour. Halligan assumed that the discussions had collapsed, but Corish replied to the contrary: getting right down to business, Cosgrave had simply offered Labour five Cabinet posts, and added 'and you can be Minister for Finance'. Corish declined Finance but accepted the five Cabinet posts, which were proportionally greater than Labour's nineteen seats would have merited. Halligan believed that Kenny would approach coalition talks with a similar sense of generosity. I had my doubts.

Enda and I had been TDs together for twenty-two years. We knew each other well and had always been on friendly terms, often exchanging banter when our paths crossed on Leinster Lawn or in the corridors and lobbies of Leinster House. But, crucially, we had never actually worked together. We had never served on the same committees, never been spokespersons of the same portfolios, and never travelled together on delegations. We had, therefore, never developed the kind of rapport that we each enjoyed with other colleagues with whom we had worked on a cross-party basis. As opposition leaders, we often competed with each other, and our level of co-operation and contact was minimal. I was partly to blame for this, as Kenny had made some attempts to discuss co-operation, which I had rebuffed as I sought to assert Labour's separate identity.

The very first political dealing we had, after I became Labour Leader in September 2007, did not bode well. New Dáil committees were being formed. As seat proportionality does not always divide neatly into the number of committee places, a little co-operation, flexibility and sometimes ingenuity is required by the parties and political groupings to ensure that every group and TD is reasonably satisfied with their committee allocation.

On this occasion, a problem arose over the composition of the Justice Committee. For some reason, there was no automatic place for the new Labour Justice spokesperson, Pat Rabbitte. The obvious solution was for Fine Gael to surrender one of its two places and for Labour to surrender a place to Fine Gael on some other body. Our Whip, Emmet Stagg, came to me to report that Fine Gael would not agree to the swap and that I needed to speak directly to Enda Kenny. I thought it would be a relatively straight-forward matter, as these kinds of practical arrangements are made all the time. I rang and was surprised to discover he wouldn't agree. I was quite taken aback at his inflexibility. I pointed out that the position was for my predecessor as Labour Leader, who of course had worked closely with Enda, and who had, despite considerable resistance within the Labour Party, agreed the pre-election Mullingar accord with Fine Gael. Kenny still would not budge. The following morning, as the Dáil was assembling, I spoke with the Fianna Fáil Chief Whip, Tom Kitt, told him my problem and suggested that the Government increase the size of the committee to facilitate Pat. He replied simply: 'I will speak to the Boss about it'. I saw him walk around the lobby of the chamber and down the steps until he sat beside Taoiseach Bertie Ahern. I watched as Bertie held his head sideways to Tom, like a priest in confession, and after a while he looked out from under his brow until he found me and caught my eye and nodded his assent. For Ahern, no big deal about a relatively small housekeeping matter.

In August 2008, Enda and I were both in Denver, Colorado to attend the US Democratic Party Convention, which nominated Barack Obama for President. Staying at the same hotel, we inevitably fell into conversation about Irish politics. One morning, over breakfast, we talked about the prospects for forming a government after the next election. My predecessor, as Leader of the Labour Party, Pat Rabbitte, had negotiated a formal pre-election agreement with Fine Gael, known as 'The Mullingar Accord', and I was anxious to avoid any such arrangement. So I told Enda, that while I was open to a Fine Gael/Labour coalition after the election, there would be no pre-election pact, that Labour would campaign on its own policies and that he should understand that this might often put Labour and Fine Gael at odds in opposition. In any event, the next election was probably four years away, and who could now predict the circumstances in which it might be held.

Enda and I did not ever again discuss the prospect of governing together, until that Tuesday morning when we met in Leinster House, after the 2011 Election was over, and in a climate of crisis, we were now obliged to put together a national government.

While among the public, in the media and within the two parties, it seemed to be practically taken for granted that a Fine Gael/Labour coalition would be formed on 9 March, these episodes stuck in my mind as I prepared to meet Enda. I did not expect any great generosity, and I expected the negotiations to be tough. He was, though, full of bonhomie at the start, as we exchanged congratulations and shared a few anecdotes from the campaign. Getting down to business, he proposed, as expected, that Fine Gael and Labour form a coalition government, and that we should form negotiating teams of three members each to prepare an agreed Programme for Government. I responded that before negotiations could commence on such a programme, he and I would need to have a clear understanding about the make-up of this Government and how it would operate. I was careful to point out that this would be the first time a coalition would be made up of the two largest parties in the Dáil – something of a national government– and that, therefore, key decisions would have to be made on a joint basis and the composition of the Government would have to reflect that. I proposed that Labour should have six Cabinet seats and hold the Ministry for Finance. Kenny instantly rejected this, pointing out that Fine Gael had twice the number of seats that Labour had, and that, therefore, in Cabinet, there should be ten Fine Gael Ministers and five for Labour, and that Fine Gael would insist on holding Finance.

I pointed out that, in previous governments, particularly the last one, the nucleus of power was between the Taoiseach and Finance Minister, and that Labour couldn't possibly accept a coalition arrangement in which the key decision making was centred on two Fine Gael figures. If we could not agree to a model of shared decision making between the two parties, I concluded, then I could not recommend the Government to my Party, and therefore there was no point in establishing negotiating teams. Unless there was going to be shared decision-making, especially on the economy, I was not going to agree.

Throughout the rest of the day, there was continuous contact at different levels between Fine Gael and Labour. Mark Garrett and Mark Mortell, in particular, worked hard to find a way forward. With my knowledge and approval, they worked on a new proposal, which Kenny confirmed when I met him again the following morning. The Department of Finance could be split to create two

Finance departments, one each for Fine Gael and Labour, and considering the seriousness of the crisis, a top-level economic committee should be formed to make the key economic decisions. While commenting on the proposal, Enda spoke a lot about joint decision making, about the two parties working as a team, and about the importance of he and I working closely together considering the enormity of the challenge we were facing. I felt that there was in all this a basis on which we could work, and I therefore agreed to the commencement of talks between the negotiating teams. I felt the economic committee idea could be developed into something more substantial, new and relevant for these crisis times.

The negotiations on the Programme for Government began on Wednesday. Enda nominated Michael Noonan, Phil Hogan and Alan Shatter for the negotiating team. I nominated Joan Burton and Pat Rabbitte, with Brendan Howlin to lead the negotiations for Labour, on the basis that he had chaired Labour's policy committee in the lead up to the election and was therefore the most familiar with the full range of our policies. He also had previous experience of negotiating a Programme for Government. They were joined on the negotiation team by Colm O'Reardon, with Jean O'Mahony providing policy support. We had compiled, prior to the election, a policy comparison manual, listing each Labour and Fine Gael policy and comparing their detail and emphasis. This document would guide our negotiators in their work.

While they worked on the policy programme for the new Government, Enda and I met several times over the two days, to plan its composition, structure and modus operandi. There would be a Department of Finance and a Department of Public Expenditure and Reform. The latter would have responsibility for the estimates process and for the public service. I was wary of Fine Gael's attitude to the public service, and considering Labour's tradition of commitment to the delivery of good public services and respect for those who work in the service, as they were proposing to achieve three-quarters of the budgetary adjustment by expenditure cuts, it seemed to me critical that Labour would hold the expenditure portfolio. At this time of crisis, the best way to protect public services, in my mind, was to have a Labour minister in charge of the public service.

Most significantly, considering the nature of the challenges the coalition would face, we refined and clarified the idea of an economic committee at the centre of government. This committee developed into the Economic Management Council (EMC), which would act as a kind of war cabinet for the economic crisis. It would be chaired by the Taoiseach, while the Tánaiste would be responsible for its management and for its agenda. A new Secretary General, reporting to the Tánaiste, would be appointed to oversee this work. I later nominated Geraldine Byrne Nason (now Ireland's Ambassador to France) for the role. In addition to the Taoiseach and the Tánaiste, the Ministers for Finance and for Public Expenditure would be its other two minister members. Its meetings were to include the secretaries general of the Departments of Finance, Public Expenditure and Reform, Taoiseach, Foreign Affairs and Trade, as well as the economic advisors to the four ministers and key officials from government departments and State agencies as the occasion required.

This new structure at the heart of government would consider the key economic decisions on banking, budgets, economic strategy, and relations with the Troika and with the European Union. It could meet sometimes in political format (ministers only or ministers plus advisors) or more usually in full format in the presence of the secretaries general and officials. It would, of course, report to the Cabinet where government decisions were made.

The establishment of the EMC, ensuring that both parties in government shared equally in the key economic and strategic decisions, was key to the formation of the new Government. It provided a political space where differences over budgets or economic strategy could be ironed out, and it provided the centre point in government for the weaving together of all sections of government required to secure economic recovery.

Furthermore, while Labour was outnumbered around the Cabinet table, at the EMC we were on equal terms. This would turn out to be critical in later battles over budgets, banks and economic policy. There were many issues, including the ratio between expenditure cuts and new tax measures, that were not finally settled in the Programme for Government, and which had to be worked out in practice through the EMC. The establishment of the EMC ensured that all the key economic decisions in government would be made jointly by Labour and Fine Gael.

Meanwhile, there were significant differences in policy being teased out in the broader negotiations. Every party in the election, even Sinn Féin, was agreed that the budget deficit had to be reduced to under 3 per cent of GDP. The differences emerged in relation to when and how that was to be achieved. Fine Gael wanted it under 3 per cent by 2014; Labour by 2016. The compromise was 2015. Fine Gael wanted 75 per cent of the budget adjustment to be achieved by spending cuts on public services and just 25 per cent by taxation. Labour wanted a 50/50 split. The Programme for Government did not resolve this, though it was generally understood that the compromise was to be around 2:1.

There were also differences over Fine Gael's intentions for compulsory redundancies in the public sector; over dealing with the Croke Park Agreement which the previous Government had negotiated with the public service trade unions; over the sale of

State assets; over the extent to which the bailout programme could be renegotiated; and over a range of other policy areas such as the Irish language, European defence, abortion and same-sex marriage. The negotiating teams exchanged drafts on all the main areas of policy and worked through them each day, reporting respectively to Enda and me each evening.

I recall the Labour team being shocked at the joint briefing which the negotiators from the two parties received from the Department of Finance. We would be facing into government in circumstances where the State was rapidly running out of money.

The Department of Foreign Affairs and Trade advised us that the perception of Ireland within the EU 'was not as good as in the past', and that at the two European Council meetings coming up, on 11 March and on 24/25 March, Chancellor Merkel and President Sarkozy were likely to advance a Franco-German Competitiveness Pact. This, we knew, could have serious adverse implications for Ireland. In preparation for those meetings, the European People's Party (EPP), to which Fine Gael is affiliated, and the Party of the European Socialists (PES), to which Labour belongs, were having leaders' meetings in Helsinki and Athens later in the week. Enda Kenny and I recognised the degree to which Ireland's international reputation had been damaged and that no time could be lost in seeking to regain it. We needed to rebuild trust and confidence among other European governments. We agreed that even though it would take both of us away from the Government negotiations for most of Friday and Saturday, we should both attend these meetings and bring a positive message to European Prime Ministers, Foreign Ministers and Party Leaders about the results of the Irish elections, our intention to form a new government, and of our determination to get out of the crisis. We were both well briefed by the Departments of Foreign Affairs, Taoiseach and

Finance before setting off.

In Athens, I had a private meeting with George Papandreou, the PASOK leader, who was then Prime Minister of Greece. He was trying to work Greece out of its crisis, and I believe that if he had been properly supported then by European leaders, Greece would have recovered like Ireland, and the Greek people would have been spared the hardship which they are now enduring.

I got back from Athens on Saturday afternoon and went directly to Government Buildings. It was as if the previous regime had fled. Enda was already ensconced in the Taoiseach's office at the end of the corridor on the first floor. The negotiating teams were hard at work in the Sycamore Room. My team had set up base in the Rooms 301 and 308 upstairs. The Labour Party had convened a Special Delegate Conference for the following day, Sunday, in the O'Reilly Hall on the UCD Campus, and Fine Gael had arranged a similar meeting. Both meetings would have to approve the Programme for Government, and again, this could not be taken for granted.

We were all, therefore, working against the clock. The final compromise on some texts had to be agreed between Enda and me, and we had to settle on the composition of the Cabinet and on the distribution of portfolios between the parties. To resolve the issue over Cabinet numbers, Enda proposed that Labour would get a 'super junior'. This was a status initially created when the Fine Gael/Labour/Democratic Left Government was formed in December 1994, whereby a Minister of State would be allocated a particularly substantial and important portfolio and would attend Cabinet meetings with all the supports to which a Cabinet member is normally entitled. I had expected this offer, and therefore had in mind a portfolio for this office: housing and planning. Previously held by Progressive Democrat Bobby Molloy, I saw it as a role that was now critically important in addressing some of the fall-out from the property bubble: the unfinished housing projects or 'ghost estates', for instance, and the risks to family homes from a new banking regime. I felt a Labour minister could have a very positive impact in this role.

I was not, however, satisfied with that alone, and held out for a sixth Cabinet post. Enda and I were deadlocked on it. Pat Rabbitte and Phil Hogan came up with a solution. Labour would nominate the Attorney General. Now we had to conclude on some difficult policy differences, but eventually in the early hours of Sunday morning, Enda and I shook hands on an agreement to govern together.

I was satisfied with the outcome. There would be eighteen people around the Cabinet table. Eleven (including the Government Whip) would be appointed by Fine Gael, and seven including the AG, by Labour. Six of the fifteen Ministers of State would be Labour nominees. Cabinet decisions would be made by general agreement, rather than by vote. The key economic decisions would be agreed at the EMC at which the two parties had equal representation. Issues going to Cabinet would be scrutinised by advisors from each of the two parties, with our respective Chief Advisors working to resolve differences. Anything that could not be agreed would be referred to the Taoiseach and Tánaiste for resolution. The Programme for Government represented compromises in the positions of both parties, but within a short week, we had put together a solid basis on which we felt we could face the enormous challenge of governing in a crisis.

We walked down the corridor to the Sycamore Room together and thanked the exhausted negotiating teams and staff. At 4 a.m. on Sunday morning I headed home to get a few hours sleep before putting the package to my Party the next day. I was awake by eight.

1. The Parliamentary Labour Party after the 2011 General Election - the largest in the history of the Party. (Credit: The Labour Party)

2. About to start a meeting of the North South Ministerial Council in Armagh.

3. Examining old maps of Belfast with Peter Robinson and Martin McGuinness. (Credit: Fennell Photography)

4. In Tanzania, with Hillary Clinton, working on a Joint US-Ireland Hunger Initiative.

5. To mark the 50th Anniversary of John F Kennedy's visit to Ireland in 1963, we recreated the State welcome at Iveagh House. We invited Caroline Kennedy Schlossberg (now US Ambassador to Japan) and former US Ambassador to Ireland, Jean Kennedy Smith.

6. Welcoming Russia's legendary Foreign Minister, Sergei Lavrov.

7. Chairing the OSCE Ministerial Council at the RDS.

8. Meeting with Aung San Suu Kyi. (Credit: Fennell Photography)

9. Co-chairing a UN session with the Prime Minister of Bangladesh Sheikh Hasina.

10. Campaigning in Dublin South Central with Mary Upton and Rebecca Moynihan. (Credit: The Labour Party)

11. Canvassing with Senator Ivana Bacik. (Credit: The Labour Party)

12. With Joan Burton and Proinsias de Rossa at a campaign event outside the headquarters of Anglo Irish Bank. (Credit:The Labour Party)

13. Campaigning. (Credit: The Labour Party)

14. Happens on every campaign! (Credit:The Labour Party)

15. The late Páidí O Sé welcomed me to his pub in West Kerry and presented me with the jersey of An Ghaeltacht. But he was not too happy when I announced that I come from Caltra who had defeated An Ghaeltacht in the All Ireland Final! (Credit: The Labour Party)

16. Tom Cruise was enthusiastic about his Irish heritage. (Courtesy of Photocall Ireland)

17. Brendan Howlin pinning the Rose. (Credit: The Labour Party)

18. Checking the text with Cllr. Aoife Breslin.
(Credit: The Labour Party)

19. Kevin Eager provided transport services to the Labour Party! (Credit: The Labour Party)

20. Addressing the General Assembly of the UN in New York.

21. With Secretary General Ban Ki Moon, his special envoy Mary Robinson, and the Irish team at the UN.

22. With Jack O'Connor and members of the Connolly family at the annual James Connolly Commemoration at Arbour Hill. (Credit: The Labour Party)

23. In Somalia visiting a refugee camp with the United Nations.

24. At the Parliamentary Party with Chairperson Jack Wall TD. (Credit: The Labour Party)

25. With the Labour councillors in Dun Laoghaire County Hall (Credit: The Labour Party)

My first meeting at the O'Reilly Hall would be with the parliamentary party.

Only fifteen of our thirty-seven TDs had ever experienced being on the government side of the House, and that was fourteen years previously, in entirely different circumstances. The majority had either served only in opposition or had just been elected to the Dáil for the first time a mere week ago and were still adjusting to their new roles as TDs. Now, all of a sudden, they were faced with the prospect of their party entering government and taking responsibility for the country in a time of crisis, retrenchment and hardship. I presented the proposals for the new Government, and Brendan Howlin went through the details of the programme. I watched their reactions as they took in the implications of the compromises that had to be made on our election manifesto. A few raised objections. Some were irritated that they had little time to study the text of the programme (it had to be printed in the early hours of the morning), but there was overwhelming support for entering government.

As delegates from Party branches from all over the country began to assemble in the sun outside the O'Reilly Hall, I sensed that the mood was upbeat and certainly more positive than it had been at any time since the election itself. As our General Secretary, Ita McAuliffe, called out the names and introduced each of our thirty-seven TDs, the delegates responded with emotional cheering. The Party Chairperson, a former TD for Waterford, Brian O'Shea, called on me to propose the motion: 'That this Conference approves the recommendation of the Party Leader, for the Party to enter into government with Fine Gael, for the purposes of implementing the terms of the circulated draft Programme for Government.' I had not had time to prepare a script, but according to my notes, after congratulating the TDs elected and thanking the candidates who stood unsuccessfully, the Party staff for their work, and Party members for the campaign, this is roughly what I said:

> This is no ordinary time. This is no ordinary conference. The decision which we will make here today will be truly historic and will make so much difference for the people who voted for change on last Friday week. Our country's economy has been broken by Fianna Fáil, but it's not beyond repair. The morale of our people has been shattered but hope and confidence can be restored again. Confidence in our political and public institutions has been diminished, but these institutions and bodies can be reformed again. On Wednesday next, this country will get a new government for the next five years. Today, we decide whether or not Labour will take part in the government, and it is a decision which does make a difference.
>
> This is no ordinary time, because last Friday week, the Irish people blew away the parties that made up the last Government, which led our country into economic crisis, and which mismanaged it. This is no ordinary time, because the people gave Labour its biggest ever vote, gave Labour our largest ever number of Dáil seats, and made us the second largest party for the first time ever. Those who gave us that mandate did so because they want Labour to be a part of the solution. They want Labour's policies implemented in a new government and they want Labour to work for fairness and balance in that new government.

It was an outstanding election result and yet there is no euphoria or triumphalism, because we know only too well the size of the challenge which confronts us. The constitution of the Labour Party is very clear on what happens after an election. Last Monday night, the Central Council, representing every constituency and section, gave me a mandate to open negotiations with Fine Gael on the possible formation of a new government. Our negotiators, Brendan Howlin, Joan Burton and Pat Rabbitte, supported by a team of staff led by Colm O'Reardon, worked through the weekend and concluded at about 4 a.m. this morning. At times it was difficult, and at times it appeared that the negotiations might not succeed. But they produced the draft Programme for Government which is before you and we have agreed on a new structure for government and on the way decisions are made, which reflects the unique nature of the proposed National Government.

The Programme for Government is not the Labour manifesto – but much of the Labour manifesto is in it, and in every section it is driven or moderated, depending on how you look at it, by Labour thinking. But it is not the Fine Gael manifesto either, and when it comes down to it, the decision we have to make now is whether the next Government follows this blueprint or it follows the Fine Gael manifesto on its own.

I went on to deal with the details of policy and with the new structure for government and concluded by recommending the

Party's participation in government.

> I understand the challenge and I understand the risks. I understand the worry of many delegates here today, about how Labour will emerge from this Government, in light of historic experience.
>
> This is no ordinary time. We have never been here before. But what we do know is that Labour's strength has been built on taking challenges, not by avoiding them. Many still question why Labour stood aside at the historic moment in 1918. We do not want future generations to wonder why Labour stood aside in 2011 when the country faced its deepest economic crisis. We must take courage from our history. Labour modernised this society in the face of bitter opposition, some of which is in evidence again. Labour and its allies stood for peace on our island, and a resolution based on mutual respect, when others were waving their tribal flags. It was Labour which laid down the social floor, on housing, on welfare and on rights for working people. None of that was easy. It never is. So let us now face our country's greatest economic challenge. Let us take courage here today, and prepare to lead our country out of crisis and recession.

The debate lasted for two hours. Of the parliamentary party, only Deputies Tommy Broughan and Joanna Tuffy spoke against the motion. Jack O'Connor of SIPTU questioned some of the detail of the Programme for Government but supported the proposal to enter government. The main argument against entering government was that if Labour went into opposition, we would sweep to power in 2016. My response was to question where the country would be by 2016. Were we to sacrifice our country so that the Party could benefit? I argued that those who had lost work, businesses and hope, and those who were in danger of losing their homes, deserved better. They could not afford to wait until 2016. They needed the crisis solved now. I warned the Conference that this would not be easy or popular, and that, at our next conference, we might have to 'wade through a forest of placards'.

In the end, the Conference overwhelmingly approved the motion and I left the O'Reilly Hall and travelled to Herbert Park for a photo call with Enda Kenny, who had also successfully put the proposals to his parliamentary party. On Wednesday, the Dáil would be asked to approve the coalition agreement and to elect a new government with Enda Kenny as Taoiseach and me as Tánaiste.

5 THE LONELIEST DAY

Early on Sunday morning I called Máire Whelan SC and asked her if she would consider being the next Attorney General (AG). During a break in the conference proceedings at the O'Reilly Hall, she confirmed to me her willingness to serve. The appointment would not be announced until Wednesday, but speculation was already alive in the press as to whom Labour would nominate as the new AG. A number of names were mentioned, including Máire's. As attention began to settle on her, something of a campaign against her appointment was begun by a small number of senior legal figures. They lobbied colleagues, some on behalf of other possible contenders, but also just to block the appointment of Máire. There was a strong whiff of misogyny in some of the comments.

This campaign also targeted Fine Gael, and on Tuesday Enda raised the issue with me. I confirmed to him that my nominee was Máire. He didn't know her, but he expressed strong doubts about her appointment.

'She is an officer of the Labour Party!' he exclaimed. 'You cannot seriously appoint a political figure to such an important and sensitive position in government.'

I pointed out to him that Fine Gael had previously appointed serving TDs (Declan Costello and John Kelly) to the position, and that they were hardly apolitical. Through Tuesday, as we met to tidy up the issues before the re-convening of the Dáil the following day, we spoke several times about the AG appointment. Late on Tuesday night, we met in Enda's office on the fourth floor of LH2000. He paced the floor as he struggled with my refusal to consider a different appointment. Eventually, I said to him:

'Enda, we are about to start governing in very difficult circumstances. We will have to learn to trust each other. I know how important the AG's role is, and that the AG reports through the Taoiseach. I am not going to begin this Government by making a bad appointment. I believe that Máire Whelan will make an excellent AG and that it won't be long before you see this for yourself. You will just have to trust my judgement on this.'

He paused, and then held out his hand. We shook on it. It was the beginning of a new working relationship between the two of us.

Several times over our years in government together, he remarked that Máire Whelan was indeed an outstanding choice for AG, and she continued to impress all the members of Cabinet with her good advice and extraordinary appetite for the work.

With the Programme for Government agreed, all eyes now turned to the appointment of ministers. Labour's thirty-seven TDs represented a talented pool. Many of them, I knew, would make good ministers. A couple of the newly elected ones expressed an interest, but as would be expected, most attention was focused on the twenty-three who had previous experience as TDs or senators. Some mentioned their interests directly to me: Róisín Shortall as we met briefly in the RTÉ entrance lobby on the Sunday after the count; later in the week Ruairí Quinn made a passing remark about his passion for education reform; and Joan Burton told me she would be interested in the foreign affairs portfolio. Others made their wishes known through intermediaries or through formal letters from constituency organisations. In all, there were eleven ministerial posts to be filled: six at Cabinet level, including one of the ministers of state, and five other ministers of state. It was generally assumed that the three negotiators of the Programme for Government (Brendan Howlin, Joan Burton and Pat Rabbitte) would be appointed to office and probably to Cabinet. The competition for the remaining positions was intense.

Picking the team was something I had to do by myself. For obvious reasons, I could not share my thinking with colleagues who were hopeful candidates for appointment. And my staff felt that it was not their place to offer me advice on the relative merits of my own elected colleagues. In any event, I did not ask them.

For myself, I initially considered not taking a ministerial role at all, as I knew it would result in my having four jobs: as a TD for my constituency of Dun Laoghaire, as Leader of the Labour Party, as a minister responsible for a government department, and as Tánaiste in a coalition with huge cross-party responsibilities. In Northern Ireland, where admittedly government is structured differently, three of the main party leaders are not ministers. In some other countries, party leaders nominate ministers and continue to lead their parties from outside government– the Dutch Labour Party, for example. Coalition has always been electorally challenging for Labour, and I wondered if, instead of taking office, the Party Leader left government work to others and concentrated on leading and building the Party, the result might be different.

I foresaw problems with this, though. The first was that I would be out of the government loop. I would not have access to Cabinet papers or Cabinet committees and would therefore be unable to directly influence what was happening in government. Meanwhile, as Leader I would have to continue to defend the actions and decisions of ministers while being open to the charge that I had personally dodged the draft! I didn't believe this was a realistic option. I knew, though, from my experience of government in the 1990s, just how time consuming departmental and ministerial responsibilities can be: the deputations which have to be met, the files which have to be studied, the decisions which have to be thoroughly considered; so I explored the possibility of being Tánaiste without departmental portfolio. This did not seem to be constitutionally possible, and would probably have resulted in one less department for the Labour Party.

Dick Spring and his former programme manager, Greg Sparks, had both impressed on me the enormous workload there is on a Tánaiste leading a party in coalition. Every item of government business goes across the Tánaiste's desk. In effect, the Tánaiste has to do almost everything the Taoiseach does but without the infrastructure of the dedicated Taoiseach's Department. My decision was to select a department that would be compatible with the role of Tánaiste by having a whole-of-government remit. Foreign Affairs and Trade was the obvious and, in fact, the only one that fitted the bill, and at this time, I felt it was particularly relevant.

One of the new Government's principal challenges would be to restore Ireland's international reputation, work which would have to be led by the Department of Foreign Affairs and Trade. I felt there would be a significant international dimension to the recovery project, involving negotiations with international institutions and the re-building of relationships in the European Union and with individual states. Ireland would also hold the EU Presidency early in the life of this Government.

Once it was agreed that the role would have responsibility for the coordination of the Government's overall trade strategy, my decision to take Foreign Affairs and Trade was confirmed late on the Saturday night before the conclusion of negotiations on the Programme for Government.

There were other difficult decisions for me to make and the pressure was increased by the sense of expectation in the air around Leinster House. Ita McAuliffe, whom I had appointed General Secretary of the Party in 2008, gave me a useful piece of personal advice just before the general election: 'The loneliest day of your life and your most difficult day in politics will be the day the new Government is formed,' she said, speaking from experience. She had worked for the Party since Brendan Corish's time and she had been witness to the formation of many governments. She told me my colleagues would turn up that morning anxiously hoping for the call; that they would study me for any hint or signal at the prayer service before the Dáil session and at the opening session itself; and then they would wait for their phones to ring. Those disappointed at first would lower their sights and wait hopefully again for the announcement of the ministers of state the following morning. 'After that, these corridors become a sea of disappointment. You will never again have the same good relationship with your fellow TDs', she warned me.

The tension was intensified by an unexpected delay. After the vote in the Dáil, on the nomination of Taoiseach, Enda left for Áras an Uachtaráin to be appointed by President Mary McAleese and to receive his seal of office. I adjourned to a room in the adjacent Government Buildings to await his return. We had earlier agreed that to avoid any leaking of information about portfolios, we would inform new ministers of their appointments simultaneously. Though I would, over subsequent months and years, come to accept that punctuality was not the Taoiseach's strongest quality, I wasn't used to it then and felt intensely every minute of the hour delay caused by his extra time at the Áras that day.

As I waited in the Taoiseach's dining room, a small square room with a hexagonal table in the centre, just off the main corridor on the first floor of Government Buildings, I went back over the team I had chosen. Given the plight of the country, I had decided to go for experience. Ruairí Quinn had been Ireland's best ever Minister for Finance when he served in the Rainbow Government of 1994-97. He had chaired the European Council when it agreed the euro as the single currency. At this moment of financial crisis, it would have been a mistake not to harness his knowledge and track record. I nominated him to be Minister for Education and I was confident of his reforming zeal.

Brendan Howlin had, prior to the election, produced a 140-point set of Labour proposals for reform of the public service. This, together with his role as Chairperson of Labour's policy committee, gave him an understanding of public expenditure across all departments and made him the uniquely qualified candidate for this new portfolio, the Department of Public Expenditure and Reform, where public service reform would be central.

In the selection of an economic portfolio, I chose the Department of Communications, Energy and Natural Resources for the Labour Party. The Green Party's Eamon Ryan had established a strong profile in and for this department in the previous Fianna Fáil/Green coalition. In my view, this was the department from which the 'green jobs' of the future would be created. It was also the department responsible for key state-owned companies, such as the ESB and RTÉ, which I believed would need protection from Fine Gael's instinct for privatisation. I thought that Pat Rabbitte would hold the Labour line well on this. He was my immediate predecessor as Leader of the Party, is highly talented, and he and I had developed a strong bond of trust over decades of remarkably similar careers.

I anticipated that our biggest battles with Fine Gael would be over social welfare. The Programme for Government had not settled on an exact ratio of spending cuts to new taxes for the budget adjustment. There would therefore be an annual battle over the social protection budget, which I knew was firmly in Fine Gael's sights. If Labour was going to protect pensioners, the widowed, the unemployed and the poor from the worst effects of the crisis, we would need our toughest fighter as Minister for Social Protection. I valued Joan Burton's considerable abilities, and as I thought about those challenges, I felt that she would be the ideal person for the portfolio.

Unfortunately, Joan didn't see it the same way I did, and reacted very negatively when I told her. She was visibly shocked at the appointment. She asked me about the allocation of the other Labour portfolios and the answer did not quell her growing anger. She told me that I was making a big mistake in appointing her as Minister for Social Protection, that it would go down very badly in the Party. I was taken aback by Joan's reaction. The Department of Social Protection was responsible for nearly 40 per cent of all State spending. It reached into every home in the country. Every time the Party participated in government, this portfolio was always held by one of Labour's most senior figures. Any Labour Party serious about protecting the most vulnerable in society from the worst of the economic crisis would want to have control of the Department of Social Protection.

She was not the only unhappy appointee. Willie Penrose reacted furiously when I told him that I was nominating him to be Minister of State for Housing and Planning and that he would sit at Cabinet. He initially refused the nomination and left me in the Taoiseach's dining room. While I was making arrangements to send for another nominee, Máire Whelan and Pat Rabbitte talked to Willie in the corridor and persuaded him to reconsider. When he returned, I pressed him if he was now happy with the assignment, and he assured me he was.

With the new ministers all informed, we filed in traditional order into the packed and expectant Dáil chamber, led by Enda Kenny, followed by me as Tánaiste, and then each Minister in order of their length of service as Minister. I caught sight of my wife, Carol, and two of our children, Gráinne and Seán, sitting in the distinguished visitor's gallery, and smiled. It was, in many ways, a proud moment for our family, considering the long hard slog of my political life that had brought me to this point: the Deputy Prime Minister of my country.

At the same time, it was an awkward moment. I could sense the disappointment of many of my colleagues who had not been appointed to office. Ita was right. As they applauded the new Cabinet, I could see them struggle with mixed emotions on their faces. I thought of their families and how, like the families of everyone in public life, they had sacrificed privacy and time in their investment in the political project. I could imagine their feelings of hope that their spouse, or parent, or child, might be promoted to ministerial office. I could picture colleagues putting on their best threads that morning in the cautious hope of the call. I could hear the conversation of disappointment later in the day: 'Not this time.' I could understand if they were all sore with me, and felt they could do as good a job or better than those I had chosen. I felt for them deeply. I was determined to talk to each of them individually over the next few weeks, about the importance of their work in government and in the Party, and about their own futures. I felt very strongly that as Leader I must make time to motivate the individual members of the team I had been chosen to lead, to keep them encouraged and focused on the future.

When the Dáil debate on the nomination of the Government was over, we headed for Áras an Uachtaráin. Not, though, in the traditional manner. Enda and I had agreed the previous day that, in such times, a fleet of ministerial cars driving through the city was not appropriate. Instead, we all trooped onto an army bus for the journey. But it was no luxury coach. En route, I wondered to myself, what happens if we break down?

There is a sense of history about the appointment of ministers by the President. An official photograph is taken, with each Minister holding the seal of office before handing it back. The seal is in a box, so it does not really matter if Minister's are given the right one. Before handing mine back to the army officer, I glanced at it. It read: Aire Cosanta, it was: Defence!

The photograph was followed by a quick celebratory cup of tea. Carol, Gráinne and Seán had come to the Áras for this special event and they stayed on while the new Cabinet adjourned to the end room for our first Cabinet meeting.

Our very first decision was to cut our own pay. The Taoiseach's pay was cut to €181,050 post pension levy (from a peak of €272,000), the Tánaiste's to €167,092 post pension levy (from €230,000 at peak); and the pay of ministers to €153,551 post pension levy, having been almost €212,000 at peak. We followed this up with a decision to cut out state cars and Garda drivers for all ministers except the Taoiseach, Tánaiste and Minister for Justice. We agreed the Programme for Government as official policy, and decided a number of formal matters before adjourning until the following day, when we would appoint the new ministers of state.

I returned to the Radisson Blu Hotel where our Party head office had organised a social event to celebrate the formation of the new

Government. The mood was grumpy. Ita's words came back to me again. She was there and cheerily reminded me of them herself. It was around midnight when I left for home. I needed some rest. The first meeting of the EMC would be at 8 a.m. the following morning.

Twenty-four hours later, early on the morning of 11 May, I was at Dublin Airport, about to board a flight for Budapest and my first meeting of the EU Foreign Affairs Council, when I heard there had been a major earthquake in Japan. Arrangements would be made when we landed for me to speak to our Ambassador, John Neary in Tokyo. When we arrived in Budapest, I was told that RTÉ's Sean O'Rourke wanted to interview me for the lunchtime news about the earthquake. I needed to find out what our embassy could tell us about it. Were there any Irish people affected? Had contact been made with them all? Where would worried relatives get information?

Predictably, Sean did not confine his questions to the disaster in Japan; he wanted to know just as much about the political storms closer to home. 'Why was Joan Burton done down and not given Finance?' For most of the next week that was the focus of our national media. Some commentators suggested that I had been sexist in making ministerial appointments. One female journalist wrote that I had appointed Brendan Howlin to his portfolio because he was 'a safe pair of balls'! In the first two weeks of the life of the new Government, I found myself spending as much time defending my choice of ministers as I did explaining the horrendous state of the country which we were now trying to salvage.

It was a bad start. I was getting hammered in the press and I was somewhat slow in responding. I had persuaded Tony Heffernan to stay on as Party Press Officer for the election; he was now retired and had not yet been replaced. Mark Garrett had become a father

6 PROJECT RED

The first meeting of the Economic Management Council (EMC), began at 8 a.m. on the morning of 10 March 2011, the day after the new Government was formed. The EMC was conceived as a kind of war cabinet to manage the country's financial crisis. The Sycamore Room became our war room, the room from which Ireland's economic crisis was analysed and managed, and in which we strategised, planned and advanced the country's economic recovery. First, though, early on the morning of 10 March 2011, it was where we had to come to terms with the frightening scale of the economic crisis and the enormity of the job facing our new Government. Different officials briefed us on the various problems. The State was now spending €10 for every €7 it was collecting in taxes. The State's debt had trebled in just three years, from €47 billion in 2007 to €148 billion in 2010. Unemployment was heading for half a million. Over €46 billion of taxpayer's money had already been put into the banks, but it would not be enough. The banks were now in danger of collapse, and a collapse could cost the State €185 billion in guaranteed liabilities, which we could no longer afford.

How much money did the State actually have at this point? One briefing added up everything in the State's reserves, including the National Pension Reserve Fund and borrowings already drawn down. I estimated we had enough money to last five months. That was all we had to keep the hospitals and schools open, to pay pensions, public servants and social welfare, and to pay for all the other obligations. We would be able to pay teachers until the summer, but was there enough money to re-open the schools in September?

What does a country do when it runs out of money? A company goes into examinership, receivership, or ultimately liquidation. A household turns to social welfare. But there is no social welfare system for countries. In theory, a country can borrow. But since the end of 2010, no international lender would lend to Ireland. That's why the previous Government had to turn towards a bailout from the EU, ECB and IMF. And the terms of that bailout were very severe.

There are some, such as Sinn Féin, who argue that we should have repudiated the bailout at that stage. As Gerry Adams put it, 'we should have told the IMF to go home, and to take their money with them.' And then what? We could, of course, try to live within our means, and avoid borrowing. But that would have required a 30 per cent adjustment in the national budget. Was there anybody who seriously believed we could cut people's pay and pensions by 30 per cent, or increase taxes by 30 per cent?

Instead, we decided to stay within the bailout programme – our only source of borrowing, and to renegotiate the terms. At the top of our agenda was the interest rate. The ECB was borrowing at 1.75 per cent on the open market, and lending on to Ireland at around 3 per cent, making a tidy 1.25 per cent mark-up on our misery. That was Frankfurt's way, and it would have to end. So too would their insistence on cutting the national minimum wage. In the same way their intention to force us to sell airports, ports, forests, state companies and embassies to raise €5 billion for paying down national debt would to end. All this and more was about to change.

At the very first meeting of the EMC, we discussed a strategy for renegotiating the conditions of the bailout. The work was to begin the very next day, when the Taoiseach attended a meeting of the European Council in Brussels. We knew that there would be resistance to renegotiation, because the EU at that stage was becoming increasingly concerned about Spain and Italy. The view was that Europe could handle a crisis involving bailing out Greece, Ireland and Portugal, but if the contagion spread to larger member states, the crisis could get out of hand.

We also knew that some countries might look for concessions from Ireland for any easing of the terms of the bailout. President Sarkozy had publicly targeted our 12.5 per cent rate of corporation tax, blaming it for job losses in France. We were determined to defend the rate come what may, because we knew that to maintain the flow of foreign direct investment was critical for our chances of recovery.

We anticipated correctly. The following day, Sarkozy made it clear to the Taoiseach at the European Council that any change on bailout interest rates would come at a price, a change in our corporation tax rate. The Taoiseach refused.

That meeting, and my first meeting of the Foreign Affairs Council, over the same two days, taught us something else as well. Ireland's international reputation was more damaged than we had feared. Ireland now had few friends. The European institutions were unhappy that in the preceding years Ireland had ignored their advice and failed to correct the public finances. They were particularly bothered about the solo run the previous Fianna Fáil-led Government had done with the bank guarantee, and they had little sympathy for Ireland now that it had backfired. It appeared to me that other member states had sensed hubris and an arrogant swagger from Ireland, during the Celtic Tiger years, and now there was a feeling in Europe that Ireland's troubles were Ireland's own fault.

We realised that if we were to successfully renegotiate the terms of the bailout, we would first have to restore trust among the European institutions and rebuild our relationships with member states. The following Sunday, on the RTÉ Radio *This Week* programme, I announced my intention to lead a diplomatic initiative for renegotiation.

We would have to explain our case, country by country to the other member states. We would have to win allies, by displaying our own determination to get the Irish economy to recover and we would have to convince the sceptical of the justice of our case. Most importantly we would have to show that Ireland's recovery was critical to Europe's own fortunes. To persuade the European institutions to change their programme for Ireland, we needed to create political and diplomatic space. This was essentially my role as Minister for Foreign Affairs and Trade. Grandstanding with the ECB, the European Commission or the European Council was never going to work, as the Greek episode has painfully demonstrated. Instead we embarked on a slower more private process of patient persuasion.

And it worked. We succeeded in getting around a 2% reduction in the interest rate; the Troika eventually agreed to the restoration of the minimum wage; they agreed also to a jobs budget and, following negotiations with Brendan Howlin, they changed their ambition on the sale of State assets. They even finally changed their own approach to the crisis to one which was closer to the policy of the Irish Government and of the Irish Labour Party.

Our immediate priority in March 2011, however, was to sort out the banks. One of the most basic requirements of any economy is a functioning banking system. Yet when Enda Kenny, Brendan Howlin, Michael Noonan and I met for the first time as the EMC, the Irish banking system was dysfunctional, and was in danger of bringing down the entire economy. The bank guarantee had tied the financial misfortunes of the banks to the State and, as a result, the viability of the State itself was now on the line. Quite simply, we were staring at possible national bankruptcy. What a horrific moment to arrive in government! But as Bill Clinton once said, 'the only thing you can do in a crisis is to face into it.' And that's what we did.

Ireland had six damaged banks, too many to be repaired all at once. All of them were guaranteed by the State. Two of them, Anglo Irish Bank and Irish Nationwide, were already bust, but had been nationalised and merged into the Irish Banking Resolution Corporation (IBRC). The previous Government had decided to recapitalise the two banks at a cost of over €30 billion, which was to be paid by way of promissory notes, amounting to €3.1 billion euro every year for ten years. This was a cash payment from the State which would have to be made each year for the following ten years. To pay this huge sum of public money to a dead bank was not something we could stand over. We would have to deal with this before the next payment came, due again in early 2012.

Meanwhile, we had to decide what to do with the remaining four institutions, none of which appeared to be healthy. The assessment we were given of EBS and PTSB was that they were not viable on their own. The state of AIB, which had been fully nationalised, was worse than had previously been thought. The strategy for Bank of Ireland had initially been to leave it in private ownership and try to source private capital for it, but now it appeared that it also might have to be nationalised.

The banks had two financial problems: a shortage of liquidity and a shortfall in capital. The ECB was funding the liquidity shortage through the Central Bank, and by this stage, they claimed that they had used up 25 per cent of their available funds dealing with it. They were reluctant to supply any more, fearing resources would be needed by emerging banking crises in Portugal, Cyprus, and more alarmingly, in Spain and Italy. They were also deeply troubled by the capital inadequacy of the Irish banks, and they made it clear to us, through the Troika, that we had to face up to the problem urgently.

The Fianna Fail/Green Government had recapitalised the banks the previous September to achieve a capital ratio of 8 per cent, which Brian Lenihan had thought would be sufficient. It was not, and both domestic and international confidence in the Irish banks continued to erode. The Troika was now telling us that more State money was needed to bring the capital ratios up to 12 per cent in order to take them beyond the risk of future shocks. (They subsequently brought this down to 10.5 per cent.) Inside the Sycamore Room, the new Government was being told that more taxpayer's money was required for our banks to survive. Outside, the same banks were no longer lending to businesses, were losing deposits and rapidly running out of options.

How much more of the country's money would the banks need before they could perform their function in society? The initial estimate which was given to the EMC was €10 billion, but this estimate grew as March wore on. The hole in the banks' capital seemed to get deeper and wider by the day.

Allowing any of the banks to collapse at this stage was not an option, since it could trigger the State guarantee, and the State no longer had the money with which to honour that. If the State were to default on it, Ireland would be locked out of financial markets for decades and would probably be unable to borrow. The pariah status would not be confined to the State either, but would infect Irish companies and businesses too.

We needed the next recapitalisation to be decisive and final. The confidence crisis that would follow if we fell short was not something we wanted to risk. Firms of leading international banking consultants were tasked with answering the key questions of scale. These so-called PLAR and PCAR exercises were designed to tell us the 'bottom line' for the capital requirement and what we needed to know about liquidity. The stress tests being conducted by these consultants would tell us what the banks needed once and for all to get out of the mess. They were to report by 31 March.

Over the weeks leading up to the results of the stress test, the EMC discussed various plans for restructuring the banking system. We needed to slim down the Irish banking operations to become fit for purpose for the Irish economy. The IBRC (Anglo and Nationwide) would have to be worked out over time. EBS would be merged with AIB and this combined entity, along with Bank of Ireland, would be promoted as the two pillar banks of the economy. Irish Life would be sold and the proceeds used to support a renewed PTSB. A new regime on governance, on pay and bonuses would have to be enforced across the sector, since Irish people, rightly, were no longer prepared to tolerate excessive remuneration for top banking executives.

But how could we, meanwhile, minimise the impact on the taxpayer of the additional cost of recapitalisation? In March 2011, Europe was still a long way from establishing the European Stability Mechanism (ESM), which would share the burden of bank losses in the euro area. It would be fifteen more months before the

European Council would decide to separate bank debt from sovereign debt; and it would be two years before work would get underway to establish a European Banking Union. At the point when we had to make our decisions, the EU/ECB position was simple: the Irish banks were Ireland's problem. We considered playing for time on this, because we were seeking changes in the European position, but we knew that would be seen as indecisive by 'the markets'. When the stress test results were published, it would only serve to further undermine confidence in the Irish banks and lead to an even bigger problem.

Shortly after 9 a.m. on Monday 28 March, the EMC convened in the Sycamore Room to receive the results of the stress tests. The mood was tense and expectant. Ministers, advisors and civil servants queued quietly at the coffee dispenser to fill our cups. There was no banter. Nobody seemed to have an anecdote from the weekend. The Taoiseach called the meeting to order and asked Michael Noonan to lead off the discussion. He summarised the conclusions from the stress tests and asked Kevin Cardiff (who was still Secretary General of the Department), Ann Nolan and John Moran to present the details to the EMC. The bottom line was worse than we had feared. An additional €24 billion would be needed to re-capitalise the banks: not quite as bad as the €35 billion which had been pencilled in by the previous Government in the bailout programme, but far more than we wanted to contemplate. I silently cursed the Bank Guarantee. But now was not the time to fume about how Ireland had got into this mess. That would have to wait. We had to act decisively to avoid any sense of drift. I agreed with Michael Noonan that a set of proposals should be prepared and brought to Cabinet the following morning.

The Irish banking system would be restructured, and the €24 billion provided, but we would seek to minimise the impact on the taxpayer in a number of ways: €3 billion of the €24 billion would be contingency funding, which would return to the State if not required; another €5 billion would be raised by 'burning' junior bondholders. The sale of Irish Life and of non-core assets by the banks would further reduce the cost; we would continue to press for European assistance; and we would seek to burn senior Anglo Irish Bank bondholders.

Both Fine Gael and Labour wanted to secure some 'burden-sharing' arrangement with senior bondholders, but we encountered several obstacles. The first was that the overwhelming majority of bonds that had been covered by the blanket guarantee in 2008, had already been repaid so there was only a limited amount left that could be subject to burden sharing. We also knew that burning senior bondholders in the two pillar banks could be counter-productive as it would diminish the attractiveness of these banks to private capital. That left the three and a half billion euro of 'senior' debt bondholders in Anglo.

Although as a government we were determined to burn the senior bondholders in Anglo, the European Central Bank would not permit it, and as the ECB was the source of the liquidity funding for all our banks, we were not in a very strong position to argue. But we tried. Negotiations with the ECB continued through Tuesday and Wednesday. The stress test results would be released on Thursday, and Michael Noonan would have to address the Dáil with the Government's response.

Early on the Thursday morning he gave me a draft of his planned speech. It was re-drafted several times throughout the day as repeated efforts were made to get the ECB to budge. Later in the afternoon, the Taoiseach and I were scheduled to meet the Director General of the European Commission, Irish woman, Catherine Day, in Government Buildings. I arrived for the meeting before

Enda, and when he joined us he seemed uneasy, and signalled that he wished to have a private word with me. Catherine, sensing that something was awry, discreetly withdrew. Enda told me that the ECB had just communicated their final position: they would approve the bank restructuring and the recapitalisation plan, but there could be no burning of the senior bondholders in Anglo. It was the outcome neither of us wanted.

As we both made our way to the Dáil chamber for Michael Noonan's speech, the ECB refusal rankled badly with me. Michael Noonan must have felt the same. He was late arriving in the chamber as he had to change his speech one last time. In the haste, the pages were accidentally re-arranged. But nobody seemed to notice.

The decisive action on re-structuring and re-capitalising the banks worked. Confidence in Bank of Ireland began to grow and the American investor, Wilbur Ross, bought a large chunk of shares in it at a critical time. Irish Life was successfully sold, and the banks began to off-load more core assets. The withdrawal of deposits stopped and over time the banks began to recover. By the time stress tests were conducted on all European banks in 2014, the Irish banks were among the most robust.

Another positive from this episode was the success of the EMC. By the time Michael Noonan made his announcement on Thursday evening, 31 March, the EMC had planned a communication strategy: delivered internationally, through embassies; in the press, through Ministers; and in the European institutions, through Senior Civil Servants. The message was going out loud and clear: Ireland had decisively and finally got to grips with its banking crisis. The new Government was on top of the problem.

But I still felt that on this occasion, Frankfurt had got the upper hand, and I was determined that it could not be allowed to happen a second time. The next big test would be over the promissory notes. These were the bad debts which had been left to us by Fianna Fáil. Every year, for the next ten years, the Irish Government was required to pay €3.1 billion to the IBRC. There were many difficult decisions that I was willing to make, and actions I was prepared to take to put our country on the road to recovery, but this was beyond what I was prepared to do.

However, we would need time to crack the problem. First, we had to get our jobs strategy moving and get our action plan for jobs up and running. We had difficult work to do on budgets; and we had to build a confident working relationship with the Troika; restore the country's international reputation and secure as many allies as possible for what we now expected would be a big showdown with the ECB.

It was impossible to achieve all this before the next promissory note fell due in March 2012, so we devised a way of effectively postponing payment until 2013. The Bank of Ireland were very cooperative in the arrangements, enabling us to avoid paying the prom note in 2012, and buy extra time to resolve the issue before March 2013. But by that stage we would have two years promissory notes to pay, amounting to €6.2 billion. The stakes were high indeed.

Colm O'Reardon, on my behalf, and Andrew McDowell on the Taoiseach's behalf, began to exchange ideas on possible solutions. Senior officials from the Department of Finance and from the Central Bank started to explore approaches with the European Commission and the ECB. I led a long diplomatic campaign which explained the progress that Ireland was making, the sacrifices our citizens were enduring, and the hit the country was taking, not just for our own banks, but also for European banks. Slowly, we began to get some traction for the idea that something (as yet unspecified) should be done to help Ireland.

Michael Noonan and Brendan Howlin kept us up to date on the work being done to find ways of easing the burden. In late September 2012, Brendan reported to me that a proposal was being worked up and that we would need to handle it with the utmost sensitivity. Michael Noonan brought the plan to the EMC on 24 October 2012. The Taoiseach and I agreed that, because it was so delicate, discussions should be confined to a very small number of people, on a strictly 'need to know' basis. The plan was called, 'Project Red', and that label stuck until very late in the process when, perhaps for reasons of political sensitivity, it was re-named 'Project Dawn'.

The core concept of 'Project Red' was to liquidate the IBRC, with its loans being sold off to the market or to NAMA and the prom note being converted into long term bonds. This arrangement would reduce Ireland's borrowing requirement by about €20 billion over the ten years, and would benefit the national budget by about one billion each year – although not in the very first year when we would have to bear the cost of liquidating the bank. The formula had several advantages. It would remove Anglo and Nationwide from the picture. With no toxic bank, we felt that confidence in Irish banking would improve. At the same time, we would be rid of the suffocating promissory note, which would have clear financial benefits for the State.

But all of this needed approval from the ECB. They were reluctant; worried it would be interpreted as the Central Bank effectively printing money, to which they were then adamantly opposed. So we set about winning them over to the plan. Key to this was Governor of the Central Bank, Dr Patrick Honohan. He had been appointed Governor in 2009 by Brian Lenihan, and was an inspired choice. Previously a professor in Trinity College Dublin, he was the first Central Bank Governor not to have come from the Department of Finance. He was an outstanding governor and deserves much credit for the recovery of the Irish Banking System.

As Governor of the Central Bank of Ireland, Dr Honohan was a member of the governing board of the ECB and, therefore, an important conduit between the Irish Government and his equivalents in Frankfurt. Throughout 'Project Red', Dr Honohan attended several meetings of the EMC so that he could understand our intentions and relay to us the view from Frankfurt. During these discussions, we were always careful to respect his independence as Governor and his obligations as a member of the governing board of the ECB. The ECB and its governing board acts independently of the member states, but we understood that the individual governors would always be aware of the opinions of the Governments which had nominated them. We intensified our diplomatic efforts to ensure that governments and European institutions were on our side, with a simple message to Frankfurt: to help out Ireland.

I seconded some diplomats from the Department of Foreign Affairs and Trade to the Department of Finance to help that Department with the international dimensions of their work. I put in place a weekly video conference call with key EU Embassies every Monday afternoon to assess progress and to renew instructions.

In late 2012, I was chairperson-in-office of the Organisation for Security and Co-operation in Europe (OSCE), and I was also preparing to chair the powerful General Affairs Council of the EU in early 2013. I was therefore meeting senior European political figures on a regular basis, including European Council President Herman van Rompuy, European Commission President José Manuel Barroso and European Parliament President Martin Schulz, as well as Foreign Ministers and Prime Ministers of several European countries. I used all of these opportunities to drive home Ireland's message: essentially, that Ireland was working through its programme and recovering well. We expected to exit on target at the end of 2013, and were actually beginning to see some small signs of growth and of job creation. I explained that we had restructured our banking system and that we were now engaged in detailed discussion with the ECB about a critical banking issue, the outcome of which would determine whether or not Ireland's recovery would succeed. I never got into detail, but always asked: '*I hope your Government can support us in these discussions.*'

I gradually sensed I was getting a sympathetic hearing. Ireland's standing with other member states and with the European institutions had improved considerably since our Government took office.

Another significant reason for the positive reception was that, in 2012, Europe was itself in the midst of financial crisis. The very survival of the euro was at stake. The EU desperately needed a success story. At the time, Ireland seemed the most likely country to produce the goods and to lift the siege in Europe. I played on this, and made it clear to everyone I met that Ireland was heading for recovery, but that it would all collapse if we did not get a successful outcome from our negotiation with the ECB.

Back at the EMC our target was to get 'Project Red' implemented by Christmas. I wanted it done before the start of the EU Presidency. As the weeks wore on and as each fortnightly meeting of the EU passed without a decision, and as new queries and obstacles continued to be raised, I began to doubt if we would ever get the green light from Frankfurt.

As the deadline approached for the March payment we became more and more concerned that the ECB and the European side would let the clock run down on the idea, and we would be faced with a similar situation to the one which existed on the day of the bank recapitalisation. At one point, the EMC seriously considered going ahead with the liquidation unilaterally and officials prepared for that eventuality. Although we always felt it would be far better to proceed on an agreed basis, we had to be willing to go it alone.

Another pressure point was the risk that the news would leak – this would put the directors of the IBRC in an impossible position and would put the bank at risk. In fact, the EMC Ministers became aware that at least one newspaper had enough facts in their possession to deduce what was going on, even if it would require some leap of imagination to do so. For several weekends, we waited anxiously for the Sunday papers to appear or for a phone call to come through on a Saturday seeking a comment on a story that IBRC was about to be liquidated. In those circumstances, it could have been necessary to call an emergency sitting of the Dáil, and the procedures for doing so were also quietly examined and preparations were put in place accordingly.

As expected, 2013 began with a whirlwind of EU Presidency engagements. But the EMC never lost sight of 'Project Red'. Michael Noonan was talking directly with the President of the ECB, Mario Draghi, and EMC ministers were all pushing our message with their European counterparts.

On 25 January, I travelled to Santiago, the capital of Chile, to represent Ireland and the EU Presidency at a summit of EU states and Latin American and Caribbean states (CELAC). I set out deliberately to press the urgency of Ireland's cause and to increase the political and diplomatic temperature. I met several EU leaders throughout the three days of the conference. Prime Minister Rajoy of Spain and I were guest-speakers at a major investment event on the opening evening, and I took the opportunity to discuss the case with him, but I was particularly cautious not to reveal our hand because I did not want Spain to spoil our pitch. I had some good productive bilateral meetings with Prime Minister Jean Marc Ayrault of France and with Prime Minister Katainen of Finland. I discussed the issues with Jean Claude Junker, then Prime Minister of Luxembourg and President of the Eurogroup, on the margins of the formal conference.

During a reception on the Saturday, I got the opportunity to talk with Chancellor Angela Merkel of Germany. She spoke of her friendship with Enda Kenny and remarked on the stability of the Irish Government. I told her that the Government was indeed stable and that Enda and I worked well together, but that a failure to get a result for our current discussions with the ECB would de-stabilise the Government. She seemed remarkably well briefed on the issues involved. She suggested that we were being too ambitious – that fifteen years was too long for repayment and that maybe we should be thinking of three to five years. I got the impression that she was suggesting some kind of postponement of the promissory note. She urged continued discussions with President Draghi. I told her that payment of the prom note was politically impossible for the Irish Government, and would not be approved by the Irish Parliament. I stated quite clearly that the Government could fall on the issue and put Ireland's recovery at risk.

The following morning, I decided to refer to Ireland's problem in my own address to the conference itself. My officials were nervous about using a multi-lateral forum such as this to air a national and European issue, but I knew how high the stakes were. The format for the Sunday morning session was an informal dialogue with only the political leaders in the room. No civil servants, diplomats or press were permitted. Around the large conference room, on armchairs along the walls, were over fifty Presidents and Prime Ministers from the Caribbean, Latin America and Europe. Inevitably some over-ran their allotted time, so as the morning wore on, I became concerned that I might not get to speak at all. I decided to have a private word with President Piñera of Chile, who, as host, was chairing the session. I had had a warm and relatively long bilateral meeting with him on the Friday – a privilege afforded to Ireland as a result of President Michael D. Higgins' successful State visit to Chile the previous October. I suggested to President Piñera that if he was running out of time and could not accommodate all the European speakers, he should call on me at the end, as Ireland held the presidency of the EU, just as he held the presidency of CELAC. It worked, and so at the end of a long morning, President Piñera regretted that he could not find time for all the countries who wished to contribute, but that 'our European visitors should have the final word, so I now give the floor to our good friend from Ireland who holds the Presidency of the EU'.

I spoke, of course, about the opportunities for enhanced trade between the EU and Latin America, but used the opportunity to say 'failure to conclude negotiations on the promissory note would have a potentially catastrophic effect on Ireland.'

Back home, I received some criticism in the media for being undiplomatic and going too far in such a context, but at the time, I knew just how urgent and immediate was our need.

Of great importance in the decision making process were the German Governors of the ECB. Over my time in office, I had worked to develop a good relationship with the German SPD. In October 2012, I had shared a platform at the Friedrich Ebert Foundation with Peer Steinbruck, the former German Finance Minister who would be the SPD candidate for Chancellor in the 2013 General Election. He came to Dublin on Sunday 3 February and I met him privately, and asked him to help.

By early February, the tensions were ratcheting up, as another meeting of the Governing Council of the ECB was approaching, with few such meetings remaining before the March deadline for the instalment on the prom note to be paid. I made it clear to the Taoiseach that Labour simply could not continue in government if that happened, although, to be fair to him he was equally determined to resist payment.

The ECB Governing Council meeting was to happen over two days – 7 and 8 February. The EMC was gearing up in the hope that agreement would come from Frankfurt, so that we could go ahead with the liquidation. In the early afternoon of 7 February, the EMC was actually meeting when an official from the Department of Finance came into the Sycamore Room with a note for Michael Noonan – the Department press office had received a media enquiry asking if it was true the IBRC was going to be liquidated. At this point, immediate action was needed, and the meeting adjourned so that Michael could effectively take over the bank – he signed an order to vest the powers of the board in an employee of KPMG and a team from KPMG was immediately sent in to take over the bank. This gave a breathing space, but only a short one. A few hours later, in the early evening, the EMC reconvened, for an up date from Frankfurt. Here the news was bad. The matter had been raised, but no decision was taken – they were going to sleep on it! You could have cut the tension in the room with a knife. Everyone realised that this was decision time. Would we now proceed with the legislation to liquidate IBRC, or would we wait until morning in the hope that the ECB would agree to the deal? Finance officials briefed that it would be possible to hold off, now that the order had been signed. I was absolutely clear in my own mind, however, that we had to move. The Taoiseach agreed with me, and the decision was made to proceed. A full cabinet meeting was called to update the Government and agree the legislation, and Michael Noonan then went into the Dáil for an all-night session. It was an arduous task for him and his officials – the bill liquidating IBRC was signed by the President the next morning at 7a.m. Officials flew to Rome where the President was on a State visit, so that he could consider the contents of the bill on the way back.

The following day, the hours ticked by, still with no word. Finally, around noon, I got a call from Patrick Honohan. After sleeping on it, the ECB had asked for some modest amendments to the plan, which he believed were acceptable. In legal terms, what was being proposed was an action of the Irish Central Bank, so the ECB simply 'noted' it, but that was all we needed. This may have seemed like a modest enough endorsement, but in effect it was a massive step forward. After two years of tough negotiation and hard decisions, it was now clear that the financial viability of the State would be assured. The EMC then held a very brief meeting. The atmosphere had changed and the mood was now positively light-hearted! It was a real pleasure to be able to congratulate Ann Nolan, the Second Secretary General from the Department of Finance who had been in charge of the detailed management of Project Red. It was one of the shortest meetings we ever held, as we moved quickly

7 BATTLES OVER BUDGETS

For nearly two decades, budget day had always been a good news day. From the early 90s, until the crash in 2008, Ministers for Finance had announced cut after cut in taxes, increase upon increase in social welfare payments, and ever-expanding spending on public projects, to the delight of government backbenchers and the discomfort of the opposition. Even the Budget for 2008, announced by Brian Cowen on 6 December 2007 contained further reductions in taxes, general social welfare increases of €12 per week and increases for pensioners of €14 per week.

There were few under 40 years of age who had been in the workforce when a budget had last increased income tax or when cuts were made to public expenditure. But then came the 2008 crash, and subsequent recession. Tax revenues, which had relied so heavily on the property bubble, collapsed. Unemployment surged and with it the demands on the social welfare system. Ireland was now spending far more than its income and, by the end of 2010, was no longer able to borrow the balance.

The Fianna Fáil/Green Party Government began to address the sudden crisis in the public finances in July 2008, with an emergency budget which reduced public expenditure by €1 billion. Three months later, they brought forward the 2009 Budget to October 2008 and made a further adjustment of €2 billion. In just another four months, February 2009, they took out a further €2.1 billion, and just two months after that again, in April 2009, they introduced a supplementary budget for €5.4 billion in spending cuts and tax increases. In less than a year, a shocked Irish population had suffered four harsh budgets, all of them increasing the taxes they had to pay and reducing the services they relied on. This was followed by a fifth bad budget in December 2009, which took a further €4.1 billion away, bringing the total budget adjustment to nearly €15 billion, in just 18 months. But it was still not enough to prevent the country being forced into the bailout at the end of 2010. Fianna Fáil's final budget in December 2010 was for a further €6 billion adjustment.

By the time the new Government was formed on 9 March 2011, income taxes had been increased by reducing tax credits and the lowering of the standard rate threshold by nearly €4,000. The exemption limits for pensioners had been cut by €2,000. Basic weekly social welfare rates were cut by €8.50 in 2010, and another €8 in Budget 2011; child benefit was cut by €16 per month in 2010 and by another €10 per month in the 2011 Budget; and the Universal Social Charge had been introduced. In order to reduce the public service pay bill, Fianna Fáil had introduced a moratorium on recruitment and had twice unilaterally cut the pay of public servants, including the introduction of a special pension levy on public servants.

When the Fine Gael/Labour Government was formed, the people were still reeling from this succession of severe budgets which had assaulted their incomes and their family budgets, just as the recession in the real economy was causing their pay to drop or their businesses to fail, and as they were stretched to meet repayments on personal borrowing, especially those who had high mortgages on homes whose value was now halved. No doubt there were many who hoped that the arrival of a new government would immediately bring this austerity to an end, and that somehow life could return quickly to pre-crisis prosperity.

Fianna Fáil's last €6 billion budget had been put through the Dáil just before the general election and would take effect just as we were taking office, so the new Government very quickly came to own the problem. When people are struggling to make ends meet, they don't have the time or inclination to consider which government introduced the hardship, they turn to the government in office to sort it out. But, as I had said on the *Late Late Show* the previous November, the new Government would not be able to reverse these measures immediately. Indeed, we would, in time, have to do much more to prevent the country from going bankrupt.

Under European Union rules, Ireland's deficit needed to be less than 3 per cent of the country's Gross Domestic Product (GDP). Every political party, including Sinn Féin, accepted that the deficit had to be brought below 3 per cent. Fianna Fáil had agreed with the Troika that the 3 per cent target should be reached by 2014. Fine Gael agreed with this time scale. But the Labour Party had argued during the general election that the adjustment should be spread out to 2016. In the negotiations for the formation of the coalition, the compromise was 2015, and this new date was eventually agreed with the Troika. Converted into real money, this meant that by 2015 a further €11.5 billion euro in spending cuts and tax measures would have to be found. Yet, working people and families could hardly be expected to put up with more increases in taxes. Those on welfare could not endure further cuts in their allowances. Every cut hurt more and more people, and every additional tax was bringing more and more household budgets closer to breaking point. The 'low-hanging fruit' had already been plucked by the previous Government. The people were already suffering too much, and the road to recovery would result in even more pain.

I recalled that, in the run up to the election, I was often asked, and commentators sometimes wondered, if the Labour Party was capable of 'making the tough decisions.' Over the three years that followed, I would get to know all about those difficult decisions.

All my political life, I had fought for fairness and equality, and I always saw the State as having the central role in providing public services, supporting enterprise and innovation and being the arbiter of the common good. Now, in this crisis government, I would have to make and support decisions that would reduce State spending and, in turn, would damage many causes which I had always championed. This is, surely, the very essence of a tough decision: taking actions that I instinctively did not want to take, that flouted the very arguments I had been making all my life; actions that I knew would be impossible to 'sell' to many people and would be rejected by many Party members and supporters, and that would make Labour itself deeply unpopular.

It had been tempting to stand aside, of course, and to grandstand away until our time came to step in just at the right moment to play the role of hero. But I believed it would have been wrong to prolong the crisis in such a way, resulting in far worse outcomes for our people, and possibly even undermining the viability of the State, in order to better my own political standing or that of my Party.

As I commenced my work as Tánaiste in the new Government, the very viability and future of the Irish State was at risk. A bankrupt State would not be able to pay pensions to the old and widowed, or pay teachers in our schools, or pay nurses in our hospitals, or pay for all the public services, including water, which we have all come to take for granted. I knew, too, that if Ireland did not get out of the bailout and was forced into a second one, the State would be in receivership for years to come, and its ability to deliver public services, and lead public investment would be compromised for at least a generation. However counterintuitive it may have been at some level, I felt my first duty as a socialist in 2011 was to save the State.

But back then, I was not confident that it could be saved. There were few, if any, hopeful signs in early 2011. The total budget adjustment by 2015 would amount to €32 billion, or almost 20 per cent of Ireland's GDP. Could a fragile economy, already struggling to recover, withstand such radical surgery? And how much longer would the patience of the people last? Success depended on being able simultaneously to achieve an unprecedented adjustment in the public finances, keep the Troika on-side while re-negotiating the onerous terms of the bailout deal, minimising the cost to the taxpayer of bank recapitalisation, getting the economy to grow again and making sure that growth generated new jobs (which does not always happen), and to implement difficult budgets in a manner that would minimise the impact on those who were most vulnerable.

The adjustment pencilled in for the 2012 Budget, our first one, was €3.6 billion. But through the summer of 2011, the EMC got reports from the Department of Finance that this might not be enough. They now estimated that a €3.6 billion adjustment would fall short of the target and that the deficit would come in at about 8.7 per cent or 8.8 per cent. Various new figures were produced, which, at one stage, suggested that an adjustment of €4.4 billion might be needed, almost one billion more than we had expected. Michael Noonan was keen in his first budget to show that Ireland was serious about getting the deficit down. To regain market confidence, it was essential not to fall short of the deficit target. I agreed with this, but I could not agree that there should be a buffer provision in our first budget, i.e. that we should deliberately overshoot the target to demonstrate our determination to get the deficit down. I thought it would be hard enough to hit the target without unnecessarily going beyond it.

Eventually the target was agreed at €3.8 billion, of which €2.2 billion would be by way of spending cuts, and €1.6 billion in additional taxes. Fine Gael had contested the General Election, arguing for a 3:1 ratio between spending cuts and new taxes. Labour argued for a 50/50 split, and while the Programme for Government did not settle this issue, the assumption was that the ratio would be somewhere around 2:1. The outcome of several months of discussions at the EMC was a ratio of about 1.4:1. Had the Fine Gael election position prevailed, there would have been €650 million in additional cuts in the 2012 Budget. Had Labour emerged as the largest party in the election, there would probably have been up to €300 million less.

The exercise which shaped the budget ratio was the Comprehensive Review of Expenditure (CRE) which was initiated by Brendan Howlin in April 2011. Both parties had committed to a Canadian style, root and branch examination of all areas of public spending in order to identify potential savings. Brendan asked each Department to examine their own spending in detail, and to propose the cuts in their own Department and agencies which would achieve their allocated share of national savings.

Departments cooperated constructively with this exercise and the report that reached the EMC in the autumn killed off any pre-conceived idea that the Irish public service was a bloated beast, and that there were easy targets for cuts. The expenditure report confirmed that every cut would have direct impact on services and helped persuade Fine Gael to accept a ratio which was closer to that advocated by Labour.

Finding €2.2 billion worth of cuts was not easy. At an early stage, Brendan and I agreed that a significant portion (€775 million eventually) should come from the capital budget as Ireland had already been through a long period of high public capital spending, and now possessed a better infrastructure for a lower level of economic activity. Among the projects cut was the proposed A5 cross-border motorway to Derry. As Minister for Foreign Affairs and Trade, I would have the dubious privilege of explaining this to Peter Robinson, Martin McGuinness and our Northern counterparts. We would, in time, make up the contraction in the capital programme through new stimulus packages, but in the meantime we had to proceed on the basis that cuts on the capital side were preferable to even greater cuts on current social programmes.

From an early stage in the life of the Government, the Labour Ministers began to meet and consider how we would handle the budget. We went through each Department and the suggestions which had come through the CRE. The choices to be made were all of the 'least-worst' kind, but between them, the Departments of Social Protection, Education and Health accounted for over 80 per cent of all current spending, so it was inevitable that the bulk of the cuts would fall on these three areas of vital public service.

In Education, Ruairí Quinn changed the staffing ratios for small schools (bringing the minimum number of pupils for a two-teacher school up from twelve to twenty), re-absorbed guidance teachers back into the school mainstream and increased the pupil-teacher ratio in private fee-paying schools by one. (The EMC removed a proposal which had come from the Department of Education to increase the pupil-teacher ratios in all schools by two.)

The biggest challenge was in Joan Burton's Department of Social Protection. The initial target for savings in her Department was €665 million. This was an impossible figure and would have resulted in drastic cuts in social welfare. This burden would just have to be reduced somehow. The Programme for Government had undertaken not to cut basic rates of social welfare or to increase income tax on working people. At a press event in the lobby of Government Buildings, to mark 100 days of the life of the Government, Stephen Collins of the *Irish Times* asked Enda Kenny and I if we still intended to honour this commitment; we both confirmed that we did. Now the press wanted to know how we could possibly frame a budget of almost €4 billion without touching income tax or social welfare rates. A cut of €665 million could not have been achieved without cutting social welfare rates, and at one stage the Department of Social Protection itself had suggested an €8 cut across the board. The Labour Party could not agree to this. Eventually, we succeeded in reducing the required cuts in Social Welfare by €190 million to €475 million. I saw every such reduction as another part of the burden lifted from hard-pressed families, though there would still be a lot of pain in €475 million of cuts to the social welfare budget.

Some of the measures which were agreed made economic and social sense. One of these related to the State refund on redundancy payments. The statutory redundancy payment is two weeks' pay per year of service, and until now, the state repaid 60 per cent of this to the employer. This 60 per cent dated back to a time when the statutory redundancy payment was only a half week's pay per year of service. I failed to see why, when the statutory minimum for redundancy was raised, the refund was correspondingly increased. I felt it provided an incentive for employers to make workers redundant. So we cut that 60 per cent to 15 per cent, making an estimated saving of over €50 million in a full year. Another rational move was to end the payment of the 'Back to School Clothing and Footwear Allowance' for two- and three-year-old children. Two- and three-year-old children don't go to school!

There were other social protection measures which caused real and regrettable pain, and which disturbed every Labour member of the Government and probably some Fine Gael members too. They included the shortening of the fuel allowance season by six weeks and the reductions in child benefit for third and subsequent children. There were two further measures which caused particular grief, especially for Labour TDs. The first was the proposal to standardise the age for payment of the disability allowance. In general, social welfare payments start at age eighteen, but the disability allowance started at age sixteen. Reluctantly, but under pressure to find the necessary cuts, Joan Burton planned to bring it into line with other benefits, but the proposal was one of those that stirred up instant and intense opposition. On a budget night television programme, Michael Noonan indicated, without consulting Joan, that the decision could be reversed. I felt that this had been very unfair to her, and said so to him afterwards.

Another change which drew the wrath of Labour TDs and Senators was the reduction in the training and materials grants for community employment schemes. These schemes are hugely important in disadvantaged communities and their organisers are very powerful and vocal in constituencies, which local Labour representatives would have known better than most. The issue raged on for months, and was a regular topic at the weekly meetings of the Labour parliamentary party.

On the tax side, there was no increase in income tax and the main measures centred on increases in capital taxes – capital gains tax and capital acquisitions tax were increased from 25 per cent to 30 per cent; DIRT tax was increased from 27 per cent to 30 per cent; planned increases in the top rate of VAT to 23 per cent were brought forward to 2012 and the carbon tax was increased from €15 per tonne to €20 per tonne. Significantly, we agreed at the EMC to raise the threshold for the Universal Social Charge (USC) from €4,000 to €10,000, taking 330,000 of the lowest paid earners out of the USC net entirely.

Brendan Howlin had kept the Labour TDs and Senators briefed on the issues during our long budget negotiations with Fine Gael. Only two Labour TDs ended up not voting for the budget measures: Deputy Tommy Broughan, who had lost the Party Whip the week before the budget and who had, previously, lost the whip while we were in opposition; and Deputy Patrick Nulty, who had just six weeks previously become the first Government winner of a by-election in thirty years. Patrick came to my office on the day of the budget, about half an hour before Brendan Howlin's speech, and told me that he would not be able to support the measures.

Our TDs and Senators showed great courage in supporting the budget and in trying to advocate for it in their constituencies. But the Party membership and our core supporters were deeply unhappy and let this be known. I decided to address the dissatisfaction head on, and in early 2012 undertook a tour of the country, speaking at regional meetings of Party members and responding to members' questions about the decisions we had already taken in government, and about the challenges ahead. Some of these meetings, in Galway and Cork, for instance, attracted small but vocal groups of protestors. I could see that Party members were getting a tough time of it in their workplaces and communities and I tried, as best I could, to equip them with the arguments to make the case for Labour. But I don't think I fully succeeded. Many Labour supporters simply could not reconcile their Party beliefs with cutting public expenditure, even if deep down they knew that the country was facing bankruptcy and that the measures taken would be even more severe if Labour were not in government.

Though I didn't air it much at the time, I knew better than most what a single-party Fine Gael government might do. During our budget negotiations, Enda Kenny had shared the results of research among Irish voters which his Party had commissioned from Greenberg, Quinlan and Rosner, a firm of American political consultants. It showed that the most acceptable cuts would be 'halting overseas aid to developing countries until the public finances are fixed', 'cuts in public sector numbers', 'cuts in public sector pay rates' and a variety of cuts in social welfare. If Labour hadn't been in coalition, this is an indication of what Fine Gael would have implemented in the 2012 Budget alone. Yet, there was no credit for the cuts avoided, just criticism for those that were implemented.

One of the reasons the 2012 adjustment had to be increased from €3.6 billion to €3.8 billion was because the return from the sale of State assets had fallen short of expectations the previous year. Now, at each quarterly review, the Troika was hard pressing the Government to accelerate privatisation according to what they saw as the commitment in the bailout agreement. The Memorandum of Understanding, which the outgoing Fianna Fáil Government had signed with the Troika, committed to significant sales of State assets, but the document didn't specify how much or what assets should be sold; rather, it referenced an official study on State assets and liabilities which was already underway. The review group conducting this study was chaired by Colm McCarthy and it reported in April 2011, just after the new Government took office. It stated that 'the net asset-value of commercial company assets whose disposal is recommended is about €5 billion'. This then became the Troika demand: sell €5 billion worth of State assets to reduce debt; and they presented it as what the previous Government had signed up to. At every quarterly review they piled on the pressure to privatise.

Our Programme for Government committed to the sale of €2 billion worth of 'non-strategic' state assets, but that was a long way short of the Troika demand. Once Budget 2012 was finalised, the EMC began to consider the issue of privatisation in earnest. Officials from the Departments of Finance and Public Expenditure and Reform, reflecting their discussions with the Troika, put forward a list for our consideration. It included the possible sale of 49 per cent of ESB; 49 per cent of Bord Gáis; 49 per cent of the Dublin Airport Authority (including the airport); the complete sale of Dublin Port; the sale of Bord na Móna, Coillte and the Irish Aviation Authority, as well as the State's remaining shares in Aer Lingus. It also proposed the sale of buildings in State ownership, such as courthouses, prisons and embassies abroad. It was estimated that our three most valuable embassies would net €50 million between them.

I knew from my first meetings with the Troika that we would

have to fight a battle over privatisation, but I feared we might lose it. There were some in Fine Gael who were very keen to privatise. I had taken the precaution of placing two steadfast defenders, Pat Rabbitte and Alan Kelly, in the key departments on which the attack would first be launched. When Rabbitte realised the seriousness of the threat, he called to see me to tell me he would 'do a Frank Cluskey on it', rather than preside over the sale of ESB. (The late Frank Cluskey had resigned from Cabinet in the early 1980s over the sale of the Dublin Gas Company). Pat resisted the agreement in the Programme for Government that the ESB should be divided, which he saw as a Trojan horse for privatisation.

We were by now fighting such battles on several fronts and I needed to buy us some time. Brendan Howlin went to Brussels to negotiate with the Commission on asset sales and on how the proceeds of any such sales might be used. The Troika had been insisting that all proceeds should go to debt reduction. Brendan managed to negotiate a new agreement, which set a minimum of €1 billion as the amount of sales now required. Provided we achieved the minimum, and had a target of €3 billion, we would be permitted to use half the proceeds for re-investment in the Irish economy. With the sale of the National Lottery licence, and part of Bord Gáis, the €1 billion minimum would be met. Now we would have to slow down other sales.

Pat successfully saw off the move on the ESB. I was strongly opposed to any sale of airports or ports. If these were not strategic assets, what were? I considered that they were outside the terms of the Programme for Government. Likewise, I was not prepared to countenance the sale of our forest lands, which were enjoyed by hundreds of thousands for walking and hill climbing, but was open to the idea of selling harvesting rights to the timber. This idea was explored but eventually abandoned by Simon Coveney because the price was too low. Price was also the main factor in seeing off the threat to state owned buildings. The bottom of the property market was hardly the best time to consider such sales.

As we had hoped, the pressure for asset sales gradually began to abate; and Labour's presence in the Government prevented a large sell-off of State assets. Furthermore, the proceeds from those that were sold could now be used to fund a stimulus programme thanks to the work of Brendan Howlin. For instance, the money from the sale of the lottery licence was ear-marked for the new Children's Hospital; other monies would be used to build the new DIT campus at Grangegorman and to fund the building of schools and primary care centres. Even in these difficult times, with the correct policies and strategies, we could find ways to build new infrastructure and, of course, to generate job opportunities in their construction.

2012 was a difficult year. The crisis had widened to Europe, and the euro itself was at risk. Recovery was slow, but I was determined that Labour's legacy for these difficult years in government would be nothing less than economic recovery.

The annual Labour Party Conference was held in Galway. It attracted a large body of protestors, some of whom attempted to storm the conference centre. In my address to the Conference, I told delegates that the Government was making progress on the road to economic recovery, and I predicted that we would succeed in getting out of the bailout and away from the Troika in good time, but that it would take two more difficult budgets.

The EMC began to prepare for the first of these, in 2013, by meeting in Ministerial-only format in late summer/early autumn. We considered, at first, setting out in the 2013 Budget all of the measures which would get us out of the bailout. But this plan came unstuck when Fine Gael sought to trade off movement on income tax in return for reductions in social welfare payments, specifically the €188 per week for unemployed people, which they wished to reduce. I was not prepared to allow the basic unemployment payment be brought below €188. For those who are involuntarily unemployed, and struggling to find work, a benefit to live on is a cornerstone of the Irish welfare state. €188 is damn hard to live on and I was not prepared to see it cut even further.

The Fine Gael push on the social welfare rate ended up being tied to Labour's wish to increase the rate of USC for those earning over €100,000. Self-employed people earning over that amount were paying 10 per cent USC, while those in PAYE employment were paying 7 per cent. Labour sought to increase this to 10 per cent for those over €100,000. At first, Fine Gael appeared to be willing to move in this direction, but as we approached budget day, they retrenched, and were only prepared to move on it if Labour was willing to cut the basic rate of social welfare.

Discussions on the 2013 Budget took place over several weeks through October and November 2012, between the Taoiseach, Michael Noonan, Brendan Howlin and me in the meeting room just off the Taoiseach's office. Sometimes they ran into the early hours of the morning, which did nothing to improve the mood and temperament of the four of us, as we were often already tired from a hard working day. We were also at this time dealing with the prom note. Relations between Michael Noonan and I became particularly strained during this period, and there were a number of testy exchanges between us. The budget adjustment required in the year to get the deficit below 7.5 per cent was €3.5 billion, an enormously difficult challenge for a Government which was almost out of options and in a country whose people were becoming exhausted with harsh budget measures.

Budget Day was set for Wednesday, 5 December. By the Saturday beforehand, 1 December, there was still no agreement on the measures, and the Taoiseach called a special Cabinet meeting for 5 p.m. on the Saturday. Before that, he and I would be attending Dublin Castle to launch the Constitutional Convention, and would return to Government Buildings to meet with Michael Noonan and Brendan Howlin. By this stage and despite the efforts of Colm O'Reardon and Andrew McDowell there was stalemate over the USC proposal and welfare cuts. I told the Taoiseach that, as we had failed to reach agreement on the budget at the EMC, I would meet separately with the Labour ministers, and that the Cabinet meeting could not proceed until we had broad agreement.

Gathered in the Tánaiste's office, just across the quadrangle from the Taoiseach's, were Joan Burton, Pat Rabbitte, Ruairí Quinn, Jan O'Sullivan and my advisors, Mark Garrett, Colm O'Reardon, David Leach and Jean O'Mahony. Brendan Howlin and I briefed them on the state of discussions in the EMC. There were three options. To hold our line on USC and refuse to budge on welfare and risk the collapse of the Government; to bargain a reduction in the rate of Jobseeker's payments for the increase in the USC; or to accept that we could not make progress on the USC and to negotiate a more robust package of capital taxes. The USC increase would bring in about €70 million, whereas a package of wealth taxes had the potential to yield about €500 million. Financially, this would be the most productive route to take, but surrendering on the USC increase would be politically damaging for the Labour Party, because it had already been trailed in the media as a Labour red line. The six Labour Cabinet ministers discussed the pros and cons of each option. There was no disagreement. We agreed unanimously that the best course was to drop the USC demand, to negotiate a better tax deal and to reduce the proposed cuts in welfare. Colm, Brendan and I went back to meet the Taoiseach, Andrew McDowell and Michael Noonan.

Through the evening, we continued the discussions with Enda Kenny and Michael Noonan. We agreed to reduce the cuts initially planned for both the Departments of Social Protection and Health by €150 million. We agreed a package of taxes on wealth, including an increase of 3 per cent on capital gains tax, capital acquisitions tax and DIRT. We agreed to end tax reliefs for pension pots which yielded pensions in excess of €60,000 per annum, and we agreed changes to the property tax including a reduction in the tax to 0.18 per cent for properties valued at less than €1 million, and an increase in the property tax to 0.25 per cent for properties over a million.

When we eventually went to the Cabinet room to begin the Government meeting, we discovered that our colleagues had ordered in pizza but there was none left for the EMC. When the meeting ended, a few of the exhausted Ministers and advisors headed to the Merrion Hotel for a nightcap (some to Foley's). I just went home.

Before my election to the Dáil in 1989, I had worked for eleven years as a trade union official, and I had always, over that time, sought to negotiate the best possible deal for my members. I knew that night that the deal Brendan Howlin and I had just concluded in the Sycamore Room was the very best possible in trying circumstances. We had reduced the cuts to less than €2 billion in a package of €3.5 billion (about 56 per cent) and the tax measures would fall on those who had most. But I also knew that we would get little credit for those battles, when all the bad news was announced in the budget on Wednesday.

Though every cut in that budget was hard to make, some were

particularly painful. We had to agree to a cut of €10 from child benefit, something we had committed not to do during the General Election. The telephone allowance had to be halved (though, at least some of this loss was offset by extra money for home security for elderly people). The duration of jobseeker's benefit was to be cut back by three months. The cut that attracted most media attention was the reduction in the respite care grant from €1,700 to €1,375. This was an annual payment made to carers to help defray the costs of a holiday, and no matter how Joan Burton tried to explain that holiday costs had come down during the recession, the cut was seen as an attack on carers, and by extension, on people with disabilities.

All of the Labour TDs were troubled by some aspects of this budget. Six were deeply so and they met with me in my office. I continued to meet with them over the days between the budget announcement and the crucial vote on Joan's Social Welfare Bill. We worked out solutions to their principal concerns, and so I believed that there would be no Labour casualty on this difficult budget as I entered the Dáil chamber at 2 p.m. on Tuesday 13 December for the final vote.

Sitting beside Deputy Leader Joan Burton, I watched the electronic panel, as the Government side lit up green and the opposition side lit up red. There was, however, one red light to be seen on the Labour benches. At first I was not alarmed, because sometimes TDs just accidentally press the wrong button (or even mischievously do so only to change over in the last remaining seconds). However, this red light did not change, and I turned to our Party Whip, Emmet Stagg, who was sitting immediately behind me. 'Who is that, Emmet?'

'Keaveney,' he replied.

I was very surprised. The recently elected Chairperson of the Party had, like other TDs made some public noises about the budget, but as recently as that morning on a radio programme, he had confirmed his intention to vote for the Social Welfare Bill. The previous evening, he had attended a meeting of the Party's management committee at which the Party officers, including Keaveney himself, had discussed ways of managing the political fallout from the budget. He had not informed Joan Burton whose bill it was, or the Party Whip, or me, that he intended to vote against it. He, therefore, automatically lost the party whip. At a parliamentary party meeting later that day, TDs and Senators felt he had let them all down.

The slow burner issue in the 2013 Budget was the property tax. In an extraordinary election winning stroke in 1977, Fianna Fáil had decided to abolish domestic rates. In doing so, they undermined the financing of local government and shifted the burden of taxation onto PAYE workers, which in turn, contributed to the huge PAYE tax marches in the early 1980s and the demand for tax reform. Every independent examination of the Irish tax system since then concluded that the tax base needed to be broadened, and that the introduction of a property tax was critical to this. But no government had ever had the courage to introduce it. The Fine Gael/Labour Government in the 1980s introduced a modest residential property tax, but it was abandoned in the mid-90s following a media campaign calling for its abolition.

At the General Election in 2011, every political party promised to introduce a property tax, although most were careful not to call it that. Some talked in vague terms about 'wealth' taxes, which inevitably would have to include property. The Labour Party called it a 'site value' tax. The Troika, however, were very clear that the early introduction of a property tax was a price Irish people would have to pay if their State was to get emergency funding from other European countries, all of which already had quite high taxes on property. Under the bailout deal, the property tax was to have been introduced in 2012, but no preparation had been made for it, so we decided to introduce an interim solution, the 'household charge', in 2012, with the intention of replacing it with a fully worked-up property tax in 2013.

The administration of the household charge was a mess. Arrangements for paying it were not properly worked out and this led to confusion and to high levels of non-payment. There was enormous frustration in the Labour Party that repeated efforts by Environment Minister Phil Hogan to sort out the mess only appeared to make it worse. It was also a bad prelude for the new property tax.

An expert group, chaired by the former Secretary General of the Department of Education, Dr Don Thornhill, was asked to design the new tax. The group recommended that the property tax should be dedicated to the provision of local services, that it should be based on house value, and that 65 per cent of the tax should be retained by the local authority for the area in which it was collected. I was initially concerned about basing the tax solely on property values. A modest terraced home in parts of my constituency of Dun Laoghaire might have a value much higher than a large dwelling twice its size in another part of the country. The EMC discussed this, and Colm O'Reardon and Andrew McDowell were asked to explore if some kind of hybrid basis for the tax could be devised from both values and property size. This proved to be impossible because of the variations in property prices and sizes throughout the country.

I therefore came at it in a different way. If the tax was to be based on property values alone, then the benefit should accrue to the community in which it was collected. I sought and obtained an increase in the portion to be retained by the local authority from

65 per cent to 80 per cent. Since this would give rise to considerable variance in the revenues of the local authorities concerned, we decided to permit the newly elected councils to vary the level of the tax up or down by 15 per cent. The idea was that an urban authority with high property values and high densities could reduce the tax by up to 15 per cent, whereas a county with large dwellings but low values could increase the tax by up to 15 per cent, thereby rebalancing the revenues of the councils concerned.

In order to provide a degree of certainty, we also agreed to freeze property values, for the purposes of the tax at their 2013 level, for a period of three years.

By mid-2013, when the EMC's attentions began to turn to the budget for 2014, a fragile economic recovery was beginning to take hold and unemployment was coming down. The budget adjustment pencilled in for 2014 was €3.1 billion, to take the deficit to 5.1 per cent. But as the year progressed, as revenues improved from increasing economic activity and as pressure on the Department of Social Protection began to ease with lower unemployment, it became increasingly apparent that it would not be necessary to do the full €3.1 billion. At last, we could see a flickering glimmer at the end of the tunnel.

In a series of interviews just before the summer break, I made it clear that Labour was willing to do enough to reach the percentage targets, but no more. Commentators quickly calculated that Labour was targeting a €2.5 billion adjustment. For the first time since the Government was formed, the budget battle would be conducted somewhat in public. The Fiscal Advisory Council, the European Commission and a number of academic economists suggested that we should do the €3.1 billion anyway. But I felt that we had been prisoners to deficit reduction targets expressed in percentage terms for so long, it made no sense to depart from percentages now, just when it turned slightly to our advantage.

In the EMC discussions, Brendan and I succeeded in getting agreement to a €2.5 billion adjustment, which by budget time would yield a deficit of 4.8 per cent in 2014. That year, much of the expenditure reduction would be achieved by further reductions in public sector pay, arising from the Haddington Road agreement which Brendan had negotiated with the public sector trade unions. The 'ask' from the Department of Social Protection was, once again, reduced by €150 million.

On the tax side, two of the measures introduced by Michael Noonan attracted considerable criticism and opposition. The first was the One-Parent Family Tax Credit. Up to now, separated working parents could both claim this credit, and the budget proposed to limit the credit to the parent who had custody of the child. The loss was mainly experienced by working separated fathers who mounted a vigorous campaign against the measure. The second was the decision to limit tax relief on health insurance premiums of up to €1,000 for an adult and €500 for a child. In his budget speech, Michael Noonan said that tax relief would no longer be available for 'gold-plated' health insurance, a phrase which angered many working people who struggled to meet health insurance payments for their families.

This was the budget which would clear the way for Ireland's exit from the bailout. Because recovery was beginning, the adjustment was less than originally expected. For the first time since the recession began, a budget was able to make provision for some new social spending. New classroom and resource teachers, numbering 1,250 in total, could be recruited. A book rental programme could be introduced in primary schools. €37 million was provided to commence the roll out of free GP care – initially for children aged five and under. There was money for a new round of sports capital grants, for the Wild Atlantic Way tourism project and an allocation for some 1916 commemorative projects.

But agreeing this budget was not all plain sailing. There were considerable difficulties in the Department of Health. No public service is more unpredictable than health. A bad winter, or an unusual health epidemic can put unexpected demands on hospitals in particular, and it is therefore difficult to predict with accuracy the budgets which will be required from year to year. In each of the previous two years, health had overspent, and there was ongoing tension between Brendan Howlin and James Reilly as to the reason why.

On the Sunday before budget day, the health estimate had still not been resolved. A meeting was held in the Taoiseach's office, chaired by the Taoiseach, and involving Brendan Howlin, Michael Noonan and me, together with James Reilly and his senior officials. The Department of Health wanted more money. The Department of Public Expenditure and Reform wanted Health to identify their share of budget savings. The meeting broke up and reconvened several times before a package of savings was agreed, which included '€113 million from a review of all medical cards to remove ineligible and redundant cards'. This measure arose from a report the Department had, which showed that medical cards still existed for patients who were dead, had emigrated, or who, for a variety of reasons, no longer needed the card. Meanwhile, doctors were being paid for them, and considerable savings could be made if these cards were weeded out of the system. The clumsy and inept implementation of this decision would plague the Government through the first half of 2014, would contribute to Labour's heavy election losses in May, and ultimately to my own resignation as Labour Leader.

8 GLOBAL IRISH JOBS

A quarter of a million Irish men and women had lost their jobs in the three years before Labour and Fine Gael formed a new Government on 9 March 2011.

On that day there were 442,000 on the Live Register and it was growing steadily. The biggest job losses were in construction, and not just on the building sites. Architects, engineers, surveyors, estate agents, conveyancing solicitors, builder's providers – an entire sector of the economy was being wiped out. The economic collapse saw the fall of personal spending, massive business closures, and huge job losses across all retail activity. The economy appeared to be in freefall, and it had to be halted.

Labour and Fine Gael disagreed repeatedly over budgets and social policy. But there was one issue on which we were absolutely united for our entire time working together: the imperative to halt unemployment and create jobs. While tackling the debt crisis was a priority for the country, getting people back to work was the obsession of this Government. There was never a Cabinet meeting at which the jobs agenda, in some form, was not addressed. It dominated the work of Cabinet sub-committees and of every department. In our private discussions about the formation of government, Enda Kenny and I repeatedly talked about the jobs crisis and how we might tackle it. We spoke about the need for joined-up strategies across the whole of government, involving every department, every State agency, every local body as well as the private and voluntary sectors. We understood the damage that unemployment does to individuals and families and communities. We knew, too, that every additional unemployed person cost the state about €20,000 a year in lost taxes and in social welfare payments.

We had no blueprint for the jobs crisis. The traditional Keynesian approach of increasing government spending was not available to us because of the crisis in the public finances. We had to pioneer non-Keynesian solutions, with government providing the leadership and opportunities, but with the private sector delivering the jobs. We knew from the 'jobless growth' of the late 1980s and early 1990s that getting the economy to grow would not in itself be sufficient.

The Action Plan for Jobs, led by Richard Bruton, Minister for Jobs, Enterprise and Innovation became the flagship for our jobs effort. Every department contributed to it. It had about 300 action points across all sections of Government, some relatively small, but taken together, very effective. We launched the action plan on 13 February 2012, and, as I made my speech from the podium, I could not help reading scepticism in the faces of the assembled press. We were telling them that the plan was intended to generate 100,000 net new jobs by 2016. The press had, in fairness, heard all this before. The previous Government specialised in launching big initiatives which rarely delivered. In contrast, by the time I left government in July 2014, it was clear that the target would be reached early. (I met Richard Bruton at the corner of St Stephen's Green in mid-May 2015, and he told me that on that very day, the one-hundred-thousandth job had been created since the launch, a year ahead of target.)

The idea behind the Jobs Action Plan was to focus each minister on job creation. Each department had a quarterly target for actions to be undertaken, and each quarter, the Taoiseach and I, together with Richard Bruton, presented an update on the plan to a press conference.

This was complemented by another initiative, the 'Pathways to Work', which was led by Joan Burton and her Department of Social Protection. 'Pathways' was a concerted effort to prepare unemployed people for returning to work. Given how prolonged unemployment can undermine an individual's confidence and how quickly an unemployed worker can become de-skilled, the message was that an unemployed person's first day out of work was also his/her first day on the way back to work. The strategy advanced a range of labour activation measures, including education and training to equip the unemployed for work. To meet this need, Ruairí Quinn, in turn, re-organised further education and training, by abolishing FÁS and the VECs, and setting up SOLAS and the Education and Training Boards.

We knew that in recessionary times jobs would not be created without the active intervention of government. Our first major action in that respect was a jobs budget, announced by Michael Noonan in May 2011. We had to get the Troika's agreement for this initiative, and they insisted that it could only be funded with new money. Michael Noonan proposed a levy on pension funds, which generated the money to reduce VAT in the hospitality sector. This, we thought, would boost the tourism industry and give us a relatively quick win, both in terms of increased tourism numbers, and added jobs in hotels, restaurants and attractions. The plan worked, and in 2013 it was decided to keep the 9 per cent rate for tourism and to reduce the travel tax to zero, which further boosted tourist numbers.

We had been told that one of the obstacles to tourism was the difficulty in getting a visa to visit Ireland. Alan Shatter and I discussed this, and in June we launched an initiative to accept British visas for people travelling to the UK for the 2012 Olympics. In each successive budget, a series of such small, low-cost initiatives was undertaken to boost business and create additional jobs. These included the Living City Initiative to encourage refurbishment activity in construction; a retro-fitting scheme for energy conservation, led by Pat Rabbitte; and tax concessions for trade promoters abroad and for companies to attract specialist skills to Ireland.

One of the big obstacles to business, in the early stages of this Government, was the limited availability of credit from the banks. As part of the recapitalisation plan, we set lending targets for the banks and questioned them about their performance during meetings between the banks and EMC. At local level, the old County Enterprise Boards were revamped as Local Enterprise Offices, bringing together the expertise of both local authorities and Enterprise Ireland to encourage start-ups and to support entrepreneurship.

My principal role, as Minister for Foreign Affairs and Trade, in the drive for jobs, was to take our case to the wider world. We export 80 per cent of everything we produce, we are heavily reliant on foreign direct investment, and a large part of our domestic economy, including food and tourism, is dependent on international good will. I pursued a form of economic diplomacy aimed at creating and sustaining jobs at home.

My first economic mission was for the St Patrick's Day celebrations in New York, just a week after taking office. Normally the Dáil does not meet during St Patrick's week, but the Taoiseach and I felt it would send out a very bad signal to adjourn the Dáil on the very first week of the new Government, so we scheduled a debate on the Programme for Government. This meant that both of us had to attend and speak in the chamber on Tuesday 15 March, and as a result, I could not take a scheduled flight to New York. My programme of engagements was due to start at 7 a.m. the following morning, so I travelled on Tuesday night in the government jet with the Taoiseach, who was going to Washington. At close to midnight (US time) we were met at Andrews Air Force Base by Ambassador Michael Collins and Director General Niall Burgess. The Ambassador took the Taoiseach to his DC hotel, and Niall Burgess and I took the embassy car for the long drive to New York, arriving at Fitzpatrick's Hotel at about 4 a.m. I got two hours sleep and then it was up and out to a full day of speeches, briefings, media interviews and meetings – all communicating the message that Ireland had a new government, that we were determined to recover, and that the country was open for business. At every event I attended, I was conscious that Ireland's reputation had been damaged and that sharp American business people were trying to judge if investment in Ireland (or indeed anywhere in Europe) had a future.

Among my meetings that day was one with the senior executives of Morgan Stanley – the multinational financial services corporation – one of whom was their Co-President of Institutional Securities, Irishman Colm Kelleher. They grilled me on Ireland's intentions and offered some advice. About a month later, they published a welcome report on the Irish economy, which was far more optimistic than anything else at the time. In it they said:

'We continue to believe that Ireland is fundamentally different from the other peripheral countries in that it is a fully de-regulated, fully liberalised, market economy. As a result, it should be able to adjust to the crisis more quickly. True, the challenges are somewhat bigger than elsewhere – notably in the banking sector. But Ireland is among the few euro area countries that have historically managed major turnarounds in fiscal policy (and the wider economy) and it is already showing signs of the smart cyclical upswing in the manufacturing sector.'

It was the first commendation we received at a time when ratings agencies were continuing to downgrade Ireland's credit worthiness and their outlook for our country. Morgan Stanley (and Colm Kelleher) should be given credit for being the very first financial institution to correctly predict that Ireland would recover.

Colm was one of several Irish leaders in world business who came to Ireland's assistance at this difficult time. Others emerged from an initiative of the previous Government that I adopted and developed.

In September 2009, the then Minister for Foreign Affairs Micheál Martin, convened the first Global Irish Economic Forum at Farmleigh House in the Phoenix Park. David McWilliams had suggested to him the idea of getting together Irish people who were now corporate presidents or CEOs from around the world to harness their thinking on how Ireland might tackle its sudden economic crisis. The then Taoiseach, Brian Cowen, invited me to attend as Leader of the Labour Party, and I participated in a number of the discussions. I thought it was a great idea, and felt that in these one hundred or so corporate leaders there was a unique resource waiting to be tapped.

On my appointment as Minister for Foreign Affairs and Trade, I decided to convene a second Global Irish Economic Forum for early October. The initial response was not encouraging. Some of the senior business figures who had attended the Farmleigh event felt that their advice had been ignored and that there had been little follow-up to the first forum. I set about re-assuring them that we meant business for the next forum and I asked the UCD Smurfit Business School to help design and moderate a more focused conference. We wanted to draw workable solutions from this forum and to follow through with them. The message got out and it soon became apparent that the attendance would far exceed Farmleigh's capacity, so we moved the venue to Dublin Castle.

Among those who contacted me about the arrangements for the event was Minister Alan Kelly's brother, Declan Kelly, who had recently established a company called Teneo – a US based corporate advisory firm – in which former US President Bill Clinton had an involvement. He told me that President Clinton would accept an invitation to attend, and it was eventually agreed that Clinton would make the closing speech at the event, on the Saturday afternoon. This, of course, also carried the advantage that everyone would stay until the very end. After two days of meetings and workshops, involving every government minister, all the economic state agencies and some of the world's leading business people, the 300 or so attendees crowded into St Patrick's Hall for the closing speech.

The Taoiseach and I met President Clinton at the main entrance to Dublin Castle and escorted him to the Connolly Room where we held a brief meeting and presented him with his Certificate of Irish Heritage. He got an ecstatic welcome from the crowd in the hall, and we were joined on the stage by Bono. Clinton made a rousing speech in which he expressed his friendship and affection for Ireland, and pledged to organise an investment conference for Ireland in New York in February. The first major follow-up to the forum was already set in motion.

The Clinton investment event was held at New York University on a bitterly cold February morning. The Taoiseach and I got there early for a shivering photo session in Washington Square. Back inside, we waited at a service elevator for – thanks to American security – the unspectacular and discreet arrival of Clinton.

The event was in two parts. The first was a private meeting of about thirty leading United States' business leaders, personally invited by Clinton, most of whom had no previous relationship with Ireland. Clinton introduced the Taoiseach and me, telling them that we were the leaders of Ireland's two largest political parties and that we had joined together to form a coalition government to deal with the economic crisis. To murmurs of approval, he remarked, 'I wish we could see a bit more of this on Capitol Hill'. The Taoiseach and I then spoke and answered questions about Ireland's recovery for over an hour.

The second part of the event was a much bigger lunch-time session at which Clinton gave the address. He expressed his confidence in Ireland, saying, 'Right now you would be mad not to invest in Ireland'. It was a rousing and powerful endorsement for the country, picked up extensively by the media, at a time when we so badly needed international investment.

Declan Kelly never sought any credit for his key role in making these events happen, but deserves to have his massive contribution recorded.

I followed up the forum in other ways too. We organised the participants into a global Irish network, with branches established in various countries and regions. These small groups of key influencers would work with our embassies to promote Ireland's cause and to look out for Irish opportunities. I met them regularly on my travels abroad. Typically a one-day visit to a capital city would include a private meeting with the members of the network, at which they gave me their assessment of the business mood of their country and the business perception of Ireland, and I would give them an update on Ireland's progress.

We also put together an advisory group, drawn from the network members who met with me periodically in Iveagh House. I recall one early meeting at which they discussed the negativity of some of the Irish media. I had come to take media criticism as part of the job, but these business people felt it went far beyond the normal critique of government in other countries and that it was probably costing jobs from possible new investment. Some members organised other special investment events. For example, Irial Finan, the Vice President of Coca-Cola, organised one in Dublin on the weekend of the Notre Dame vs. Navy American football match in the Aviva Stadium.

One of the most enthusiastic and active members of the Global Irish Network was Loretta Brennan-Glucksman, the New York businesswoman who was chairperson of the Ireland Funds for many years. During the crisis years, she was like a godmother to Ireland, and gave generously of her time and friendship. So too did John Fitzpatrick the hotelier from Killiney in my own constituency, who succeeded her as chair of the Ireland Funds.

Ireland owes a lot to its sons and daughters who have done well abroad. They have never forgotten their roots, and I saw first-hand how they worked with our embassies to open doors for the IDA, Enterprise Ireland, Bord Bia and Fáilte Ireland, to encourage overseas investment in Ireland, and to help Irish exporters. In 2014, for instance, United States foreign direct investment to Ireland increased by 40 per cent, over a period when it declined by almost 20 per cent in the rest of Europe. Some of the credit must go to the business network we have built among our diaspora.

That diaspora, of over seventy million people throughout the world claiming Irish heritage, is uniquely influential, and not just the leaders in politics, culture and academia among them. The Irish tend to be liked and respected all over the world, and that in turn translates in real economic terms. Given the fact that growth in our economy has always been closely linked to exports, having an Ireland friendly population abroad helps to sustain existing markets and to open new ones.

One of the keys to securing existing jobs and creating new jobs was to grow our exports. In forming the new Government, Enda Kenny and I agreed that trade functions should be added to the responsibilities of the Department of Foreign Affairs and that I should take the lead in mobilising and coordinating the national effort to increase exports and to develop new markets.

We, therefore, established an Export Trade Council which I would chair and which would include the Ministers for Jobs, Enterprise and Innovation; Transport and Tourism; Agriculture; and Education and Skill; as well as the key trade agencies. We also decided to include representatives of the private sector such as IBEC, the IFA and the Irish Exporters Association, as well as some individual exporters.

The Council oversaw the implementation of the export trade strategy, which had targeted twenty-seven strategic markets. In each of these countries we had a Local Market Team, headed by the ambassador who coordinated the work of the agencies, of exporters, and where needed, of the members of the global Irish network. These teams prepared trade visits – which were usually led by a government minister – aimed at helping to open up new opportunities for exporters or seal the deal for projects that were already underway. Every few months, Richard Bruton and I reviewed the list of potential trade visits and decided which minister would be asked to lead which visit. I led some myself, including those to Japan, Korea, Turkey, Russia and France.

International trade is a highly competitive arena, and every country strives to win foreign direct investment, attract tourists and sell its products abroad. That's how jobs are sustained and created in the modern world. In this competitive space, Ireland has one unique opportunity every year – St Patrick's Day. There is no national day of any other county that is as widely recognised and celebrated throughout the world as is Ireland's. Every 17 March, the Taoiseach presents a bowl of shamrock and has a formal meeting in the White House with the President of the United States. The Prime Ministers of no other country get such an annual meeting. The St Patrick's Day Parade on Fifth Avenue, with its enormous disruption of Manhattan traffic, is now the only such event which is allowed to take place on a weekday. More recently, in countries all over the world, iconic landmarks are lit up green to celebrate the culture of this small island of six and a half million people. It is the ideal opportunity to promote Ireland for trade, tourism and investment. But it has to be thoroughly planned to maximise its potential.

Each autumn, I requested that our embassies submit proposals for ministerial participation. By Christmas, they had submitted their outline programmes for St Patrick's Day events, with an emphasis on the business and trade opportunities. From these, I would select about twenty of the most promising and seek approval from Cabinet to designate ministers to the various locations. Sometimes, the programme itself indicated which minister should attend. A big food fair, for example, could justifiably request a visit from the Minister for Agriculture.

St Patrick's Day travel invariably attracted a degree of media scepticism at home. Press queries usually concentrated on the numbers travelling, the cost, the hotels at which we stayed, and the menu for any dinner attended. In the past, some ministers had spent a full week (sometimes more) on St Patrick's Day travel. I cut this down to a couple of days, with a strict trade focus in the programme. This meant two or three days of intense meetings, discussions and briefings, from about 7 a.m. in the morning until late at night for visiting ministers. In general, ministers travelled economy class, stayed either in the embassy or at a modestly priced hotel, and kept costs to a minimum.

The great Irish diaspora is not entirely composed of the financially successful. Many, especially in Britain, the United States and Canada, are now elderly men and women who emigrated from a jobless Ireland in the 1950s and 1960s. Many had raised families abroad and, in some cases, are now in poor and often lonely circumstances. In the main Irish centres like Birmingham and Boston, voluntary organisations are working to provide services and support to these emigrants, and the Department of Foreign Affairs and Trade provides about €10 million a year in funding to assist their work. It was always a particular honour for me to visit the Irish Centres abroad, to meet Irish emigrants, and to praise the great work being done by volunteers. One of these volunteers, Nora Higgins from County Galway, spoke eloquently at the opening of the third Global Irish Forum in Dublin Castle in October 2013, saying, 'We emigrants believe Ireland is a great small country and for us, a great place to visit, and especially to call "home" wherever we live. We never say we are going on holiday to Ireland – we always say we are going home.'

Ireland's waves of emigration always coincided with periods of economic hardship at home. The 1980s had been bad, but many of those who emigrated then acquired skills and experience abroad which, on their return home, helped build the economic success of the nineties and noughties. The 2008 recession had given rise to another exodus. This time the profile was much younger and the destinations more widespread and not so focused on the UK and

USA. Australia and Canada seemed to be preferred by young professional emigrants in the twenty-first century. We needed to find ways of helping our young citizens as they made the choice to go abroad. Of course, we hoped it was would be short-lived, but we couldn't pretend in the meantime that it wasn't happening and that we didn't have some responsibility for their wellbeing.

In Canada, during the St Patrick's Day events of 2012, I negotiated with the Canadian Immigration Minister Jason Kenney an increase in the number of visas to be made available to Irish emigrants. They were quickly snapped up when they became available through the Canadian embassy in Ireland.

The Australian Minister for Labour visited Ireland and met me in Iveagh House where he outlined the shortage of qualified tradespersons, especially in Queensland and the Northern Territory. I asked Ruairí Quinn to see what could be done to align Irish trades' qualifications with those of Australia. The increase in the number of Irish emigrants put an additional demand on Ireland's embassies and consulates and they worked closely with emigrant support organisations to provide advice and help to the new wave. We provided funds to help open new emigrant support offices, such as that in Toronto, which I officially opened during their St Patrick's celebrations in 2012.

It saddened me to see young Irish people having to travel abroad to find work, which should be available to them at home, and every time I met an Irish emigrant, I resolved to redouble our efforts to attract investment and jobs to Ireland. There are many technical measurements for economic recovery, but for me, one of the most important measures would be these young people returning home, if they wished, to new job opportunities. And yet, this new wave of emigration was different to what I had witnessed before. The new emigrants were in constant touch with home, family and friends through Skype and social media. Among the many I met, I encountered little, if any, sentimental pining for the emerald isle.

The GAA invited me to officially open their Asian Games in Suwon in South Korea in October 2011. Thirty-eight men's and women's mainly Gaelic football (though, some hurling) teams assembled there from all over the Asian continent for a weekend tournament to decide who would be the champions of Asia. The hotel was swarming with hundreds of young Irish men and women decked out in their club's colours. It was one of the happiest events I have ever attended. The captain of the Mongol Khan's Gaelic football team from Ulan Bator was a young man from Ballymacward, not far from my own home place in County Galway. His team was comprised mostly of engineers working in construction in Mongolia. All of the teams were a mixture of teachers, nurses, IT specialists, finance advisors – mainly young Irish professional workers, enjoying the experience of working in the growing economies of Asia. I admired their patience as the opening ceremony had a long series of speeches from me and GAA officials – including the Chairman of the 'Asia County Board'.

In Asia, as in the rest of the world, the GAA is a key network for Irish emigrants and often the first point of contact for new arrivals. Not only is it a cultural home-from-home for young emigrants, it is also giving all things Irish a wider international reach and helping to broaden our unique 'brand'. That is why I decided to allocate significant funding to the GAA to assist in its work abroad. I saw it very much as part of our recovery efforts.

Unemployment in Ireland peaked in early 2012. As it began to fall, tentatively at first, all of us in government hoped that the trend would continue. And it did: new jobs continued to be created. By mid-2013, our confidence was growing that we could exit the bailout on time and that we would succeed in creating the jobs we needed for our people. I went to Labour Youth's Tom Johnson Summer School in Kilkenny on 15 June 2013 with a new message: the Irish economy is recovering. We are going to exit the bailout. We have been tied long enough to targets set for us for deficit reduction. Now we need to set our own targets. Why not full employment? Why not now aim to achieve full employment – always a Labour objective – by 2020?

There were some who thought this overly ambitious, but when the Government turned its attention to a post-bailout medium-term economic strategy, I put full employment on the agenda. Economists say that full employment is reached when the rate of unemployment drops below 6 per cent. After some argument, agreement was reached at the EMC to commit to bringing unemployment under 6 per cent by 2020. In the 2015 spring economic statement, that target has now been brought forward to 2018. As I write, unemployment has fallen to 9.4 per cent, and at this rate of progress we may have full employment by the end of 2017. A job for anyone living in the country who wants to work, and for the talented and highly educated young Irish people who have emigrated but who may yet come home. The battle for jobs is being convincingly won.

There is however one group of Irish people who cannot yet benefit from all of this progress: the 50,000 or so undocumented Irish people who are living a twilight existence in the United States.

Many of them emigrated in the 1980s and remained in the US beyond the period covered by visas. They have no official status and can be arrested at any time and deported, or possibly banned, from entering the USA again. Yet they have made a life there. Many have formed families and have children, who unlike their parents are entitled to US citizenship. Most are working, though their status as workers is awkward. Many have done very well, and through partnerships with legally resident compatriots have developed successful businesses. But they cannot travel home to Ireland to see aging parents, to meet relatives, or even to attend family funerals.

The Irish embassy in Washington, together with the consulates around the US, have been campaigning for years to regularise the 'undocumented'. They cooperate with Irish-American organisations and lobby groups in speaking to American politicians at every level, in an effort to resolve the problem. But it is not easily resolved. The 50,000 undocumented Irish are but a tiny fraction of the total number of immigrants in the US whose status is regarded as illegal. It is estimated that there are now eleven million people living in the United States who do not have visas, cannot work legally, and who can, at any time, be deported.

Immediately on becoming Minister for Foreign Affairs and Trade, I took up the cause. On my first official visit to the States, I met with the Irish groups who are campaigning on the issue and I met many of the undocumented themselves. The Taoiseach and I discussed the matter with President Obama, both during his visit to Ireland in 2011 and again in the White House on St Patrick's Day in 2013. I discussed it on a number of occasions with Secretary of State Hillary Clinton, and with her successor John Kerry. President Obama and Secretaries Clinton and Kerry were all sympathetic to the plight of the Irish. When I mentioned to John Kerry, whose State of Massachusetts was home to many Irish and Irish Americans, how many undocumented Irish there were, he quipped, 'Just 50,000? I must know them all!'

The difficulty is that the Irish problem cannot be resolved on a stand-alone basis. Legislation is required to deal with all those who are living in the United States, and this can only be passed by the US Senate and House of Representatives. Over the years, various attempts have been made, but it has never succeeded. The best opportunity, in my term, arose just after the Presidential Election in 2012.

Democrats tended to support immigration reform. Initiatives to bring forward legislation on this occasion were led by politicians like Senator Chuck Schumer and Dick Durbin. I kept in regular contact with them. A particularly good friend on the issue was Senator Pat Leahy, the senior Democrat senator for Vermont. Every time I spoke to him about it, his warm response was, 'Eamon, you're in your mother's arms!'

Obama's re-election in 2012 was attributed in part to Republican opposition to immigration reform. Some in the leadership of the Republican Party began to surmise that a republican could not win the White House again until the immigration issue was dealt with. Among them was Congressman Paul Ryan, who had been their candidate for Vice President in 2012, and whose ancestral roots are in County Kilkenny. I met Paul a number of times in Washington and I concentrated on shifting the focus of our lobbying efforts onto the Republican side. Among the Republican Party politicians whom I met over the issue were Senator Rubio, from Florida the former Senator from Massachusetts Scott Brown and Senator John McCain. Senator McCain was responsible on the Republican side for getting immigration reform legislation through the Senate, but it has to be passed too by the House of Representatives, and although there is probably a majority in the House in favour of such legislation, the deeply partisan nature of politics there is preventing progress.

The Democratic Party leader in the House was Congresswoman Nancy Pelosi who had been enormously helpful to the Irish effort. During my very last visit abroad as Minister for Foreign Affairs and Trade, in June 2014, I met her again, and met other Congress leaders in our final push on behalf of the undocumented Irish in the United States.

That work continues, in the US, led by Ireland's Ambassador Anne Anderson. I believe it will eventually pay off. But Ireland's own attitude to immigrants in Europe will shape the outcome. Republican politicians in the US, who are reluctant on immigration reform, will pay close attention to the political rise of the new right in Europe, who are, in turn, hostile to the new immigrants entering our own continent. They will take their cue on how to treat immigrants who have crossed the Atlantic from how we in Ireland treat those who have come over the Meditteranean.

CHAPTER

9 SAVING THE EURO

In August 2011, Carol and I returned from holiday to a depleted fridge. I was dispatched to the village for milk and bread. I found a parking space just outside Brady's pub and saw the man himself stepping outside for a smoke. He had spotted me too, and as I manoeuvred into the space, he nonchalantly took up position on the footpath covering my route to the ATM and the shops. This looked like a medical card problem, I thought to myself; or a house for his daughter, maybe; or a back-to-school issue for a grandchild. I reluctantly reached across for my notebook and pen, struggling to adjust from holiday mood to constituency mode. But I need not have worried. This time I did not need to take notes. 'Eamon,' he asked, 'can you tell me, is the euro safe?'

The financial crisis was, by then, Europe-wide. Throughout the summer, there had been several meetings of the European Council and bi-lateral meetings between Chancellor Merkel of Germany and President Sarkozy of France to help stabilise the turbulence. It seemed now that the future of the euro had displaced the resumption of the English Premiership as the subject of conversation over mid-afternoon pints in Brady's of Shankill.

Greece was put into a bailout before Ireland. Portugal followed us in early 2011. Then there was talk of serious problems in Cyprus's banks, and more worryingly, concerns that Spain and possibly Italy would also need rescuing. Europe could manage the smaller member states, but what would happen if a large country, or worse still, two large countries, needed assistance? If Ireland alone needed 25 per cent of the European Central Bank's available resources for its bank liquidity, how could the ECB possibly afford crises in Spain and Italy? And if the ECB could not hold back the tide, then how could the euro survive?

In Ireland, some commentators were questioning the wisdom of remaining in the Eurozone, and were suggesting that leaving the common currency was the best solution for our problems. Similar voices were being raised in other euro countries. Before long, media speculation turned to a possible break-up of the currency zone.

The public mood in Europe's AAA countries, including Germany, the Netherlands, Austria and Finland, was beginning to harden against the 'profligate peripherals'. Bailouts cost money and taxpayers in the stronger European economies were beginning to question why they should pay for 'ouzo-drinking Greeks' who didn't pay taxes at all, and the 'reckless Irish' who had lost the run of themselves building and buying property on borrowed money. While Irish media commentators were questioning the euro in relation to Ireland's national interest, commentators in the bigger euro economies were questioning if their countries should continue to support the currency. After all, if a big EU member state like Britain could manage with its own currency, why couldn't Germany?

These views were finding expression, not only in the media, but also, with each passing election strengthening the euro-sceptic parties in several member states, in parliaments and governments too. While the governments of all the Eurozone countries publicly declared continued confidence in the currency, the possibility was growing that, at some point, some very big member state might decide that the cost of continuing with the single currency was becoming too expensive, and their national interest might be better served by going it alone and returning to the DM or other national currency.

In Brussels, at a Foreign Affairs Council meeting, I was asked by a journalist out of the blue if the Irish Government had a 'plan B' in the event of the euro falling apart. I dismissed the question, because even to entertain in public the possibility of break up would be irresponsible, as it could damage confidence in the currency and possibly even contribute to its destabilisation. But behind closed doors, we did consider the matter very seriously.

As the European financial crisis deepened, the four ministerial members of the Economic Management Council did contemplate the question: what if the currency falls apart? We did not want to be caught off-guard by a sudden decision elsewhere or sudden break-up. We therefore gave the go-ahead for contingency plans to be made.

The euro as a concept and as a currency was unprecedented. Never before had 17 countries with 17 different currencies come together to integrate their monetary policies so closely as to be able to join their markets under one new currency. Francs and punts, deutschmarks and liras, drachmas and pesetas would all disappear into the euro. It happened in stages over time, with initially just a fixed exchange rate between the various currencies (the ERM – European Exchange Rate Mechanism), then a shadow style currency (the ECU – the European Currency Unit) and eventually the euro was released while each of the national currencies was 'stood down'.

The euro came into circulation on 1 January 2002. That evening, I joined my stepfather Tommy Keane for a pint in Keary's in my native village of Caltra. At the bar were three elderly men, in their winter caps and overcoats, holding up the new notes and working out what each was worth in real money, i.e. punts and pence. I could picture similar scenes in cafes and bars from the Peloponnese to Brittany, as similar confabs came to terms with the new currency and reminisced about the old money. The euro had indeed become the most tangible expressions of Europe's union.

Another pub was sometimes mentioned as the euro faced its time of crisis some ten years later. The final agreement on the new currency was made at an ECOFIN meeting held in Dublin during the Irish EU Presidency in 1996. It was chaired by Ireland's then Finance Minister, Ruairí Quinn, and when the meeting was over, he took his European counterparts for the Dublin pub experience at Kitty O'Shea's on Grand Canal Street. Now some sceptics were quick to quip unfairly, 'What can you expect of a currency dreamt up late at night in a Dublin pub?'

While a monetary union had been formed to underpin the euro, there was to be no fiscal union to accompany it. The Eurozone countries agreed a set of stability and growth rules to govern the euro, but those countries were free to draw up their own budgets, set their own taxes and determine their own economic policies. And, as would be expected, all of these varied widely, across the large, strong economies like Germany's to the weaker and smaller economies such as Greece's. Sharing the same currency meant all the economies that were participating affected all the other economies in a very direct way, and there were always going to be up-sides and down-sides for everyone involved.

When this down-side crisis came, the stronger countries banded together to contain the fallout. The relatively small, peripheral economies of Greece, Ireland and Portugal were forced into EU/ECB/IMF bailouts and put into effective isolation to stem the 'contagion'. Ireland was told to solve its own banking crisis, and because it had, in 2008, pre-emptively and unilaterally guaranteed all the banks, it was now in a weak position to resist.

The policy of containment did not work. The contagion spread, and when Spain and Italy began to display symptoms, European leaders knew that more was needed. But the response from the European institutions was slow, indecisive and insufficient. In particular, the conclusions of the European Council meeting of July 2011 fell so far short that instead of calming the situation it undermined further market confidence in the EU's ability to deal with the crisis.

There were several flaws in the EU's response to the crisis in early 2011, when the Fine Gael/Labour Government took office. The first was a misdiagnosis. The dominant EU view at this point was that the banking element was a national problem for each individual State to deal with, and that it should not be mutualised. The new Irish Government disagreed. My message, and that of my colleagues, at all the meetings attended in Europe, was that 'Ireland's problem was Europe's problem', and we argued strongly for the Europeanisation of banking. We argued that the ECB needed to build a stronger firewall against bank failure in Europe and that a common European banking policy needed to be developed. Over time and with increasing evidence for its need, we succeeded in persuading our European counterparts to establish the European Stability Mechanism (ESM) based on a fund of €700 billion, established with contributions from the Eurozone Member states.

The June European Council meeting in 2012 decided to 'break the link' between bank debt and the State. This was a critical change in Europe's position on the banking crisis. Arising from that decision, it was agreed to establish the European Banking Union, with a single European bank supervisor. Michael Noonan would do much to progress this during the Irish EU presidency in 2013.

Unfortunately, while we were succeeding in bringing about major changes to the EU/ECB position on banking, we were not yet directly benefitting from them at home. If the ESM and the new European policy of separating bank debt from the sovereign had been in place in March 2011, we would not have been left on our own with the responsibility to finance the recapitalisation of the Irish banks. We set out to highlight this point to our counterparts in Europe, to leverage it in our efforts to get a better deal on the promissory note, and we hoped in time to get agreement on retrospective ECB recapitalisation of the Irish banks. We were encouraged in these efforts when the European Council, in June 2012, agreed to reference Ireland in its conclusions, effectively acknowledging that we were a special case.

The second major failure in EU policy at the early stage of the crisis related to the prescription. The various crises in Ireland, Greece, Portugal, and later in Spain and Italy were seen by the dominant European leaders as arising from public spending. The theory was that these countries were spending too much, and that the solution was to cut public expenditure and reduce budget deficits. An 'austerity only' policy was adopted and was being forced on the bailed-out countries in particular. There was little or no consideration being given to the need to create jobs and to enable these economies to grow again. Such was the opposition to a growth agenda that, as late as May 2012, a senior German official responded to us, 'What does growth mean? Not your debt-fuelled growth, anyhow? We won't sign up for that.'

The mistakes in European policy at the early stages of the crisis were political and ideological in origin. At the beginning of Ireland's new Government in March 2011, most of the EU Governments leaned to the right. Most Prime Ministers were affiliated to the European People's Party (EPP), to which Fine Gael belongs. Two of these were Chancellor Merkel and President Sarkozy, who worked a Franco-German axis at the heart of Europe and were driving the austerity agenda from the right. This right-wing dominance of the European Council was mirrored in the European Commission, where only six of the twenty-seven commissioners were of the centre-left Party of European Socialists (PES). The PES Presidents – Paul Rasmussen, a former Prime Minister of Denmark, and his successor, Sergei Stanishev, a former Prime Minister of Bulgaria – convened regular meetings of the leaders of the EU's Labour and Social Democratic Parties. I attended the meetings at which a strong critique of the dominant conservative approach to Europe's crisis was made and from which repeated calls were made for measures to enhance growth and generate jobs. But the overwhelming majority of the PES leaders were in opposition and could, therefore, do little to advance an agenda to counter-balance the austerity policies of the right.

One of those was Sigmar Gabriel, the leader of the German SPD. Shortly after my appointment as Tánaiste, he came to Dublin to talk with me. He asked, in particular, about PES preparations for European Council meetings, and he appeared taken aback when I told him that there were no formal PES meetings, because by then there were only three Prime Ministers from our political family who attended the European Council of twenty seven. We conceived the idea of a meeting of PES Prime Ministers and Deputy Prime Ministers which should be held before each European Council meeting. The first was convened before the December Council meeting. There were just six of us, three PMs and three DPMs. At successive meetings we were joined by the President of the

European Parliament, Martin Schulz, who attends the beginning of the European Council; and by PES members of the European Commission. Our main objectives at this early stage were to 'Europeanise' the banking crisis and to advance the jobs and growth agenda.

Happily for me, both of these were in perfect harmony with Ireland's national objectives. Our Programme for Government did not echo the 'austerity only' approach of the European right, but strongly emphasised jobs and growth. It recognised that the flight to recovery would never be made on one wing. This stance of the Irish Government was remarked upon at an early meeting of this PES group. One Prime Minister said that 'Kenny speaks more like the PES than the EPP!' This compliment was earned thanks to the Taoiseach's adherence to the Programme for Government, and to the EMC's preparations for the European Council, but also to his own personal belief, which he shared with me, in a jobs-led recovery.

Support at the European Council for our two-pronged jobs and growth strategy would grow over the two years that followed, particularly as new elections increased the number of Labour and Social Democratic parties participating in governments across the continent. Our small group of Prime Ministers and Deputy Prime Ministers grew with the election of Helle Thorning Schmidt as Prime Minister of Denmark; Francois Hollande as President of France; Prime Ministers Lette and later Renzi of Italy; Prime Ministers Fico, Ponta and Muscat of Slovakia, Romania and Malta; Frans Timmermans as DPM of the Netherlands, Elio di Rupo as PM of Belgium and eventually Sigmar Gabriel as the new DPM of Germany. By the time I left office in July 2014, there was PES representation in half of the governments of the EU member states. The political balance on the European Council was now similar to that in the Irish Government, and not unlike in Ireland, the Council began making its decisions by negotiation between the two main political groupings, the PES and the EPP. The Austrian Chancellor Werner Feymann had once said to me the Council meets 'just to hear the decisions which have already been made at the EPP group meeting in the morning!' This was now no longer the case.

With the Irish Government now having a foot in both of the main political groupings, Enda and I worked closely together to maximise the benefits of this situation for Ireland. Normally we would both travel together to Brussels on the morning of European Council meetings, and be briefed by officials on the government jet. On arrival in Brussels, Enda would be taken to the EPP meeting and I would go to the PES event. We would both lobby our respective political colleagues for a position favourable to Ireland's needs and we would talk again to compare notes and refine the strategy for the Council meeting itself. This collaboration worked particularly well for the crucial June 2012 meeting, which separated bank debt from the sovereign, and which referenced Ireland's unique case in a positive light. On that occasion we met in the Irish delegation room and our debriefing helped Irish officials to significantly influence the later drafting of the final conclusions of that Council.

One aspect of the EU response to the crisis would eventually require change to the European treaties, and therefore, the prospect of a referendum loomed in Ireland. Twenty-three of the twenty-seven EU members had broken the shared Stability and Growth Pact at some stage. The EU desperately needed to show to the outside world that not only did Europe have robust budget rules, but that member states were keeping to them. Throughout 2011, two sets of enhanced budget rules were agreed by the member states – increasing co-operation on budgetary policy, providing for

European Commission pre-clearance of member states' budgetary objectives, and giving power to the Commission to issue 'country-specific recommendations' to member states in relation to their annual budgets. Despite these measures, though – known as the 'two pack' and the 'six pack' – there was continuing doubt about Europe's determination to enforce its own rules for the euro. The argument for some kind of protective 'debt brake' along with the enhanced rules for the euro being put into the European treaties started gathering support.

As Minister for Foreign Affairs and Trade, I became engaged in this European discussion at an early stage. My first concern was the content of what was to be agreed, and my second was whether or not a referendum would be required in Ireland. My initial view was that the EU could enhance the budget rules without changing the existing treaties at all. I felt that the provisions of the Lisbon Treaty were sufficiently flexible to permit the European Council to make whatever decision was needed in relation to a member state. However, both Merkel and Sarkozy appeared determined to enshrine the new rules in the Treaty and to require countries to adopt the debt brake as a provision of their own constitutions. To me, this was unnecessary and excessive, and I went to work on watering down the language in the new proposed international agreement.

I sought changes based on three principal concerns. The first was that Ireland was already in a bailout programme, involving intense external supervision. Would the new treaty impose an additional layer of supervision on us? It was eventually agreed that the terms of the new treaty would not apply to countries in a bailout until they were out of the bailout. My second concern related to the calculation of the structural deficit, which I felt would be difficult for a high exporting country like Ireland. Again, we succeeded in getting significant country-specific qualifications put on the calculations of the structural deficit. The third was the idea of including a debt brake in our constitution, which I felt was no business of the European Union's. This idea was watered down and eventually expressed in these terms: 'Through provisions of binding force and permanent character, preferably constitutional...' I hoped that the word 'preferably' would remove the obligation to change our own constitution, and therefore that another referendum could be avoided.

Irish officials from the Departments of Foreign Affairs and Trade, Taoiseach and Finance worked on the text through Christmas and New Year of 2011/12, a final draft being agreed at the European Council meeting of 30 January. The following day I sent the draft to the Attorney General for her advice as to whether or not a referendum would be required. I was at a meeting of the EU Foreign Affairs Council in Brussels on Monday 27 February when I got word from her office that she had completed her advice and that it would be available for the Cabinet meeting the following morning. I first saw the advice when I arrived home at about 11 p.m. that night. As always, she had given my question thorough and comprehensive consideration, but on this occasion she gave the answer I did not want to hear: on balance, a referendum would be required.

I was in Government Buildings at 8 a.m. the following morning and spoke with the Taoiseach about Máire Whelan's advice. We agreed that I should bring the issue to Government; that we should make the decision at Cabinet level to hold the referendum and at least have the advantage of surprise. The likely opponents of the Treaty had, we supposed, presumed that the AG would have advised the other way, and that the Government would not hold a referendum on this proposal.

I knew that winning this referendum would be very difficult. The referenda on the two previous European Treaties, Nice and Lisbon, had been initially defeated and were passed only after some new concessions were won in renegotiation. Whatever cases could be made for Nice and Lisbon, there was little positive that could be said about this treaty. Indeed, if we got into arguments about the structural deficit and the complexities of the debt brake, I felt we would probably lose. I also knew that the referendum campaign would mobilise as a bloc all those who had always been opposed to the EU and to the euro, and all those who were campaigning against the Government's budgetary strategy, providing them with an opportunity to send that familiar 'message in the ballot box' to the serving government.

I decided that we should keep the issue simple: 'This is about the euro, our own currency … a set of rules to restore stability and secure the future of the currency'. It was a strong, simple message designed to persuade the man in Brady's pub. To underline the message, I decided to shorten the title of the document to the Stability Treaty, and to make it clear that the Government did not regard it as a panacea for our own or Europe's economic ills: 'This treaty will help to stabilise the currency while we implement the growth strategy to create the jobs necessary for recovery'.

The rules governing referenda require that the government can only spend public money on advocacy provided it allocates an equal amount to the campaign opposing the referendum. However, these rules only apply to the period of the referendum itself. So before the enactment of the referendum bill, and the setting of the date for the referendum, I believed that I was permitted, as Minister for Foreign Affairs and Trade, to communicate and explain the terms of the proposed treaty to the public. If the Government had negotiated an international agreement on behalf of the Irish people,

I believed that it had the right, and arguably the duty, to spell out what it meant to the people. I therefore set up a unit in the European Division, under Secretary Geraldine Byrne Nason, tasked with explaining the Treaty to the public before the commencement of the referendum process. We published leaflets and booklets, all of which I personally approved, explaining what this treaty contained. We were, however, careful not to advocate how people should vote in the referendum. One small problem arose, nonetheless, when the website associated with this information campaign featured the speech which I had made in the Dáil, including a call to vote 'Yes'. We were obliged, with some slight embarrassment, to take it back down.

There were, of course, complaints that we were breaking the 50/50 rule and there were threats of legal action. One of these threats arrived just as the final leaflet was about to be distributed a couple of days before the making of the referendum order by the Minister for the Environment. I was a little worried about it, but the threat never materialised; nobody went to court to stop the information campaign.

Meanwhile, the Minister of State for European Affairs, Lucinda Creighton and I met with those who would lead and coordinate the 'Yes' campaign. They initially included Brendan Halligan, the chairperson of the IIEA; Brigid Laffan of UCD; Pat Cox; Danny McCoy of IBEC; Patricia Callan of the Small Firms Association; and trade unionist Blair Horan. There were many others, and from the outset, we decided to involve people who were not associated with previous European referendum campaigns. Among those who came to our assistance was Norah Casey, businesswoman and broadcaster. She agreed to join me on the 'Yes' side in the main television debate with Declan Ganley and Mary Lou McDonald. Norah won the debate hands down. She was sensible and sensitive and she was able to present the arguments in very accessible language. The Labour Party itself mounted a vigorous campaign on the ground. We produced an effective poster, and in most constituencies, public representatives and members took the case to the doorsteps. I also decided to get out on the campaign in the constituencies; I attended public meetings, events in workplaces and did countless local radio interviews.

My door-to-door campaigning was not without incident. I joined Ciara Conway TD and some of our councillors for a canvass in Waterford City. Within minutes we attracted a small but loud and aggressive group of protesters, who followed us along the street, shouting abuse at us through a megaphone. The evening had started to get very wet and, in normal circumstances, we might have called off the canvass, but we were not going to be intimidated by a gang of loudmouths. So we persisted, walking up driveways to the echoes of the most vile and vulgar remarks from the sidewalk. But the behaviour of the protestors was being entirely counter-productive for them. At one door, a woman told me that she had intended to vote 'no', 'but now that I see what you are up against, Mr Gilmore, I think it'll be a "yes".'

In the end, we achieved a convincing win, with the 'Yes' side getting just over 60 per cent of the votes cast. I took quiet personal satisfaction in becoming the first Minister for Foreign Affairs in fourteen years to get a European referendum passed on the first attempt.

The Taoiseach and I spent the day of the count on the phone to European leaders, to build on the goodwill which the referendum win would give us. We gave a press conference on the steps of Government Buildings at which we welcomed the results and interpreted it as a mandate to push for a growth agenda in Europe.

This, in turn, had just received a big boost following the defeat of Sarkozy and the election of Francois Hollande as President of France. Hollande had caused some difficulty for us during the referendum campaign when he spoke about renegotiating the Stability Treaty. I telephoned Pierre Moscovici, who was managing the Hollande campaign, and explained our problem. He assured me that the intention of the French Socialists was to seek a jobs and growth pact in Europe, and hold off on ratifying the treaty until there was agreement on jobs and growth.

The Irish Government enthusiastically supported the French efforts on growth. Mark Garrett and I travelled to Paris for Hollande's victory and to join the celebrations of our French Socialist comrades. We were hosted by Hélène Conway-Mouret, a Professor at Dublin Institute of Technology who represented the French diaspora in the Senate of France. A few days later, she was appointed by President Hollande as a Minister in his first Cabinet. She is also a member of the Dalkey branch of the Irish Labour Party, and on the day of her appointment she called me to tell me the good news. It was just before the weekly meeting of the Parliamentary Labour Party and I enjoyed relating the news: 'I have an important announcement to make. There is a new Labour Cabinet Minister!' And as they tried to figure out if they had missed the reshuffle, I explained that I was referring to the new French Cabinet. Hélène did great work in cooperating with Ambassadors Paul Kavanagh and Rory Montgomery in Paris, building Irish relations with the French Government, and of course, in constantly reminding me of the Labour commitment to build the new DIT campus in Grangegorman!

She accompanied President Hollande and me at Stade de Frances on Saturday 15 March 2014, when Ireland beat France to win the Six Nations. It was Brian O'Driscoll's last game for Ireland, and to mark the occasion I went to the team hotel to make a small presentation to him on behalf of the Irish Government. To the annoyance of my press team, I insisted on doing it privately, without any press. I always thought there was something gaudy about politicians trying to catch some reflected glory from our sports stars, and I still recoil at the pictures of Charlie Haughey 'winning' the Tour de France for Stephen Roche!

The compact for jobs and growth, promoted by Hollande, and strongly supported by Ireland, was agreed in mid-2012. It would mobilise €120 billion in initiatives to reboot the European economy and create jobs. Among the measures was an enhanced role for the European Investment Bank (EIB), which was of particular benefit to Ireland in putting together funding for a major €2.2 billion stimulus package, which Brendan Howlin assembled and announced later in the summer.

Ireland played a key role in advancing the growth agenda, partly thanks to the coincidence of our holding of the rotating six-month presidency of the EU in the first half of 2013. As Ministers from the Presidency country chair Council meetings, and Presidency civil servants chair and coordinate the many committees and working groups in Brussels, we knew we could make a lot of progress in that time.

Decision making in the European Union is now very complex. It is never easy to get agreement from 28 member states, with many of them having conflicting or competing national interests. The European Parliament, now with a very diverse political complexion, has an increased role in decision making. A good and effective presidency will pull together the European Commission and the other institutions, will work the room at Council meetings to get compromise decisions, and will negotiate an outcome with the European Parliament. It requires considerable planning, political skill and diplomatic effort.

Ireland already had a good reputation for running effective presidencies. This would be our seventh, and expectations across Europe were high. We began to prepare for it over a year in advance. The previous Irish presidency was in 2004, and had cost over €100 million to organise. In keeping with the mood of the times, I decided to cut the cost and budgeted to run the presidency for just over half the cost in 2004, and for about half the costs incurred by the presidencies of other member states. I decided that the practice of Ministers hosting expensive informal ministerial meetings in their own constituencies should end. The biggest cost associated with these events was the setting up of translation facilities, press centres and security arrangements at big local hotels. There would be one conference venue, I decided: Dublin Castle. We would fit out a new conference facility there in the old Revenue Stamping Building. We would use one hotel; the contract we tendered was won by the Westbury. We would cut down the fleets of black cars with Garda motor outriders running to and from Dublin Airport. Instead we would use buses. The limited number of cars to be used would be provided on a sponsorship basis by a motor company. We would cut down on entertainment and gifts, deciding on a well-designed tie and woollen scarf, both of which were in big demand. We cut out most of the trappings and concentrated on the business end.

The theme of the Irish presidency was 'Stability, Jobs and Growth', and we saw our role as pushing the jobs and growth agenda at every Council formation. The Common Agricultural Policy was now much about jobs in food production and Simon Coveney succeeded in getting a new agreement there. Michael Noonan got agreement on banking union; Pat Rabbitte got agreement on energy; Richard Bruton got a mandate to start the transatlantic trade talks with the US; Joan Burton secured agreement on the youth employment guarantee; and Seán Sherlock made excellent progress on research and innovation.

In Dublin, all of the work was coordinated at ministerial level by Lucinda Creighton and me, and at civil service level by Geraldine Byrne Nason and her team. Geraldine produced a presidency progress book – a folder with colour-coded objectives for each Department. In Brussels, Rory Montgomery and Tom Hanney led a team of enthusiastic and hard-working officials, some of whom were recruited specifically for the duration of the presidency.

I chaired the EU General Affairs Council (GAC) during the presidency. This council prepares the agenda for the EU summits, so from mid-2012 I met regularly with Commission President, José Manuel Barroso; with Council President, Herman van Rompuy; and with the Parliament President, Martin Schulz. I also met with most of the Commissioners and with the Chairs of key European Parliament committees. Lucinda Creighton spent considerable time at the European Parliament, both before and during the presidency, building up the relationships which would be essential to getting agreement on various portfolios.

One challenge for me as Chair of the GAC was the plan for EU enlargement. Croatia was due to become the twenty-eighth Member State of the EU on 1 July 2013, but there were still some issues to be finalised, mainly to do with allocation of EU funding. I worked closely with the Croatian Foreign Minister, Vesna Pusic, to resolve this and she invited me to speak at the outdoor accession ceremony in Zagreb at midnight on 30 June 2013 – the very last minute of the Irish Presidency.

Serbia was anxious to start negotiations for membership, but could not do so until it had resolved its dispute with Kosovo. Cathy Ashton, the EU High Representative on Foreign Affairs and Security, brokered an agreement between Pristina and Belgrade which enabled the GAC to approve the opening of formal accession negotiations with Serbia. Iceland, too, had been making solid progress toward EU membership. There were major difficulties, however, over fisheries, and following their general election in April 2013, Iceland suspended its accession talks.

Accession talks with Turkey had been stalled for over two years. Cyprus, which held the presidency immediately before Ireland, was hostile to Turkish accession, so I felt that in the Irish presidency, accession talks should be recommenced with Turkey. I visited Turkey in April, and in talks with Foreign Minister Ahmet Davutoğlu, President Gül and other Turkish leaders, I got a strong sense that Turkey believed that Europe was not really serious about Turkish accession. I realised that this would send Turkey to look elsewhere for allies and trading partners and that Europe needed to send a strong signal that it was still in favour of Turkish membership. My efforts to re-open negotiations with them met strong resistance from Germany. Before the critical June General Affairs Council, I spoke by phone with Davutoğlu and with German Foreign Minister, Guido Westerwelle. I felt that Westerwelle himself was closer to my position, but that his apparent instructions from Berlin were to block progress. I insisted and eventually worked out a formula that allowed for the reopening of some Turkish chapters by October.

By far the biggest challenge for me, though, and indeed for the entire Irish presidency, was to get the 2014 – 2020 Multi-Annual Financial Framework (MFF) agreed. This amounts to a seven-year European Union budget plan, covering all areas of spending by the EU, including the Common Agricultural Policy, rural development, spending on roads and other infrastructure, research and innovation, and on foreign policy areas such as humanitarian and development aid. The European Commission had initially proposed a seven-year MFF of €1,033 billion, all of which would have to be contributed by member states. A number of states, including the UK and Germany, wanted this reduced. They argued that, at a time when national governments were being forced to cut their own spending programmes at home, they should not be increasing the spending of the EU, for which the member states would have to pay over time. Two internal groups of member states developed: the so-called 'Friends of Cohesion', mainly Eastern European States, who were net recipients of EU funding and who wanted a large EU budget to fund infrastructure projects of the kind the EU funded for Ireland in the 1980s and 1990s. The second group were the 'Friends of Better Spending', mainly the net contributor countries to the EU who wanted a smaller budget more effectively deployed.

By the time we took on the presidency, the European Council had agreed to reduce the MFF to €960 billion, but still a very large sum, which would help generate economic activity and jobs. Those wishing for an EU stimulus plan need look no further. Here was a stimulus budget amounting to almost a trillion euro. But first, the Union would have to agree to it. My job was to get agreement on how much should go to each budget heading and how it should be spread out over the seven years. I needed to secure the agreement of three institutions: the European Commission, still smarting because their draft budget had been cut by almost €100 billion; the twenty-eight member states, each of which had its own different national priorities; and the European Parliament of 760 members, of which 380 would have to vote in favour for the budget to be passed.

At the beginning of 2013, the prospect of European Parliament approval did not look promising. It passed a resolution effectively rejecting the €960 billion as inadequate. There was little sympathy for its position at the General Affairs Council, where many Ministers felt that members of the European Parliament had the luxury of passing or rejecting such a large spending budget without having to take responsibility for raising the money. Funding the European budget was the responsibility of the individual member states whose governments would have to raise it in taxes.

The lead negotiator for the Parliament was the highly experienced French MEP, Alain Lamassoure, a member of Sarkozy's UMP Party. In early 2013, he came to Dublin to talk with me about how we might handle the negotiations. He felt that, although the Parliament considered the €960 billion to be insufficient, members might be persuaded to accept provided they could be assured of a few things: that all of the €960 billion would eventually be spent, that there be flexibility across budget headings, that the MFF could be revised mid-term, and that there was at least a future possibility of the EU raising its own tax resources.

Lamassoure explained that while it would be difficult to get over half the MEPs to vote for this budget now, it would be even more difficult after the summer when their minds would turn to the parliamentary elections of May 2014. If we failed to get agreement during the Irish presidency, therefore, there might not be a seven-year plan at all. EU budgets would then have to be decided upon on a year-to-year basis, making it impossible for the likes of universities and industries to plan research, or for governments and local authorities to plan spending on roads and big infrastructure projects. Some countries might not be unhappy with such annual EU budgeting because less would eventually be spent. As well as saying a lot about the EU's capacity to make decisions, these negotiations would have considerable impact on work and jobs, and so they were very important for me, and for Ireland.

The negotiations would take the form of three-way meetings, known as trilogues, between the Commission, led by Polish Commissioner, Janusz Lewandowski; the Council, led by me; and the Parliament, led by Lamassoure. It was hard going just to get the meetings started. We eventually arranged the first for 11 April, but that was cancelled because the Parliament wanted outstanding discussions on the 2013 Budget completed before they could start negotiations on an MFF commencing in 2014. Another trilogue arranged for 25 April was again postponed. I spoke on the phone with Lamassoure and Martin Schulz, the President of the European Parliament, in an effort to get things moving. It was, after all, the end of April at that stage, and there were only two months left to negotiate an extremely complex file.

I had first met Martin Schulz in 2004 when I was Labour's National Director of Elections for the European Parliament elections and he was Leader of the Socialist Group in the EU. We met many times after that, including during several visits by him to Ireland, and we formed a good friendship. This bond would be critical in these negotiations, but I had to be careful that Lamassoure did not form the opinion that I was going around him.

Schulz suggested that he, Barroso and the Taoiseach should meet with me, Lamassoure and Lewandowski to kick-start the discussions. This meeting took place in Brussels on 6 May. Enda made it very clear to everybody that I was leading the negotiations for the European Council and that he did not intend to become directly involved. It was a position he maintained right through the talks and it convinced the other institutions, helpfully, that there was just one Irish presidency negotiator.

Following this meeting, the trilogues eventually got underway properly on 13 May and continued intensively through to the very end of June. To maintain institutional balance, each successive meeting had to be held in the Berlaymont, the Parliament and the Justus Lipsius Building, home to the Council. In the latter, we were in the presidency offices on the fifth floor, appropriately decked out with Irish furniture for our six months.

Lewandowski was accompanied by a team of officials from the Commission. I was accompanied by senior officials of the European Council, led by Jim Cloos and by a team of Irish officials, led by Rory Montgomery, Ireland's Permanent Representative to the EU, and by Lorcan Fulham from the European Division and Emma Cunningham from the Department of Finance. Lamassoure was accompanied by an MEP from each of the political groupings in the European Parliament, and they, in turn were accompanied by an official from each group.

The early meetings were a series of speeches from each side, with separate speeches being made by each of the MEPs, presumably for the benefit of their political groupings back at base.

I operated on the basis that the substance of speechmaking is quite different to that of the actual negotiations, so I set about meeting each of the main participants separately to map out a 'landing zone' on each of the main issues.

My own personal sympathies were largely in line with those of the Parliament. I too wanted a better budget, more flexibility, more potential spend on valuable programmes and the opportunity to revisit the MFF when economic circumstances improved. But I was constrained by the General Affairs Council, where twenty-eight member states had widely differing opinions on the budget. I was, meanwhile, also being lobbied at home by farming organisations, who wanted to defend the CAP and secure funding for rural development; by industries and universities, who wanted to increase the budget for research and innovation; by trade unions, who wanted more done on jobs, especially on youth unemployment; and by a range of NGOs, who wanted to ensure a strong development aid budget. Among those who came to meet me in Iveagh House was Bill Gates, whose Bill and Melinda Gates

Foundation works closely with the Department of Foreign Affairs and Trade on projects in the developing world. Over breakfast he encouraged me to protect the EU Aid Budget, especially as the EU and its member states account for about 55 per cent of all the world's aid programmes.

Over the course of the trilogue meetings it became increasingly apparent to me that the individual MEPs had perfectly reasonable demands, but unfortunately they could not agree a common position from which to negotiate because they were each saddled with mandates from their political groups, which they could not be seen to abandon in the presence of their opponents. I came to the view, therefore, that the only route to an overall agreement was for Lamassoure and me to agree a compromise, which I would recommend to the General Affairs Council and he would recommend to the Parliament.

After a full day of side meetings, Alain and I came to an agreement. I could sense that when we announced the details to the reconvened trilogues, some members of his delegation were voicing resistance to it, but I was not unduly alarmed by this, since I knew their own red lines. I informed the press that Lamassoure and I had an agreed set of proposals which we would recommend. This was, unfortunately, though not unexpectedly, interpreted by many as a deal on the MFF, and was reported as such by the media. The following day all hell broke loose.

Some of the MEPs on Lamassoure's delegation publicly opposed the compromise and had harsh words for my role and my style of negotiation. To my amazement, the following morning the *Irish Times* ran an editorial that was strongly critical of me. Normally editorials like this do not appear until a few days after the event. This one was well-informed, full of detail and used accurate EU jargon, and was not entirely in harmony with the paper's own reports of the negotiations. I sensed, and suggested as much to colleagues, that it had come from inside our own tent and possibly from somebody with a score to settle. I now faced the possibility not only of no agreement on the MFF, but that the whole thing would blow up in my face politically. I spent the weekend on the phone to Lamassoure, Schulz, MEPs, officials, and other European ministers in a desperate effort to save the negotiations and to finalise a deal before the Irish presidency finished at the end of the following week.

Schulz once again suggested a meeting of the four presidents for the morning of Thursday 27 June, ahead of the European Council meeting, which was due later that day. I travelled on Sunday night, 23 June, to Luxembourg for the meeting of the Foreign Affairs Council. I used my time at that meeting to sound out ministers on what additional tweaking to the MFF might secure parliament agreement. The following day, at the General Affairs Council, which was attended by Council President Herman van Rompuy, I asked for and got a mandate for one last effort to conclude the MFF. I travelled to Brussels that evening to meet the leader of the Socialist group, Hannes Swoboda, whose support would be essential for eventual agreement.

Back in Dublin, I spent Wednesday 26 June on the phone to several of the key players and spoke with Schulz again on a number of occasions. That evening the Taoiseach and I left Baldonnel for Brussels, arriving at around 11 p.m. As we both sat into the back of the lead car, I noticed I had two missed calls from Schulz. With the Taoiseach sitting beside me, I returned the call on the drive from the airport to the hotel. Martin and I agreed the very final changes to the MFF during that twenty minute call, and when we arrived at the hotel I told our exhausted officials the nature of the final compromises. Around midnight, they went off to meet their Council and Commission counterparts to draft the changes before the formal meeting at 8 a.m. the next morning. But all was not yet solved.

The Commission, led by Barroso, began to fight a last minute rear-guard action on elements of the allocation for the Commission's own administrative budget. Fortunately, with officials working furiously behind the scenes on final re-drafting, it was all resolved by lunchtime, and we were able to hold a joint press conference to announce the good news. The European Union would have a seven year budget plan up to 2020.

That afternoon, the Taoiseach went to the European Council meeting, where each of the heads of state and government congratulated Ireland on a very successful presidency, now just crowned with an agreement on the MFF. I went to the offices of Ireland's permanent mission to the EU, where Rory Montgomery had assembled all the Irish Brussels-based staff who had worked on the presidency. Over tea and cake, I thanked them for their valiant and tireless work over the six months, which had delivered such positive results for Ireland and for Europe. My only sadness was that so many of them who had been employed on contracts would be finishing up the next day. I hoped that, in time, many of them would re-join the Irish public service.

There was only one more hurdle for the MFF: the vote in the European Parliament itself. That was set for the following Thursday, 3 July, in Strasbourg. I couldn't risk anything going wrong at this final stage, so I travelled out for it, missing an important speaking opportunity in the ICTU Conference in Belfast. The MFF was passed by 474 votes to 193, with forty-two abstentions.

It was not the only vote of interest to Ireland that day: Emily O'Reilly was elected by the Parliament as the new Ombudsman for Europe. And as I congratulated her and her family, I reflected on how much Ireland's reputation had improved over the previous two years.

10 THE GOODEST COUNTRY

For a time, every article about Ireland in the international press seemed to be illustrated with a photograph of a scrawny, forlorn-looking pony in a 'ghost estate'. All the coverage of Ireland's crisis years told the same story: the Celtic Tiger is finished; millionaire property tycoons are now bankrupt; highly bonused bankers are under investigation; businesses are closing; housing developments are abandoned; families are struggling to pay mortgages now twice the value of their homes; the pubs are empty; the people are sad; even the horses are hungry!

Sadly, the reality actually matched the newspapers' colour features. The unthinkable had happened. Ireland, once one of the world's most successful economies, was now in an IMF bailout. Irish debt was considered to be junk by financial ratings agencies. We were considered to be one of the problem peripheral countries of Europe – the PIGS, as in Portugal, Ireland, Greece and Spain. We had few friends around the European table. Those who were sympathetic to us kept it to themselves. Others were not reticent about declaring that we had it coming. The arrogant swagger of some Irish political figures and celebrity businessmen during the

Celtic Tiger years may have created envy, but it won few admirers and even fewer friends. We were on our own now, and in boardrooms all over the world, company directors wondered about Ireland, delayed making the investment decisions and were cautious about trading with us. Ireland's international reputation was at its worst in living memory.

If we were to turn things around from this grim scenario, save jobs, resume business and get the economy to recover, we needed to restore Ireland's good name and do it fast. That is why I chose to be Minister for Foreign Affairs (and to add the Trade responsibility to the Department in order to give a clear economic focus to the work). The message needed to get out quickly that Ireland had a new government, and this Government was serious about getting to grips with the economic crisis, and determined to lead Ireland back to recovery. I wanted to be to the fore in delivering that message.

So, as soon as I could, I invited all the ambassadors from other countries who are resident in Ireland to Iveagh House in two groups – first, those from EU member states, and then, those from outside the EU. Later, on our National Day of Commemoration in July, I hosted a lunch for the 'non-resident' ambassadors, most of whom are based in London. All got the same message: 'Ireland will recover and here's what we are doing to make it happen…' I knew that each ambassador would send a confidential note of the briefing to their respective foreign ministers.

I then called back to Dublin all of the Irish ambassadors abroad, and over two days in the ballroom of Iveagh House, they were briefed by me, the Taoiseach, by Michael Noonan and Brendan Howlin, and by the State agencies on our plan for recovery. Each of them would return to their mission, newly mandated, and equipped with a renewed and consistent Irish message. This was followed through with a coordinated series of ministerial and trade visits to as many countries as possible. These visits included not just official meetings with other governments and their ministers, but also business events and briefings for foreign journalists and opinion-makers. Consistent message books were prepared for such visits.

Ireland was re-launching and re-promoting itself to the world again.

This re-launching of Ireland benefitted greatly from the back-to-back visits of Queen Elizabeth and President Obama in May 2011. I was in the car, between campaign stops during the general election that January, when I got a phone call from Brian Cowen. No, he wryly assured me, he was not ringing to wish me well in the election! He reminded me that both President Mary Robinson and Mary McAleese had cultivated a relationship with Queen Elizabeth, and that President McAleese believed that the time had now come for the first ever State visit by a British monarch to an independent Ireland. The dates being considered were in May, and if that were to happen, the invitations would have to be issued in February. Cowen wanted to clear the invitations with Enda Kenny and me. I readily agreed, as did Enda.

The preparations for the visits were, therefore, well under way in the Department of Foreign Affairs and Trade, when I took up office. The visit of Queen Elizabeth would be the most significant visit to the country since the late President John F. Kennedy in 1963, or perhaps Pope John Paul II in 1979. The Head of Protocol, Kathleen White, was overseeing a complex set of practical arrangements, including where Queen Elizabeth would stay, how she would travel, what events she would attend, who would accompany her, who would be invited, and how we would manage the inevitable enormous press entourage.

Relations between Britain and Ireland had improved over the

years, and since the Good Friday Agreement in Northern Ireland, there had been more than a decade of peace. Nevertheless, our biggest concern for the visit was security. Dissident republican groups were still active, and just one, even acting alone, could destroy the visit. These concerns were not groundless or excessive by any means: on the morning of the visit, in fact, a suspected explosive device was discovered on a bus coming from Longford; and Baldonnel Air Force base, where the Queen would land, had to be 'swept' following a bomb threat, which turned out to be a hoax.

As Foreign Minister, it was my duty, and that of my wife, Carol Hanney, to meet and greet Queen Elizabeth and Prince Philip on their arrival at Baldonnel. I left that Tuesday morning's Cabinet meeting early for the drive out to Baldonnel. I had spent much time in the previous days doing interviews, mainly for British and other overseas media, about the importance and the historic nature of this visit. I was still worried that something might go wrong, including that the public would react negatively to the severe traffic restrictions, which, for security reasons, were being imposed throughout Dublin.

It was only on the way to the airport that it dawned on me: I would be the very first person to welcome Queen Elizabeth to Ireland. A little moment of history in the making. But I was also conscious of the weight of our long and complex history with Britain, and I was clear that the welcome should be nothing more and no less than it would be for any Head of State: no bowing, no curtsying, no deference; but a warm, generous and genuine welcome. The mixed feelings, perhaps, of any democratic republican welcoming a British monarch to Ireland.

As I stood at the bottom of the steps leading from the RAF plane, which had just arrived from Northolt, my mind turned to the

Queen herself. My image was of the stiff, formal, somewhat cold figure, largely in sync with the recent Helen Mirren portrayal. The first thing that struck me as she stepped out of the plane was that she had chosen to dress in a bright green suit. That wasn't expected! But the implied signal of respect was most welcome and would, it turned out, set the tone for the rest of the visit.

As she and Prince Philip gingerly made their way down the steep steps, it occurred to me that they were both about the same age as my late mother and late step-father would have been, and I was momentarily concerned simply that they would make it safely to the bottom. When she reached the bottom of the steps, the Queen turned and beamed a smile at me, and I stepped forward to shake her hand and welcome her and Prince Philip. She exuded warmth and friendship and goodwill, and she expressed her delight in being in Ireland at last. She seemed a little excited at her new adventure, at finally being able to visit her nearest neighbours. I had expected the occasion to be awkward, but it was so relaxed that I felt I could be chatting with any older person in any part of my constituency. I introduced the visitors to Carol and then they moved along the line to speak to the dignitaries, including the British Ambassador Julian King, and his wife Lotte, and representatives of the Irish Defence Forces.

I walked and chatted with the Queen along the customary red carpet, at the end of which stood nine-year old Rachel Fox, a pupil from St Anne's School in Shankill, who presented a bunch of flowers. The Queen lingered to chat with Rachel. Late in the preparations, an official in my Department thought it might be a good idea to include a child in the welcoming ceremony, and I asked School Principal Jim Halligan, who had taught my sons at St Anne's, to nominate a pupil for this role. Rachel performed the honour to perfection.

Getting into her car, the Queen turned to me and asked, to my surprise, 'Are you not coming with me?'

'No,' I replied. 'I'll be travelling after you, but we will meet again at the President's lunch in Áras an Uachtaráin.'

After lunch with the President, short speeches and some music, we travelled to the Garden of Remembrance for the first public part of the visit. The Garden was built to commemorate the Irish patriots of 1916 who had been shot by an indignant British Empire, then in the midst of the First World War with Germany. It is close to the GPO, where the Irish Republic was proclaimed that Easter Monday, and it is just around the corner from Moore Street, where Padraic Pearse surrendered, and from the Rotunda Hospital, where the surviving Irish volunteers were first imprisoned. Laying a wreath in memory of Ireland's 1916 heroes, Queen Elizabeth bowed. In that one simple, solemn, silent moment, she declared loudly that the relationships between Britain and Ireland had changed utterly, into a new confident friendship between two close neighbours.

Sinn Féin planned a protest for this event. They intended to float black balloons over the Garden of Remembrance while the ceremony was taking place. However, nature had other ideas, and the breeze blew in the opposite direction, taking their black balloons off away from Parnell Square. (At least they learned from it to judge more carefully which way the wind was blowing, as, in April 2014, the Sinn Féin Ard Comhairle decided to allow Martin McGuinness to attend President Higgins' State visit to Windsor Castle, and in 2015, Gerry Adams effectively invited himself to shake the hand of Prince Charles at a function in NUI Galway.)

The State visit by Queen Elizabeth surpassed all expectations. The commemoration event at Islandbridge involved Northern Unionists; her speech at the State Dinner in Dublin Castle was eloquent and historic; her visit to Trinity College, the Guinness

Storehouse, stud farms, the Rock of Cashel and the Tyndall Institute showed the breadth of her interest in Ireland. By Friday, the final day of her visit, as she mingled with crowds of well-wishers in Cork, the 'Rebel City', it was clear that the Irish people had warmed to her, as I had on the first morning. Relations between Ireland and Britain had been moved onto a new plateau.

While the Taoiseach was saying goodbye to the Queen and Prince Philip at Cork Airport, I was back in the Department of Foreign Affairs and Trade, preparing for the next big visit. President Obama and his wife Michelle were due to arrive at Dublin Airport on Air Force One early on Monday morning, for his first visit to Ireland.

On St Patrick's Day, two months previously in the White House, the Taoiseach had invited President Obama to visit. Nobody expected it to happen quite so soon, but the President had planned to visit Britain and Europe in the week beginning 23 May, and decided to add Ireland to the beginning of his itinerary. One State visit is a challenge for any Foreign Ministry; two in the space of a week – particularly of such huge significance – required an exceptional effort.

The security arrangements for the President's visit were very different, though. The British left security to us. Whatever British security presence was around the Queen was very discreet. But the Americans roll differently: flying in their own secure cars; an army of secret service officers, arriving in advance – with their close-cropped hair, their ear pieces and their lapel mics – and practically 'taking over'.

At Dublin Airport, their briefing notes apparently said that only two cars could go plane-side for the welcome. We had three, so the occupants of the third had to pile into the two cars carrying me and Ambassador Rooney. On the Irish side, there was some satisfied amusement later in the day when the President's long limousine got stuck on the ramp at the US Embassy in Ballsbridge. One senior Garda mused to me, 'Now, if they had left that to us, we would have had the good sense to test drive that big thing over the ramp before he came!'

One thing no security could protect us from was the weather. On the morning of Monday 23 May, the skies opened. Dark skies, heavy rain, strong winds and bone-chilling cold assaulted us from every direction as Carol and I took up duty at the steps of Air Force One. Coming straight from a sweltering Washington, Barack and Michelle Obama were lightly clothed and shuddered at their first experience of the Irish weather. The President took personal care to ensure that Ambassador Rooney, who suffered from a back complaint, got the most comfortable seat on the helicopter taking them to Áras an Uachtaráin.

The Taoiseach and I had a formal meeting with the President at Farmleigh House, at which we discussed a number of international and European issues, Ireland's prospects for recovery, and the plight of Ireland's undocumented in the US. As was very widely covered at the time, the President travelled to Moneygall to meet his cousins and sip a pint in their bar, before returning to the Bank of Ireland building on College Green, where we met briefly again before he went out to address the huge crowd stretching from the walls of Trinity College all the way up Dame Street.

As always, the President was accompanied by a large entourage of important US officials, from the White House, the State Department and other US Government agencies. Officials in our Department of Foreign Affairs and Trade had anticipated that these important people might be at a loose end when the President retired to his suite in the Merrion Hotel that Monday night, so they organised a session for O'Donoghue's pub on Merrion Row. Some well-known Irish musicians were assembled and a little food and drink organised for what was, of course, seen as an opportunity to socialise with, and have a word in the ear of, some key US Government people.

Unfortunately, the President's visit had to be cut short suddenly. Air traffic was being affected by the ash cloud from an Icelandic volcano, and he was taking no chances with his visit to Britain. But with all the guests rushing out to Dublin Airport to catch up with their President, a senior civil servant asked me what we would do now about O'Donoghue's.

'We're going ahead with it,' I replied. 'After what you've all done for Ireland in the last week, you deserve to celebrate a little'. It was too late to cancel it, anyway.

The two visits, especially that of Queen Elizabeth, attracted media attention all around the world. We had expected big coverage in the English speaking world, but the interest was much wider than that. Our embassies all sent back reports of the first really good news story from Ireland for a very long time. An article, which the British Foreign Secretary, William Hague, and I co-authored, was published in thirty-two countries and in several languages. The attention and publicity provided us with a great opportunity to promote Ireland, and to tell the world that we were on the way back.

We deliberately set out to exploit the visit for trade purposes. The British Minister accompanying the Queen was Foreign Secretary William Hague, whom I had got to know at the EU Foreign Affairs Council. On the first day of the visit, he and I launched the British-Irish Chamber of Commerce. We were both surprised that although Britain is Ireland's largest trading partner, and Ireland is Britain's fifth largest, and although about one billion euros' worth of goods and services are traded between the two islands every week, there was no formal joint Chamber of Commerce.

We both followed up on the visit with another meeting in London, as did the Taoiseach and Prime Minister Cameron, who agreed a formal statement of the new British-Irish relations. We continued to build on the visit, as trade, business and job opportunities emerged from our strategy.

I also set out to develop the Ireland-US relationship, which was already very strong. That US companies employ over 100,000 workers in Ireland was well-known, but less well-known was the fact that Irish companies employ almost as many in the USA. The economic, political and personal ties between the two countries have long worked to mutual advantage, but perhaps, I thought, the time had come for Ireland and the US to work together, not just for ourselves but for others.

At the previous United Nations General Assembly in 2010, Ireland and the USA had launched a joint aid package called the '1,000 Days' initiative, aimed at tackling hunger and nutrition among very young children in Africa. When I met Secretary of State, Hillary Clinton, in Washington on 18 March, we talked about the potential of this initiative, and I agreed to provide some funding from the Irish Aid Programme for her 'Cookstoves Initiative'. We agreed to meet again in Tanzania in June to promote the '1,000 Days' initiative there with the Tanzanian Government. It went from strength to strength and was eventually mainstreamed by the United Nations as its Scaling Up Nutrition (SUN) movement, which has contributed enormously to reducing infant mortality and enhancing conditions for children in developing countries, especially in Africa.

While on that visit to Tanzania, I performed the official opening of a village grain centre which had been built with the assistance of

Irish Aid. The locals had decided to make me an honorary member of the Maasai tribe and so before my alarmed advisors could do anything about it, I was wrapped in a Maasai shawl, and a spear and colourful shield were thrust into my hands. Back home, the resulting photograph provided great glee for the tabloids, and some ammunition for those in my own party who were beginning to mutter that I was spending too much time out of the country.

As I saw it, Labour's policy was that Ireland's jobs recovery should be export-led. In the lead up to the general election, we had published a policy document which emphasised the need to grow Ireland's trade presence in the emerging economies, especially the BRICS – Brazil, Russia, India, China and South Africa. We followed through on this in government under my watch. Minister of State, Joe Costello, accompanied President Higgins on a very successful visit to Brazil which resulted in increased business for Irish education. Minister Leo Varadkar visited India for St Patrick's Day, capitalising on his own family connections with the sub-continent to the benefit of Ireland. In October, I travelled to Moscow, accompanied by a team of officials from the Departments of Agriculture, Jobs, Transport and Tourism, to chair a meeting aimed at reviving the Joint Economic Council between Ireland and Russia.

While in Russia, I had my first meeting with Foreign Minister, Sergei Lavrov. Lavrov is a legend among foreign ministers. He had begun his long, distinguished career in the Soviet diplomatic service and had served at a senior level for every Russian leader since, including, most recently, for Vladimir Putin. I had called him some months earlier to sympathise personally with him on the sudden death of the Russian Ambassador to Ireland, Mr Mikhail Timoshkin. He appreciated the gesture. When we met he had with him Ambassador Timoshkin's successor, Mr Maxim Peshkov, who, he proudly informed me, was a great-grandson of the great Russian writer, Maxim Gorky. We had a bilateral meeting lasting several hours and continuing over lunch. Lavrov proposed the first toast, 'To Ireland'. After that we toasted Russia, the friendship between our countries, the United Nations, peace, poetry, love and eventually, towards the end, there were several toasts to Aidan McGeady, the Irish footballer who was then playing with Lavrov's team, Spartak Moscow, and of whom Sergei was a fan.

Fortunately, the Secretary General of the Department, David Cooney, had given me good advice on how to cope with this Russian ritual of mid-day toasting with vodka: 'Throw the first one back,' he said. 'Don't sip. Empty the glass. Then refill your glass with water and repeat. After each toast, throw it back and refill again with water. That way the waiter can put no more vodka in your glass.' It was good advice. By the time the lunch ended, Aidan McGeady's feats were improving with every toast, but I was still stone-cold sober.

China accounts for one-fifth of the population of the planet and is one of the world's fastest-growing economies. A number of significant Chinese visitors came to Dublin in 2011, including the Chairman of the Chinese Investment Corporation. I met each of them in Iveagh House and at each meeting we discussed ways of increasing trade between Ireland and China. In early 2012, I was informed that the then Vice President of China, Mr Xi Jinping, intended to visit. It was being speculated that at the Party congress later that year, he would be elected as General Secretary of the Chinese Communist Party, and would, in due course, become President and Leader of the country. His visit at this time would therefore give Ireland a unique opportunity to develop a relationship with somebody who could be a major world leader for the next decade or more. We understood that the only other countries which he was visiting on this tour were the United States and Turkey.

On Saturday 18 February, I travelled to Shannon Airport to welcome Xi Jinping to Ireland. We had discussed the programme for the visit with the Chinese Embassy and it was tailored to meet their wishes. I took him to visit the Shannon Development Company, which the Chinese had used as a model for the development (on a much larger scale) of their own airports and industrial centres. That evening, at the request of our guests, we had dinner in Bunratty Castle, and sitting at the long benches, I chatted with Xi Jinping about our respective rural backgrounds. His family had been sent into the countryside during the Cultural Revolution and he had experienced the hard physical work of subsistence farming. I told him about my growing up on a small mixed farm in County Galway, and we had plenty of anecdotes of rural life to share. He was particularly interested in the transition which Ireland had made over the decades from a mostly rural economy, and how urbanisation and modernisation had changed our society and culture.

The following day, Simon Coveney took him to a farm in County Clare, where he was presented with a calf; and Joe Costello took him to Croke Park, where he displayed an innate aptitude for Gaelic football. The Taoiseach and I held a formal meeting with the Vice President and his delegation in Dublin Castle before going to Belvedere College to see a performance of particular resonance for both our countries.

Riverdance is phenomenally popular in China, and Xi Jinping wished to see it performed in its native Dublin. No problem, we thought … until we discovered that the show was not on anywhere in Ireland at the time. The only solution, for such a guest, was to arrange a special performance. One of the most elaborate productions ever produced in Ireland, and the State would have to pay for the entire thing! I felt the expensive gesture would pay for itself many times over in the long term and so I asked some of the associated State agencies to chip in and I allocated funding from the Department's budget, and a special, for-one-night-only performance of Riverdance was staged.

I sat beside Xi Jinping in the concert hall in Belvedere, and can vouch that he certainly enjoyed it. Moya Doherty turned up, one of the creators and producers of the show, and Xi was delighted to meet her. The following morning before his departure at Dublin Airport, he spoke to me about his sincere wish to strengthen and develop the relationship with Ireland. A job well done, I felt, and we took him up on it.

The Taoiseach visited China a few weeks later and signed a Strategic Partnership Agreement between the two countries. This was followed up by a succession of ministerial visits which led to the opening up of the Chinese market for Irish fish products, Irish beef, and the growth of exports for other Irish foods, pharmaceutical and software products. I saw, at first hand, the great strides being made in trade between the two countries and the enormous business potential when I visited in July 2013. (And, to my amazement and delight, I saw Chinese dancers perform a piece from Riverdance at an event in Shanghai at which I launched the Chinese video of the Wild Atlantic Way!)

These meetings with Chinese and other leaders were not, of course, confined to trade issues. We also always discussed a range of international and political matters, especially relating to human rights. Ireland follows a values-based foreign policy, and while we remained focused on trade and economic relationships, we never pulled back from our obligations to promote human rights. Ireland's reputation as an advocate for human rights, strengthened by Mary Robinson's role as UN Commissioner for Human Rights, was put to the test in an important United Nations election.

Immediately on taking office, the Department briefed me on the upcoming election for the UN Human Rights Council (HRC) in November 2012. Three countries were to be elected from a pool of countries, which included some from western Europe and others such as the USA, Canada, Israel, Australia and New Zealand. Five countries had declared their candidacy: the US, Germany, Sweden, Greece and Ireland. If it were football, this would be known as the 'group of death'. I was asked by officials, should we even stay in the race? We could pull out and seek election in another year, or we could stay in and risk the first ever defeat for Ireland in a UN contest. The stakes were high, but I felt our chances were good enough, considering our unique track record, and decided to stay in the contest.

A level playing field? The United States and Germany had enormous global influence, and resources, of course. Sweden was one of the few countries to exceed the UN's Aid target of 0.7 per cent of GNP, and had a very active foreign policy. Greece was highly respected and active. Of the five, Ireland had by far the smallest diplomatic service, and due to the economic crisis at home, we were not in a position to appoint special envoys or additional staff to carry on a campaign. However, we had great reputation for aid, peace-keeping and standing up for human rights to refer to, and we also had a highly respected ambassador at the UN, Anne Anderson, with a very talented, hard-working team around her.

We decided to campaign country by country, canvassing them individually and setting out what Ireland stands for in the world. Every minister, no matter what the purpose of their engagement with another country, was instructed to put the UN Human Rights Council on their agenda. Phil Hogan, who relishes electioneering, came back from an environment conference in Rio de Janeiro with good news: 'Eamon, I got you loads of votes in Rio'!

At every international meeting I undertook a series of bilaterals to secure votes for Ireland. At the UN General Assembly in New York in September, I held twenty-five such meetings. Every one of the 193 member states of the United Nations, big and small, would have a vote in the elections. This would be a real measure of Ireland's standing in the world. In time I came to realise that Ireland's greatest assets in this high-level election were its people. At almost every meeting I held with the leaders of other countries, there was a favourable Irish-people connection of one sort or another. They had been taught by an Irish nun or priest; they had been treated by an Irish doctor or nurse; they had worked with an Irish volunteer; they admired an Irish sports star or musician; or, very often, they simply valued the company or friendship of an Irish man or woman. The Polish Foreign Minister, Radislav Sikorski, for instance, who was not known for being open to flattery or small-talk, spoke to me in gushing terms about the humour and good behaviour of Ireland's soccer fans at the European Championships in his country. The campaigning reputations of Mary Robinson and Bono were frequently mentioned to me. Both helped enthusiastically with our campaign for election to the HRC. Bono agreed to join me for a final push with UN ambassadors at an event in New York organised by Ambassador Anderson for Monday 29 October, the October bank holiday in Ireland. Unfortunately, it had to be abandoned because Hurricane Sandy hit the East Coast of the US. Manhattan had a post-apocalyptic feel of desertion as I got the last flight out on the Sunday night.

Another invitation which Ambassador Anderson secured for me was to deliver an opening speech at a conference of small island states which was held during the UN General Assembly. This would be an ideal opportunity for Ireland to connect with and hopefully win the support of these tiny, vulnerable states, many of which are located in the Pacific. To my surprise, a rival in this election, US Secretary of State Hillary Clinton, had also secured an invitation to speak. When I met her just before the event I joked, 'Since when did you become a small island state?'

'Eamon, I'm here because everybody loves the Irish too much,' was her cheerful reply.

As voting day approached, each of the five countries intensified their efforts. A defeat for any of the five would be embarrassing. We began to hear that one of the oldest campaign tricks was being played against us: a message was abroad that, apparently, 'Ireland doesn't need your vote'. Ambassador Anderson supplied the Taoiseach and me with a final targeted list to telephone for a final push. I briefed the Cabinet on the election and tried to dampen expectations. Then I waited anxiously for Anne Anderson's call from UN Headquarters.

The United States of America: 131 votes; Germany: 127 votes; Greece: 78 votes; Sweden 75 votes; and Ireland: 124 votes. It was a dream result, better than we had ever dared to hope. My first thought was what an emphatic vote of confidence in and sign of respect for Ireland from the countries of the world! What a cause for pride it would have been to the patriot Robert Emmet, who, after his trial in 1803, famously said, 'When my country takes her place among the nations of the earth, then, and not till then, let my epitaph be written.'

The Foreign Minister of Germany, Guido Westerwelle, was the first to ring to congratulate me. He had expected the US and Germany to be elected in the first round of voting and thought as the campaign progressed that Ireland was getting the edge on Greece and Sweden for the third place in a second round. But he had never thought it possible that Ireland would end up jostling his own country and the US to head the poll. He couldn't but be impressed.

It had probably helped that, on behalf of Ireland, I had been Chairperson-in-Office of the OSCE since the beginning of the year. The Organisation for Security and Cooperation in Europe had its origins in the Helsinki Final Act of 1974, which was intended to reduce the tensions of the Cold War, and included every country, all across Europe and North America. By 2012 it had fifty-seven participatory States from, as they put it, 'Vancouver to Vladivostok'. Chairing so many widely different and differing countries was one thing; doing so when every decision had to be made by consensus was quite another. Just one country withholding its agreement can block a decision in the OSCE. This was probably easier in the organisation's earlier days, when the Soviet Union and the United States agreeing on anything was probably enough to make all the other countries fall into line. In more recent times, however, the organisation included all the former Soviet States, the countries of Eastern Europe and the Balkans, as well as the now more multiple interests of the Western European and North American countries. Many had recent histories of conflict with others and there were still several unresolved conflicts.

During my year, I tried to help tackle a number of conflicts: to get peace negotiations resumed between Moldova and Transnistria; between Georgia and Russia; and between Armenia and Azerbaijan over the Nagorno-Karabakh region. I visited these latter two countries in the south Caucasus in 2012 and came away very concerned about the fragility of the peace and the potential for devastating conflict in that region. I felt that the experience of the Northern Ireland peace process might provide some inspiration and guidance for those still affected by conflict and seeking to resolve it. I therefore organised a special international conference to which I invited George Mitchell and Finnish Nobel Peace Prize laureate, Martti Ahtisaari, who had helped broker the Northern Ireland peace deal. I also invited Peter Robinson and Martin McGuinness. Every conflict being different, the idea was not to offer an Irish template for conflict resolution but to enable other countries to learn lessons from the Irish experience, straight from those who were directly involved.

One issue, which the Irish perspective helped to resolve, related to the Serbian parliamentary elections. The Serbian population of northern Kosovo is entitled to elect MPs to the Serbian Parliament in Belgrade, but there was a problem over how such elections were to be organised. Imagine if Dublin attempted to organise elections to the Dáil in nationalist areas of Northern Ireland: could the Tricolour fly over the polling stations? Could An Garda Síochána go across the border to provide the security? Could civil servants from Dublin conduct the ballot? Such were the contentious issues in this fraught area. The Kosovan Government was opposed to Serbia doing any of this, and the possibility of disturbances and even violence breaking out during the elections was very real. After months of mediation, I managed to get agreement from both sides, which enabled the OSCE to effectively administer the Serbian election in northern Kosovo. The election was duly held over two successive Sundays, without any serious incident.

Freedom of expression is one of the OSCE's founding principles, and in the internet age some countries' attempts to limit or censor online expression have been a considerable problem. The question of where, if at all, a line should be drawn on freedom of expression on the internet was at the heart of an international conference I hosted on internet freedom in the Mansion House in Dublin. This involved governments, journalists, media outlets, NGOs and the internet companies based in Dublin. Google sponsored and co-hosted the event.

Despite the OSCE's many achievements, some of the participating states were beginning to question its value. Over the years, with field missions in several countries, it made an enormous contribution to restoring and keeping peace across the continents, building and bolstering democratic institutions, upholding rule of law and human rights. The annual budget for the organisation is less than the cost of a single war plane, yet some countries, who spend much more on such armaments, were now complaining about the financial contribution they made to the OSCE. I recognised that so much had changed over the decades since its foundation; the time had come for significant renewal and reform. At the ministerial meeting of the OSCE in Dublin, I secured approval to initiate a review of its mission, with work to be completed by the fortieth anniversary in 2014 of the Helsinki Final Act. We called it Helsinki Plus 40. It was not a moment too soon. Within two years, the OSCE would have to play a vital role in the country that succeeded us in the Chair: Ukraine.

The crisis in Ukraine, and even more so, the tragedy of Syria shows just how fragile is peace. From the beginning, I tried to draw national and international attention to Syria. I was appalled at Assad's attacks on his own people, at the deaths and at the refugee crisis, which had begun long before refugees started to pour into Europe. I visited a refugee camp in Turkey, which had good facilities but where the Syrian refugees were already frustrated and angry at the West's disinterest in their plight. That was three years ago, when Turkey, Jordan and Lebanon were taking the bulk of the displaced.

One of the most memorable, but sad duties I had to perform in Foreign Affairs was to attend, with President Michael D. Higgins, the funeral in South Africa of Nelson Mandela. As a young TD, I had met Mandela briefly when the late Kader Asmal – a close ally in Mandela's South African cabinet - introduced me to him during his visit to Ireland in 1990. As preparations were made for the funeral, it occurred to me that those Irish who most deserved to pay a last tribute to Mandela were the courageous women who took strike action in Dunnes Stores in 1984 to enforce a boycott on South African goods. I invited the Dunnes Stores strikers to attend the funeral, and with the help of the union, Mandate, they attended the service in the FNB stadium with me.

Ireland has a strong relationship with South Africa, and this was cemented when both countries were asked in 2012 to co-chair the preparations for the United Nations review of the millennium development goals. President Zuma and I addressed the opening session of the review at the UN General Assembly in September 2013. The selection of Ireland for this prestigious role at the UN is due to our country's strong track record on development aid. Ireland's reputation in the Third World dates back to the missionary work of Irish nuns, priests and brothers, and has continued through the formal Irish Aid programme operated by the Department of Foreign Affairs, by the great work of Irish NGOs, and by the enormous generosity of the Irish people at times of disaster, famine and humanitarian need.

By the time I arrived in Iveagh House, the budget for Irish Aid had been cut by almost 30 per cent as a result of the financial crisis. I didn't want to see it fall any further. The Programme for Government committed us to continue to strive for the UN target of 0.7 per cent GNP. In the crisis economic environment we could not increase aid, but I determined to hold the level. Fine Gael were looking for cuts in aid, but I would not agree to pass the consequences of our financial crisis onto the poorest in the world. Neither could I cut the Department's diplomatic activity, which we desperately needed in our fight to restore Ireland's reputation abroad. And I was not prepared to sell embassies, and certainly not at the bottom of the market. But as Tánaiste in a Government where every Minister had to make difficult choices, I could not entirely eschew cuts in my own Department. So in a least-worst approach, I decided to close some embassies. It wasn't an easy decision, and I knew I would not necessarily save a lot of money, but it would make a loud statement, I felt, and hopefully get the cuts pressure off my Department, and especially away from the aid budget.

I asked Secretary General David Cooney for an assessment of each embassy, with particular reference to their role in our trade strategy. Based on his report, I selected three embassies for closure: Timor-Leste (East Timor), Iran and the Holy See. The embassy in Timor-Leste had been supporting an aid programme which was now almost complete; trade with Iran had not lived up to expectations down the years; and while the Holy See was regarded as an important listening post, much of our listening was now conducted at the multi-lateral missions, such as the UN and the EU. I recognised, of course, the significance of the Vatican Embassy for the Irish Catholic Church, so I telephoned Cardinal Sean Brady and Archbishop Diarmuid Martin before I made the announcement. They were both understandably saddened and disappointed by the decision, and I sought to re-assure both that the resumption of a resident embassy in the Holy See would be reconsidered when economic circumstances improved. To emphasise that we were not breaking off diplomatic relations with the Vatican, I appointed David Cooney, the Secretary General of the Department, and the country's most senior diplomat, as the non-resident ambassador. Such measures, however, couldn't halt the criticism. Though not in any way related to it, the closure of the embassy coincided with the Government's criticism of the Vatican's handling of child sex abuse investigations. Following the publication of the Ryan Report, I had called in the Papal Nuncio and told him of our deep dissatisfaction with the Vatican's role, and the Taoiseach spoke about it, in the strongest terms, in the Dáil.

Some criticism went further and suggested that the embassy was closed because I was pursuing a secular agenda which was hostile to the Church. That was utterly false, and when the opportunity arose nearly two years later to open new embassies, I included the Holy See, though this time on a one-diplomat basis and no longer based in the Villa Spada, which, by now, had been recast as the Irish Embassy to Italy.

Throughout my time as Minister for Foreign Affairs and Trade, I was criticised, both from within the Labour Party and from outside it, for having 'chosen the wrong Department', for being too pre-occupied with overseas events, and for spending too much time abroad. This is despite the fact that many of those making such comments would agree that international work is more important to Ireland than it is for many other countries. We are such an open trading economy that our reputation among those countries with which we trade is vital. Furthermore, our standing in the international community determines what kind of a hearing Ireland gets when it needs something from the EU or other international bodies; how fast the door is opened for new Irish business; how willing tourists are to visit our country; and how confident investors may be to plant their money here to create jobs. In terms of aid, feeding the hungry, relieving distress and helping poor countries to develop is the right thing to do morally, which makes it enough to justify our policies and missions in that area. But, it also makes good economic sense for Ireland.

Under the new Africa Strategy which I launched, for instance, Ireland's aid effort is now opening new doors for trade in the rapidly growing economies in that continent. Our agencies harvest jobs for Ireland right around the world. Our international reputation helps us to access new markets quicker than many others and to locate allies when Irish people have difficulties abroad. It is also beneficial to our 70-million strong diaspora, who can be proud of their Irish heritage while making lives and building communities around the world. Thanks to our international work, Ireland is, despite its size, now one of the most 'global' countries in a world where business, transport and communications are all now globalised.

The Taoiseach used to say he wanted 'to make Ireland the best small country in the world in which to do business.' Over time he has expanded that mission to, 'do business, raise a family and grow old with dignity' due, I would like to think, in no small way to the influence of his coalition partners. But even that falls short of the strength of Ireland's position and influence in the world.

Just as I was being replaced as Minister for Foreign Affairs and Trade in mid-2014, political scientist Simon Anholt published *The Good Country Index*, in which he ranked countries based on their contributions to science and technology, culture, international peace and security, world order, planet and climate, prosperity and equality, and health and well-being. In a TED talk on 24 June 2014, he announced that the 'goodest country in the world' is Ireland.

If we are seen that way then it is due mainly to what must be the best diplomatic service in the world. Ireland is fortunate to have a small, but highly talented team of officials in the Department of Foreign Affairs and Trade. We have less than 400 diplomats serving abroad. Other countries of our size have twice or even three times that number. Several Irish Ambassadors and Consul-Generals abroad work as one-person missions, flying the flag for Ireland and dealing with whatever comes at them, day or night, ranging from potential crises to assisting Irish citizens in need. Even in some of our larger embassies, such as Washington D.C., we have a grand total of just eight diplomats. The French and British have more diplomats in their embassy press offices than we have in our entire embassy. I regret not having been able to serve in the Department in better economic times, so as to have been able to build it up.

But on the 23 May this year, as I stood in the courtyard of Dublin Castle, and a sea of rainbow flags danced with the Tricolour, and tens of thousands proclaimed their joy that Ireland had become the first country ever to approve same-sex marriage by popular vote, I felt privileged to be living in that 'goodest country in the world', and proud too of my own small contribution in getting us there.

26. Arriving at the very first Global Irish Economic Forum in 2009 with Eamon Ryan and Brian Lenihan (Courtesy of *The Irish Times*)

27. Tea and scones for the Lisbon Treaty with Brian Cowen and Olivia Mitchell in Dundrum Shopping Centre. (Courtesy of *The Irish Times*)

28. Celebrating the Marriage Equality Referendum result with Labour TD John Lyons in Dublin Castle (Credit: The Labour Party)

29. Celebrating International Women's Day with Women for Election, Senator Jillian van Turnhout and US Senator Kirsten Gillibrand from New York (Credit: The Labour Party)

30. Signing an Ireland-UK agreement with Nick Clegg (Credit: Maxwell Photography)

31. With John Major and Dick Spring at an event to remember the Downing Street
    Declaration on Northern Ireland. (Courtesy of Photocall Ireland)

32. Launching the Wild Atlantic Way in China with Ambassador Declan Kelleher.

33. Greeting the Chinese Vice President Xi Jinping (now President) on his arrival at Shannon Airport in 2012 (Credit: Maxwell Photography)

34. Danish Prime Minister, Halle Thorning Schmidt, who was confronted with a long teachers'
    strike, asked me to explain the Haddington Road Agreement to her.(Credit: PES)

35. Sharing experiences with President Francois Hollande of France.(Credit: PES)

36. The Taoiseach has a warm welcome for Chancellor Merkel (Courtesy of Photocall Ireland)

37. Arriving at a PES Leaders Meeting with Sergei Stanishev, President of the PES and former Prime Minister of Bulgaria. (Credit: PES)

38. Carol and I join President Higgins and Sabina, on the receiving line at Áras an Uachtaráin.
   (Courtesy of Photocall Ireland)

39. Boris Johnson welcoming President Higgins and me to his Mayoral office
   (Courtesy of *The Irish Times*)

40. Sorting things out with Enda Kenny. (Courtesy of *The Irish Times*)

41. On a snowy day. (Courtesy of *The Irish Times*)

42. Welcoming Queen Elizabeth II and Prince Philip at Baldonnel at the start of their historic State Visit to Ireland. (Credit: Maxwell Photography)

43. Rachel Fox, a student at St. Anne's School in Shankill, presents flowers to Queen Elizabeth II (Credit: Maxwell Photography)

44. With the President
of the European
Council Herman Van
Rompuy during
Ireland's Presidency
of the Council of the
European Union in
2013.

45. Greeting President
Barack Obama and
Michelle Obama
on their arrival in
Ireland. US
Ambassador Dan
Rooney is on the
left. (Courtesy of
Photocall Ireland)

46. The Liberty Hall banner.
(Credit: The Labour Party)

47. Arriving for the Special
Delegate Conference in the
O'Reilly Hall UCD with
Kevin Eager and Karen
Griffin. (Courtesy of *The
Irish Times*)

48. Preparing the script with Colm O'Reardon. (Credit: The Labour Party)

49. With Mark Garrett. (Credit: The Labour Party)

11 SOCIAL AND POLITICAL REFORM

Tom Johnson was the first parliamentary leader of the Irish Labour Party. He wrote the democratic programme of the first Dáil in 1919, and was leader of the opposition in Dáil Éireann between 1922 and 1927, the year Fianna Fáil took their Dáil seats, and Johnson himself lost his own seat in the 1927 election. Now, every summer, Labour Youth organise a weekend summer school in his memory as an opportunity for members of the Labour Party to stand back from day-to-day political activity, to reflect on political philosophy, and to hear and debate ideas. On the Saturday night, the Party Leader normally delivers a keynote speech. In my seven years as Leader, I used these occasions to try out new ideas and to set new challenges for the Party.

The 2012 Tom Johnson Summer School was held in the Newpark Hotel, Kilkenny on the last weekend in June. I needed to settle members' anxieties about the difficult decisions we had to make in government, but I also wanted to turn their minds to the wider social agenda. 'Irish society cannot be put into suspended animation while the economic crisis is addressed,' was my guiding theme. Reminding them that our movement had always led social change in Ireland, I spoke about personal freedoms, including freedom of religion, about the separation of Church and State, and about the upcoming constitutional convention, which was itself a Labour idea. I said:

'It is not the role of the State to pass judgement on who a person falls in love with, or who they want to spend their life with. That is why one of the reforms for consideration by the constitutional convention is a provision for same-sex marriage. I believe in gay marriage. The right of gay couples to marry is, quite simply, the civil rights issue of this generation, and in my opinion its time has come'.

I repeated the message, the following day, at a press event, organised by Marriage Equality, at the Oscar Wilde corner of Merrion Square. As I was now the most senior politician to declare in favour of marriage equality, the comment attracted much press coverage and the Taoiseach was asked if he agreed. He replied that creating jobs was his priority!

He was not alone in being unsure about how the issue should be handled. Some of my colleagues in the Labour Party let me know that they thought it politically unwise for their Leader to make such a strong statement about what was then considered a marginal issue while people were still suffering from the recession. But the Labour Party had given a commitment in its 2011 general election manifesto to hold a referendum on same-sex marriage. Fine Gael did not agree to holding the referendum right away, but to have the issue considered by the new constitutional convention. My concern was that the proposal would be warehoused in the convention and allowed to die. The speech in Kilkenny was intended to make it clear to Fine Gael that Labour was serious about this social reform.

When the constitutional convention recommended in 2013 the holding of a referendum on marriage equality, I raised the issue again with Enda Kenny. He agreed to hold a referendum, but did not want to do so in 2014 because it would clash with the local and European elections. I didn't want to get the two mixed up either, and based on the experience of two referenda on divorce in 1986 and 1996, I thought it prudent to use the intervening time to legislate on the issues relating to children, adoption and family relationships, before putting the question to the people. My worry, though, was that, if the referendum was not held in the first half of 2015, it would run into the general election and be put off, so we settled on May/June 2015, with the date to be agreed in time. The Taoiseach did not oppose the holding of the same-sex marriage referendum, and told me, from the outset, that he intended to campaign in favour of it.

Enda was, however, not so comfortable with the other major social issue of our time, abortion. The Labour Party had opposed the 1983 referendum that introduced the constitutional ban on abortion in Ireland, and now had a policy which favoured legislating to permit abortion in Ireland in cases where either the life or the health of the mother was at risk. In 1992, the Supreme Court had allowed a child who was suicidal to have an abortion, but in the twenty years since, no government had introduced legislation for this, the so-called 'X case'. Just before the 2011 General Election, the issue came to a head again, when the European Court of Human Rights (ECHR) ruled that the absence of such legislation in Ireland violated the human rights of the women concerned. The Labour Party committed in its manifesto to legislate for the X case. We were the only party to do so, and therefore attracted a hostile campaign of attack from those opposed to abortion. Just two weeks before election day, the *Irish Independent* published an article by David Quinn, headlined 'Why a vote for Labour is a vote for Abortion'. The Catholic magazine

Alive carried a strong anti-Labour message and drew attention to an interview I had done with Pat Kenny, at the end of which he read out a comment from a listener, 'Is Ireland ready for an atheist Taoiseach?' I had never actually said that I was an atheist, but like many of my generation, I had stopped practicing, and had previously described my attitude to religion as agnostic. Now, in the rhetoric around the elections, I was being portrayed as some kind of Antichrist who wanted to kill babies.

Though impossible to quantify exactly, the anti-abortion campaign had an impact on the Labour vote. As the election campaign progressed, many worried Labour members reported back from different parts of the country that I was being painted as an abortionist and that voters who had been leaning towards Labour were now worried that a vote for Labour would indeed be a vote for abortion. Almost every day of the campaign, I was confronted by anti-abortion campaigners, often accompanied by children with disabilities whom the campaigners claimed I would have aborted. One wet Sunday morning, such a group came all the way across a soggy football pitch in Fairview to confront me as I did a kick-about with Johnny Giles. A bus-load of people from the same camp picketed my constituency office in Booterstown, before making their way to Shankill to repeat the performance outside my family home.

Not surprisingly, Fine Gael would not agree to have legislation for the X case in the Programme for Government. The best we could do was establish an expert group to consider the implication of the ECHR ruling. I knew that the terms of reference for, and the membership of, this group would be critical to the outcome, and I asked Jean O'Mahony to give it meticulous attention. The group formed included medical and legal experts. They did a thoroughly independent job, and when they reported in November 2012, it was clear that the only realistic course open to the Government was to legislate.

Just as their report was about to be released, a tragedy occurred at University College Hospital Galway that dramatically changed the debate. A young Indian woman, Savita Halappanavar, who had been working in Ireland, died during pregnancy. She had begun to miscarry and acquired an infection. Her husband stated that she had been requesting a termination and that this was refused until the hospital was satisfied that the foetus was already dead.

Although the full facts were not yet known, there was an immediate public outcry. Why was Savita allowed to die? Why couldn't she get a termination? Why hadn't the Government already legislated for this? Ironically, I suddenly found myself responding to correspondence blaming me and the Labour Party for the failure to legislate. In the Dáil, Sinn Féin's Mary Lou McDonald relished the opportunity to give full voice to the indignation, and tried to insinuate that responsibility lay with me: 'We need the legislation. I want to know when the Tánaiste will bring it forward,' she declared.

'My position,' I replied, 'on this issue is known for a very long time. I am on the public record for more than twenty-five years as to how this issue should be dealt with. There is no doubt about it. It has not always been a popular position or one that has commanded support across all parties in this House.'

'I am familiar with the Tánaiste's public position and that of his Party. It is one we wholeheartedly share and support,' Mary Lou claimed. But in truth, they did not. The Labour Party Research Officer, Claire Power, sent me an email headed 'The Recent Conversion of Sinn Féin', in which she pointed out that there was no reference to X case legislation in Sinn Féin's 2011 general election manifesto; that Martin McGuinness had been quoted as saying 'Sinn Féin is not in favour of abortion and we resisted any attempt to bring the British 1967 Abortion Act to the North'; and Pearse Doherty was quoted on an anti-abortion website as follows: 'Senator Pearse Doherty has given a written personal commitment to oppose any legislation that would make abortion available in Ireland and supports a law to protect the human embryo from deliberate destruction.'

I felt deeply upset by Savita's tragic and avoidable death and by the terrible loss her husband, Praveen, had suffered. I concentrated my efforts on persuading the Taoiseach of the necessity to legislate sooner rather than later. I knew that there were many in Fine Gael who also supported legislating for X, including the Minister James Reilly, who said in a Dáil debate that six successive governments had failed to act and that this would not be the seventh.

But Enda Kenny was personally opposed to abortion. I respected his position, though I disagreed with him. Ultimately, on this very complex and difficult ethical issue, I believe that it is the woman's right to make the decision. We talked it over several times during December. Enda recognised that there was little option but to legislate. The Council of Europe was pressing for our response to the ECHR judgement, and my Department had to deal frequently with Strasbourg on this question. Apart from Labour's position on the X case, I could not, on my watch, allow Ireland to be found in breach of the European Convention on Human Rights. Above all, I wanted legislation to be brought forward that would protect the lives of women in pregnancy.

The aspect that caused Enda most concern related to suicide. The Supreme Court in the X case had ruled that abortion was permissible where a woman's life was at risk due to suicide. He feared that legislating on this basis would be tantamount to 'abortion on demand'. There would have to be some medical certification that a woman's life was at risk, and he suggested that in the case of suicide, there should be more than one medical practitioner involved. I wanted to press on with the legislation so I agreed to this higher level of test for suicidal intentions. On that basis we agreed to begin preparation of the legislation.

I nominated Alex White, whom I had recently appointed as Minister of State in the Department of Health, to lead for Labour in preparing the legislation. James Reilly would lead for Fine Gael. The initial drafts were totally unacceptable. At one stage, the Fine Gael side proposed six doctors to certify the suicide grounds. At another, it was suggested a court decision would be required. Exasperated, I pointed out that we were legislating for circumstances where a woman was at risk of losing her life. The Oireachtas Joint Committee on Health, chaired by Cork Deputy, Jerry Buttimer, held hearings on the issue and conducted a valuable and reasoned discussion on the topic. This fed into the drafting process. Nevertheless, by the time the draft legislation came to Cabinet, there were still problems. Some of the detail in the draft Bill would have rendered it useless. We adjourned the discussion and spent the day re-drafting. Repeatedly, drafts came back from the Department of Health that were unacceptable to Labour. By the time we were eventually satisfied, I noticed at the top of the page that we were on draft number sixty-four.

The legislation was passed in the Dáil by 127 votes to 31. (Fine Gael lost five TDs and two senators who voted against. The most outspoken was Lucinda Creighton, who lost the Fine Gael whip, and her position in Government as a Minister of State.)

After twenty years of talk, we finally had legislation for the X case. Ireland had, for the first time, passed a law permitting abortion, though only in very limited circumstances. Although I knew this would not have happened if Labour were not in government, I felt no great sense of achievement. I was deeply uncomfortable with the fourteen-year prison penalty the legislation provided for abortion in every other circumstance. During the preparation of the legislation, I questioned it, and the Attorney General's advice was that because the Constitution affords equal protection to the life of the unborn and the life of the mother, the penalty for ending the life of the unborn has to be equivalent to the penalty for killing the mother. Where does that leave a young woman who takes the abortion pill, I wondered? Where does it leave her doctor if she presents with complications? I hope the next Government addresses such questions as a matter of urgency, and I hope too that the infamous eighth amendment will be repealed in another referendum, carefully prepared and planned for, so that this fundamental gender equality issue can be dealt with comprehensively.

Abortion might not still be the contentious issue that it is, if there were more women in the Dáil. Ireland, at 15.6 per cent female participation in Parliament, is only in 109th place in the world, way down the bottom half of the league table. Afghanistan is sixty places ahead of us.

From my very first day as a TD, I have been acutely aware of how unnatural the working environment of the Dáil is. The overwhelming male composition of its membership and the sometimes macho nature of the exchanges remind me of boarding school. It is odd that in the twenty-first century, our robust democracy and our fair electoral system should produce such a gender imbalanced parliament. The problems start at a much deeper level of society than politics; they are structural. How to get more women TDs elected has been the subject of debate for decades.

Without a list system, it would be impossible to try positive discrimination. Our variable multi-seat constituencies are not suitable for gender quotas. The best solution, which I had heard, came from Labour Senator, Ivana Bacik, who prepared a private members bill on the matter, was to place to responsibility on the political parties to nominate enough women in the first place. Now that we have a system of State financing for political parties, an obligation could be placed on parties to nominate women as a certain proportion of their total candidates, and if they failed to do so, they could be penalised by reducing their State funding.

Ivana's proposal was included in Labour's manifesto for the 2011 General Election, and got into the Programme for Government. At the first opportunity, the measure was included in an electoral bill from Environment Minister, Phil Hogan, and was duly passed. At the general election next year, a minimum of 30 per cent of the candidates of each political party must be female and any party which fails to reach that threshold will lose 50 per cent of its State funding. At the following general election (probably 2020 or 2021, if not earlier), the threshold goes up to 40 per cent, so that by the time this State is 100 years old, the benches in Dáil Éireann should, I hope, comprise roughly equal numbers of men and women, unless, of course, the voters insist on electing a lot of Independents to whom this gender balance does not apply. Every time I pass the Leinster House portrait of Countess Markiewicz – the first woman ever to be elected to a parliament on these North Atlantic islands – I think it would be a fitting way to mark our centenary and a great legacy for the Irish Labour Party.

Reform had been one of the main themes of Labour's general election campaign. In opposition I had asked Brendan Howlin to chair a small group which drew up a comprehensive set of reform proposals, which Labour would seek to implement in government, starting with political life itself.

The sitting times of the Dáil were increased by almost 50 per cent, and a regular Friday sitting was introduced which gave an opportunity to opposition TDs and government backbenchers to introduce their own legislation. We held a referendum in autumn 2011 in an attempt to set up a public enquiry into the banking crisis, although the proposal was defeated following the intervention of some senior lawyers who claimed it would amount to a kangaroo court. Instead, we legislated for more robust forms of parliamentary inquiry, the first of which is the Committee of Inquiry into the Banking Crisis, which is being chaired by Ciarán Lynch TD.

The corrupting relationship between private political funding and political decision making was examined by both the Mahon Tribunal and the Moriarty Tribunal, with the latter lasting for over a decade. Both of these tribunals reported during the term of our Government. Following on from those reports, we reduced the amounts of money, which both individuals and companies, could contribute to politicians and political parties to €1,000 and €2,500 respectively, and ensured that, in all cases, these contributions would have to be publicly declared through the Standards in Public Office (SIPO). Every January, every politician and every political party now has to fill out forms, detailing what monies, if any, they have received, from whom and for what. It is all published in a public record. A far cry from those days of cash-stuffed brown envelopes being passed around. Anyone now accepting or giving such payments would be guilty of a criminal offence, punishable by a prison sentence.

Lobbying is a normal part of democratic life. But until the formation of our Labour/Fine Gael Government, it had never been regulated in Ireland. Brendan Howlin introduced the Regulation of Lobbying Bill, which ensures that lobbyists must now register with SIPO, and that the holders of public office must be a year out of office before they can lobby in their old field, all of which is giving this area of activity a new transparency.

Labour had, in the 1990s, introduced the first ever Freedom of Information Act in Ireland, but in the intervening years, it had been filleted by Fianna Fáil governments. Now Brendan moved to restore its key provisions, to widen its application, and to abolish the fee for making Freedom of Information (FOI) requests.

Fine Gael too had a reforming agenda, but some of their proposals caused difficulty for the Labour Party. Richard Bruton wished to reform the Joint Labour Committees (JLC) which set minimum rates of pay and conditions of employment for low-paid sectors of the economy such as hotels, restaurants and hairdressing. Following the High Court decision to strike down the JLCs, Labour feared that Fine Gael's intention, encouraged by some employer's group's spokespersons, was to abolish the JLCs and their registered employment agreements entirely. Fine Gael was arguing that they were no longer needed because there was now a national minimum wage and they were a hindrance to competitiveness.

Before my own election to Dáil Éireann in 1989, I had worked as a trade union official and was, for a time, a member of two JLCs. I knew that they were important for maintaining minimum employment standards in sectors of the economy which were traditionally low paid. Some reform was, however, necessary, as there were probably too many JLCs and some related to economic activity that was now in decline. I asked David Leach, then the Political Director of the Labour Party, to coordinate with the trade unions and to negotiate solutions with Richard Bruton's Department. David worked closely with Patricia King, the Vice President of SIPTU, and after seemingly endless meetings with officials from Richard's Department, and several working papers, a resolution was found, and a new law introduced which reinstated the JLCs and gave a legal basis to registered employment agreements.

With the rights of low paid workers now underpinned, David and Patricia continued their work together to land another shared objective of the Labour and trade union movement: to provide a legal framework for collective bargaining, the right to which was enshrined in the EU Charter of Fundamental Rights, part of the Lisbon Treaty. At the time of the second Lisbon referendum, I gave a public commitment that Labour, in government, would seek to give legal effect to the Charter's provisions on joining a trade union, and on negotiating collective employment agreements. Unfortunately, however, Richard Bruton and Fine Gael were not keen on it. They feared that multi-national companies from countries with little or no trade union culture would be put off by what appeared to be compulsory unionisation.

I met with representatives of IBEC, with the American Chamber of Commerce, and with individual employers, and sought to re-assure them of our intentions, pointing out that Ireland has a very good record on industrial relations and that trade unions had consistently played a constructive role in Ireland's economic development. My efforts were not helped, however, when, just before the Labour Party conference in November 2013, a newspaper article appeared which implied that I was seeking mandatory trade union recognition. With some extra negotiation and hard work, however, we did eventually secure agreement with Fine Gael on the issue, and legislation was introduced to provide protection for workers who join trade unions and a legal framework for collective bargaining.

Not all of our reforms, however, including one on which Fine Gael and Labour were agreed, met with public approval.

In early 2010, Brendan Howlin told me that his policy group

intended to recommend the abolition of the Seanad. He explained that there was a well thought-out rationale for abolition, and that as the proposal was sure to attract much publicity when published, he wanted to give me advance notice of it. But, before Brendan's document even saw the light of day, Enda Kenny unexpectedly, and to the surprise of his own senators, announced that Fine Gael intended to abolish the Senate.

Their proposal was set in the context of cost reduction. Fine Gael wanted to reduce the size of the public service, and of course, therefore, some of the trimming would have to be done on the number of politicians and political bodies. There was, at the time, some considerable public support for this approach: I recall speaking with Richard Bruton at an IMPACT conference in Portlaoise in May 2009 and being asked from the floor if we intended to cut the number of politicians.

However, the parliamentary Labour Party was reluctant to be seen to be tailing Fine Gael on the abolition of the Senate, so it decided that the future of the upper house should be considered by the constitutional convention, and that the Labour Party should recommend abolition to such a convention. Brendan's argument was that second parliamentary chambers remained mainly in countries, the UK for instance, that had to reconcile a former aristocracy, or countries, as in the USA and Germany, that had a federal state system. Generally, small modern States operated with just one parliament. De Valera, apparently, had reluctantly agreed to the inclusion of the Senate in his 1937 constitution. I agreed with this thinking and concluded that one improved parliamentary body would be better for Irish democracy than two unreformed chambers.

In our discussions after the general election about the Programme for Government, the Taoiseach made it clear that he wanted to go ahead with a referendum on the Senate, without referring it to the constitutional convention. If both Fine Gael and Labour were in favour of abolition, then why not proceed straight to a referendum, he argued. Labour had other issues that we were sending to the convention, so I agreed to hold the Senate referendum directly, on the assurance that if the constitutional convention recommended a referendum on any other issue that Fine Gael would not block it. I did not mention it specifically, but I was thinking of marriage equality.

Abolishing the Senate did not turn out to be a simple exercise, even with the support of the two largest parties in government. Bunreacht na hÉireann establishes several distinct roles for the Senate, some of which, such as petitioning the President on a Bill, are not performable by the Dáil on its own. Advisors and legal experts from Fine Gael and Labour developed proposals for the new structures which would be needed in unicameral parliament. There would be a strengthened committee system, new procedures for pre-legislative scrutiny of Bills and enactment review of legislation. The constitutional convention was to be asked to devise a new petitions system.

One Fine Gael idea, to which I was strongly opposed, was to bring outside 'independent' experts onto the legislative review committee. The original idea for the Senate itself was that it would bring experts into the legislative process through the various vocational panels. But in reality that did not happen as the political affiliation of the Senate candidates took precedence over their knowledge and experience in any given field. I felt that Fine Gael wanted to put in place some kind of unelected expert legislative panel. In my view legislators should be elected by the people. That is the essence of democracy.

The Senate referendum was defeated. Some in Fine Gael felt that Labour had made little effort to get it passed. I think Fine Gael made a strategic mistake in emphasising the savings which would accrue from abolition. In the end the people valued the work and culture of this significant, albeit imperfect, parliamentary institution, more than the savings that would be made from its termination.

Cost was also a factor in the reforms of local government advanced by Phil Hogan as Minister for the Environment. The country had about 1,600 councillors between cities, counties and towns. There was considerable overlap between county and town councils and, in many respects, the basic structure of Ireland's local government system, dating from 1899, was not fit for purpose in an entirely different Ireland. For decades there was talk of reform, but little or nothing was achieved. Phil decided to take it on. But there were some big differences in thinking between the two parties over local government reform, and I asked David Leach and Aidan Culhane, who worked successively for Willie Penrose and Jan O'Sullivan in the Environment Department, to take on discussions with Phil's people.

Labour had a strong historical affinity with the town councils, which were now to be absorbed into the county councils. To bridge the gap and maintain some distinct town identity in local government, the idea of municipal districts was developed. Composed of the councillors elected for the town area, the municipal districts would represent the towns and their hinterlands and would have the right to elect their own town mayors.

Another Labour objective was to limit the power of county managers. Veterans of local government, such as Deputy Emmet Stagg and Senator Denis Landy, wanted to restore power to the elected councils. Significant changes were made in the new Local Government Bill, including the re-definition of the county manager as chief executive of the council.

The biggest problem in this area, however, was the inequity in council representation between one part of the country and another. In some parts of rural Ireland fewer than 2,000 people were entitled to elect a councillor, while in the more urbanised areas, especially in Cork and Dublin, it took more than four times that number to qualify for a local representative. The ratio of councillor to population was one to 1,444 in County Leitrim, and one to 11,377 in Fingal. Each of these councillors, irrespective of population size, had the same status and the same voting rights in Senate elections. I wanted the inequality to end, or at least to be reduced.

David and Aidan made headway but were unable to finalise it all with Phil's advisors, so it fell to Phil and I to work out a compromise. Phil Hogan is a wily negotiator. It took several weeks and countless meetings and telephone conversations before we eventually settled on increased council sizes for the large conurbations and a floor for the small councils.

Phil was not the only Fine Gael Minister with whom I had to talk directly about reform proposals.

When Brendan Howlin secured agreement to sell the national lottery licence, the Government agreed to use the proceeds to build the long promised National Children's Hospital. During the Bertie Ahern era, the Mater Hospital, in his constituency, had been chosen as the site for the new hospital. However, that site was so confined that the architects had to design it high into the skyline, and An Bord Pleanála eventually refused planning permission. Going back to the drawing board for a smaller hospital on the same site was an option, though almost 50 million euro had already been spent on design costs for that site, and there was no assurance that planning permission would be forthcoming. The hospital would be smaller too and so not scaled sensibly to serve into the future. We would have to re-open the issue of site selection, thereby exposing the Government to a raft of medical and constituency lobbying.

James Reilly, as Minister for Health, appointed a team of medical and planning experts, chaired by Dr Frank Dolphin, to examine the site options and to report back to the Government. From the outset, Dolphin and his team argued that the optimal location would be a site that combined a major hospital, a maternity hospital and the children's hospital. But there was no such combination on any one site. For medical reasons, the Dolphin team thought that, at the very least, the Children's Hospital needed to be co-located with a major general hospital to maximise the clinical service which would be available on site to the children.

The Taoiseach and I agreed that we should now leave it to Dolphin and await his report. But the lobbying continued from hospitals, medical consultants and constituency politicians. The Children's Hospital would be a major construction project of about €600 million; it would be a very large employer and would be a national medical facility for, perhaps, the next two centuries.

Leo Varadkar and Joan Burton both separately made the case for the Connolly Hospital site in Blanchardstown. It had the land and the accessibility of the M50. But Beaumont would have to be moved out there. My view was we needed the Children's Hospital as soon as possible and complicating matters with building a second hospital at the same time would probably delay the Children's Hospital for, maybe, 20 years.

Dolphin reported directly to Minister Reilly, the Taoiseach and

I. He met the three of us in the Taoiseach's private office, took us through his report, explained his reasoning and made his recommendation. The Taoiseach, Reilly and I agreed that we would bring the recommendation to Cabinet and that all three of us would support it. The Children's Hospital would be co-located at St James' Hospital and have the added advantage of being close to the Coombe Maternity Hospital. Dublin 8 would therefore become a medical quarter, just as Dublin 7 would have the new DIT campus. Both would help regenerate these long neglected parts of the capital.

The welfare of children was a dominant theme right through Government. Frances Fitzgerald was appointed as Minister for Children to speed up the implementation of safety and welfare measures for children and to oversee a referendum to give specific constitutional rights to children. The previous Government had considered this and significant progress had been made by my constituency colleague Barry Andrews of Fianna Fáil. But there remained difficulties in getting agreement on the wording. A small sub-committee, of which I was a member, eventually produced a final text at a meeting on 30 August 2012 and the resulting referendum was convincingly passed.

Many of the children-related issues with which the Government had to deal arose from abuse and neglect in the past. There had been a succession of reports into the horrific treatment of children by clergy, and of children in care and various institutions. The plight of young women and their children who were institutionalised in the Magdalene Laundries had never been fully investigated. The new Government agreed to appoint Senator Martin McAleese to examine what had happened in the Magdalene Laundries and to recommend remedies to government. Upon Dr McAleese's request, I seconded one of the legal officials from the

Department of Foreign Affairs and Trade, Nuala Ní Mhuircheartaigh, to assist him with his work, which would involve extensive interviews with the Magdalene survivors.

Dr McAleese presented his report directly to the Cabinet at its weekly meeting on Tuesday 5 February 2013. He intended to publish the report that afternoon and it was agreed that there should be a Dáil debate on it two weeks later, after everybody had had an opportunity to study the content. However, that afternoon, the Taoiseach was asked in the Dáil if he would apologise on behalf of the State. Perhaps, because he had had little time after Cabinet to prepare for the questions, he came across as uncertain, and untypically for him, as somewhat unsympathetic. By the following morning, a demand for a State apology had built up through the media, and he had to face questions again. The email traffic was mounting, the telephone calls increasing and online comment was becoming increasingly emphatic, and some of it abusive, as the pressure mounted. This was the first Government which had seriously taken up the plight of the Magdalene women. Now it was sounding like this Government was responsible for what had happened to them.

Enda and I talked about the problem and, encouraged by Minister Kathleen Lynch, we agreed that an apology was the least that these brave women deserved. But first we would meet with them. The meeting was arranged for Tuesday 12 February in Government Buildings. For several hours, over cups of tea, the women told their personal stories: of rejection, effective imprisonment, isolation, cruelty, loneliness, hurt, exile, stigma and disgrace; of the lingering life-long effects, of still trying to come to terms with what they had endured, of separation from their children, of broken lives and broken relationships, of broken health and addiction, and of the seriousness of their needs right up to today.

This was a meeting like none I had ever attended. A group of wronged women, who had in the past been driven out of normal Irish society, and forgotten and forsaken, now reconnected with the two Government leaders. Enda and I had grown up in the stultified society which had rejected them. The Ireland of 40 or 50 years ago or more, of an insecure people desperately craving social respectability; of a heartless church whose dogmas dictated public and private morality, and of a compliant State which allowed it to do so. I was deeply moved by the women's stories.

Nuala Ní Mhuircheartaigh, who was present, and who had previously heard their testimonies, occasionally intervened to tell us a particular angle or an anecdote. Usually the women were pregnant when they were put in the Magdalenes, sometimes by their own families. One of the women who met us that day had not been pregnant. She was just thirteen when she was brought and lodged in the Magdalene Laundry. Her mother had been a single parent who worked as a domestic servant for a small town doctor. The mother and her daughter lived in the servant's quarters of the doctor's home. One evening, without warning, the doctor's wife, in her car, picked up the thirteen-year old girl from school and drove her straight to the Magdalene's. She would not have the mother's fate passed on to the next generation.

The following Tuesday, the Taoiseach gave a heartfelt apology on behalf of the State, to a full Dáil chamber, and to a public gallery packed with Magdalene survivors. I spoke next. I recalled, as a university student in Galway, walking every day past the high grey walls of the Laundry, unaware of the suffering women inside. I concluded my speech with the words: 'Never again, as a people, as a society, will we walk past a high wall and fail to ask what lies behind it.'

12 HANDS OF HISTORY

In February 1973, I was a first year Psychology student at University College, Galway. Taoiseach Jack Lynch, whose Fianna Fáil party had been in power for 16 years, called a general election. I was furious and so were my friends. The previous November, a referendum had reduced the age for voting from 21 to 18. But now, I wouldn't be 18 for another 2 months and even those of my friends who were already 18 were not yet on the electoral register. Holding an election now meant none of us would be able to vote.

A small group of us was sheltering from the dark and cold in an empty classroom, complaining about the injustice which was being inflicted on us, when word came through of a meeting in the Atlanta Hotel in Dominick Street that could give us the opportunity of getting our own back. The meeting was to launch the general election campaign of the Labour Party candidate for Galway West, thirty-one year-old Michael D. Higgins, who was known to us all as a colourful sociology lecturer, and for his fiery speeches at University debates. I immediately signed up for my first election campaign, and as I spoke Irish, I was allocated to the canvass team for Barna and Spiddal, under the late Delma McDevitt. Delma drove us to Connemara every evening in her black Volkswagen. Although our campaign was unsuccessful, the experience was a very enjoyable and important one for me. I subsequently joined the Workers' Party, but Michael D. and I remained friends and collaborators over the years.

In 2004, the September get-together of the Parliamentary Labour Party was in the Ferrycarrig Hotel in Wexford. Michael D. joined me at breakfast and asked if he could get a lift back to Dublin with me. After breakfast, he ran into radio broadcaster Mark Costigan, who presciently asked him if he would be interested in running for President. The response was so non-committally positive that Mark had his scoop. By the eleven o'clock coffee break, all the news bulletins were reporting Michael D.'s 'declaration' for the forthcoming presidential election. By the time we reached Gorey on the drive back he had been invited onto the six o'clock news on RTÉ; and as we drove through Arklow, Rathnew and by-passed Bray, the phone calls poured through to him from Labour members, from actors, artists, academics, sports people and celebrities of all kinds, pledging their support for his candidacy.

Nonetheless, the following day, the Labour Party National Executive decided, by just one vote, not to nominate a candidate. It was the right decision. President Mary McAleese was loved by the people and unbeatable as a candidate. If Michael D. had been nominated in 2004, he would have been defeated, and would probably not have stood again as a presidential candidate. But from that two-and-a-half-hour car journey, I knew better than most how interested Michael D. was in the Presidency, and what a wide spectrum of support he could attract.

It came as no great surprise to me, therefore, when sometime in 2010, Michael D. asked me if I had given any thought to the presidential election which was due in October 2011. I presumed he was interested and indicated my support for him. But first I needed to know his intentions for the general election, which might well now be held some time before the presidential. We talked about it a few times but came to no conclusion. We arranged to meet for a meal after the All-Ireland hurling final that year. Over dinner in the Gresham Hotel, we talked through the likely sequence, and Michael D. told me that he would not stand at the next general election so that he could concentrate his efforts on the Presidency. He just needed my reassurance that I would support him.

Following the general election in February 2011, Michael D. pressed for an early selection convention, but I resisted because I thought it could be counter-productive for him to announce too early. Senator David Norris was an early front-runner and his campaign eventually failed because he had been a target for too long. Mairead McGuinness MEP was the bookies' early favourite to be the Fine Gael candidate, but she eventually lost the nomination to Gay Mitchell. We held our selection convention in the Oak Room of the Mansion House on Sunday, 19 June. We had three fine candidates to choose from: Michael D, Fergus Finlay, the Chief Executive of Barnardos, and former Senator Kathleen O'Meara. I told Fergus and Kathleen that I was supporting Michael D. and both expected and accepted my preference graciously. There were, however, some in the Party who questioned my choice, and who suggested that Michael D. was 'too old'. To me, this ageism was reprehensible and should have no place in a party which professes equality and eschews discrimination of all kinds.

Michael D. comfortably won the nomination and the Labour Party quickly built a campaign team around him: Mags Murphy as the campaign manager, Kevin McCarthy from Cork as his driver, and we brought back Tony Heffernan as his press officer. Mark

Garrett and David Leach set about mobilising the Party organisation around the country and the renowned artist Brian Maguire was asked to design the campaign poster and other materials.

Throughout the summer and autumn of 2011, Michael D. and the team travelled the length and breadth of the country. At a community event in Kinvara, County Galway he suffered a leg injury getting up on a platform, and it caused him some pain throughout the campaign. Meanwhile some sections of the media were frantically searching for a celebrity president. If it couldn't be David Norris, or the Special Olympics organiser, Mary Davis, maybe Gay Byrne or Miriam O'Callaghan might go for it. Anybody, it seemed, but a politician. And it almost was!

In early September, Martin McGuinness was nominated for Sinn Féin, and showed strongly in early polls, But his campaign suffered an irreversible blow when he was confronted by the son of an Irish soldier, who was killed by the IRA during the rescue of kidnap victim Don Tidey, the then head of Tesco, in County Leitrim in 1983. As the campaign progressed, the polls showed Independent candidate Sean Gallagher to be gaining in support, and with a week to go, he was still well ahead.

Our campaign strategy was based on the fact that Michael D. was the most presidential of the all candidates. We emphasised his long political experience, his understanding of the Constitution, as well as his reputation for the cultural, artistic and sporting life of the country. By the final weekend of the campaign, we felt that the election was beginning to turn nicely in his favour. On the Saturday before polling day, we canvassed together with Joe and Emer Costello on Henry Street and the adjoining streets of the north inner city. Voters surged toward Michael D., wishing him well and offering their support. It was one of the warmest street canvasses I have ever experienced. The good mood continued through the day as we travelled on the campaign bus through counties Kildare and Laois and onto Athlone in Westmeath. The only discordant note all day came from a group of turf cutters in Naas who blamed Michael D. for the designation of their bogs as a Special Area of Conservation.

On the bus journey back from Athlone, I got a call from Mark Garrett. He had news of a poll in the following day's *Sunday Business Post*, which showed Gallagher still leading on 40 per cent. I shared the news with Michael D. and Sabina, and did my best to keep up their spirits. They were coming towards the end of a long, tiring campaign, and I felt for them. The following day, we met at the corner of Stephen's Green and did a press call outside the Gaiety Theatre. Some in the Party were urging us to go on the attack against Gallagher, but I felt that now more than ever Michael D. needed to show his statesman qualities. We canvassed through Grafton Street and then into the Westbury Hotel for a final rally of Labour members and supporters. 'Never mind the polls', I told them, 'the election is on Thursday and we intend to win.'

On Monday, Michael D. went to RTÉ to participate in the final debate. Sean Gallagher came across as uncomfortable while answering questions about his business affairs. The public responded, and by polling day an avalanche of votes swept Michael D. to victory as the ninth President of Ireland. That weekend was the happiest of my entire time in government: to see Michael D. Higgins, the best Labour had to offer, being chosen to represent us all as Head of State. At the declaration in Dublin Castle, I felt proud of our new President, and enormously happy for his wife, Sabina and their children: Alice Mary, Michael, John and Daniel. On Sunday afternoon, I stood on the steps of the Meyrick Hotel to welcome him back to the city that had repeatedly elected him to the Dáil, or as the Sawdoctors song had it, 'Michael D. Rockin' in the Dáil for us'. The thousands thronging Eyre Square in the soft Galway rain appeared now to be rocking for Michael D. in the Áras!

Protocol dictates that on the day of the presidential inauguration, it is the Tánaiste who escorts the President Elect into Dublin Castle, down the aisle of St Patrick's Hall and onto the podium to join the outgoing President, the Taoiseach, the Chief Justice and the Council of State, for the formal swearing in. It is a short, formal duty, but it meant a great deal to me personally.

One of my duties as Minister for Foreign Affairs and Trade was to nominate the ministers who would accompany President Higgins on State and official visits abroad. As Head of State, the President is above politics and when meeting foreign governments, he must be accompanied by an Irish Minister or Minister of State who can speak on behalf of the Irish Government. The only visit which I decided to reserve for myself was the State visit by President Higgins to Britain in April 2014 when he was hosted at Windsor Castle by Queen Elizabeth. This was to be the first ever State visit by a President of Ireland to the United Kingdom. Presidents McAleese and Robinson had, during their terms, visited Britain officially and built up good relations between the two respective Heads of State.

The sense of history began at Baldonnel Airport. The President insisted that Carol and I join him and Sabina on the steps of the government jet for the official pre-departure photographs. We stayed that night at the Kensington Hotel. My advisor, Niamh Sweeney, and I were driven out to Windsor for my live interview on the RTÉ 9 o'clock news, broadcast from a hotel balcony overlooking Windsor Castle. The town of Windsor was festooned with Irish and British flags. I began to sense how important this visit was for Britain, as well as for Ireland.

The next day, Prince Charles and his wife Camilla called to the Irish Embassy in London to escort the President and his party in the cortege to Windsor. At Datchett Road, on the edge of the town, Queen Elizabeth and Prince Philip waited on a dais for their Irish guests. The cars pulled up, we were assigned to our positions, and the British Army band, in colourful dress uniform, struck up 'Amhrán na bhFiann'. I felt a lump of emotion rise within me. This was going to be a very special week.

Horse-drawn carriages were pulled up to take us to the Castle. The Queen and Prince Philip were with the President and Sabina, and Prince Charles and Camilla were in a carriage with Carol and myself. The streets were lined with well-wishers, many of whom had waited since early morning, many with a Tricolour in one hand and a Union Flag in the other. At the castle, I watched and listened to the impressive military display, and again thought about how this imperial army had for centuries assaulted and suppressed the Irish, and here it was now proclaiming its respect and honouring the democratically elected President of our independent Republic.

I remembered that during the Presidential Election, a respected figure, who sometimes sent me unsolicited advice, wrote to suggest that the new President would be the first to do a State visit to Britain, and Irish people should be encouraged to picture in their minds which of the candidates would do them proud. President Higgins certainly did Ireland proud during that historic week in April. His many public appearances, including the State Banquet in Windsor, were shown live on television to huge audiences in Ireland, Britain and throughout the world. Ireland felt proud of the President.

I was privileged to see him perform at several events that week which were never broadcast: the lunch meeting with Prime Minister Cameron at which we discussed Northern Ireland; the private meetings with Deputy Prime Minister Nick Clegg and Leader of the Opposition, Ed Miliband; and a particularly memorable encounter with the Mayor of London, Boris Johnson. Boris was already in the forecourt of the Mayor's building, glad-handing and entertaining the public, when we arrived. He invited the President to join him, and he then invited a small group of us, including the President, myself and Ambassador Mulhall, whom he knew, to join him for a cup of tea in his private office.

'Mr President, would you like a muffin with your tea?' he enquired.

The President declined.

'Mr President, I hear you are a poet.'

'Yes Mayor, I have written some poems. And I understand you are a classical scholar?'

'I am indeed. Tell me, Mr President, who is your favourite Greek poet?'

The President replied and with that, Johnson fired off in Ancient Greek a line from one of the Greek poems. The President replied with the second line, Johnson with the third, and so on, as if in an intellectual duel, until eventually Johnson was quiet – though I was not clear if this was out of politeness, in defeat, or just because the poem ended at that point.

Throughout the visit, the President delivered eight speeches, each of them a masterpiece of language and oratory. Prime Minister Cameron, most of the British Cabinet, all its party leaders and hundreds of MPs and peers were already seated in Westminster Hall when we arrived for the President's address to the Houses of Parliament. If they had been expecting a predictable but worthy script on the improved relations between these islands, they were mistaken. The President traced the British parliamentary tradition right back to the Magna Carta. I watched at close quarters the awestruck faces of the British political leaders as they absorbed our President's insightful and inspiring address.

My favourite speech of his, though, was at Stratford-on-Avon. After a backstage tour of the Royal Shakespeare Company, we were ushered into the theatre for a performance of an extract from *Henry IV*. Then the President rose and stood on the circular stage, surrounded by the players, and delivered a superb address on language in theatre and the beauty of the English language, which is shared by the people of our two islands.

The final and most poignant events of the visit were later that day in Coventry. We toured Coventry Cathedral which had been destroyed by Nazi bombs in the Second World War and carried on to the City Hall for the final reception and farewell speech. Thousands of Irish emigrants, and the sons and daughters of the Irish in Britain, thronged the streets to cheer the President. Above all else, the State visit gave a new recognition and enhanced status to the Irish in Britain, the older of whom would remember very dark days when the Irish were often made to feel unwelcome there as immigrants. I was very pleased to be able to invite my own first cousin, Martin Gilmore, with whom I had little recent contact, to this event. His father, my uncle Martin, had emigrated from Co. Galway in the early 1950s. He had married Roly Murphy from Goatstown and they started a family in Coventry, where he worked all his life in the car manufacturing industry. His prize possession was a white Morris Minor which he kept immaculately, and sometimes took home on holidays. This was the last occasion on which I saw my cousin Martin alive, as he died a year later in sad circumstances. When another cousin of his and I called recently to his house to help clear up his affairs, my uncle's white Morris Minor, somewhat the worse for wear, was still parked in the garage.

One of the events which Queen Elizabeth hosted at Windsor

Castle during the visit was a special reception for Northern Ireland, to which were invited the Northern political leaders, including First Minister, Peter Robinson and Deputy First Minister, Martin McGuinness. The Sinn Féin Ard Comhairle had decided to allow McGuinness to attend the State Banquet and for other Sinn Féin politicians to attend events around the visit. Meanwhile, the Secretary of State for Northern Ireland, Theresa Villiers, and I sought to get some real business done while everybody was at Windsor. For months we had been trying to arrange a four-way quad meeting, between Peter, Martin, and the two of us. We arranged meeting rooms in one of the hotels in Windsor town, but unfortunately Peter was, once again, unable to make it because of a commitment in Belfast. When Martin discovered that Peter had taken advantage of his own absence in Windsor to make a significant jobs announcement in Belfast, he was furious. I explained to him that this kind of canny one-up-man-ship was not confined to the administration in Belfast.

The idea of 'the quad' – regular meetings between the First and Deputy First Ministers and the British Secretary of State and the Irish Minister for Foreign Affairs – was agreed between Theresa Villiers' predecessor, Owen Patterson, and myself at a breakfast meeting in the British Ambassador's residence early in my term of office. The Northern Ireland Assembly and Executive were, by now, well established, and policing and justice matters had been devolved to the Northern Ireland Executive. However, the Executive was not working very well.

In my first few days in office, I spoke with both Peter Robinson and Martin McGuinness, and it became clear to me that their relationship was strained and that the Executive was finding it difficult to make decisions, even on minor matters. In the way the institutions were set up, it seemed the Northern Ireland parties had become accustomed to sending for the Taoiseach and the Prime Minister to solve almost every difficult problem. It was about time, many felt, that the Executive stood on its own feet, managed its devolved functions and began to rely less on hand-holding by the two Governments. Steps were taken to encourage that independence, but given that we knew there would be circumstances of virtual stalemate, Patterson and I agreed to 'the quad' meetings as a method of regular dialogue between the two Governments and the Northern Ireland administration.

I was also conscious, at this early stage, that the new British Conservative Government did not appear to have the same interest in or feel for Northern Ireland as its Labour predecessor. Indeed, as time progressed, and as the referendum on Scottish Independence began to dominate British politics, the Government in London emphasised more the integrity of the Union, rather than the two-Government approach which had been the foundation for the Good Friday Agreement.

While Northern Ireland no longer attracted much media attention, I was aware that the Peace Process needed serious ongoing attention. Dissident Republicans still posed a real threat to national security and to the safety of the general public. Due to good co-operation between the PSNI and An Garda Siochána, some atrocities were thwarted. However, the dissidents did manage to murder PSNI Constable Ronan Kerr at his home in 2011, and Prison Officer David Black on his way to work in 2012.

We had reports of Loyalist paramilitaries reorganising, and of political difficulties growing at Stormont. Sinn Féin and the DUP were still finding it difficult to work together, and the other parties, the SDLP, the UUP and Alliance, complained that they were being excluded from decision making.

Helping to maintain peace on our island and to build on the

Peace Process were of paramount importance to me in my time as Tánaiste, but because in this phase of the process I felt that quiet assistance was more effective than public pronouncements, much of the work was low key and often went unreported. Apart from 'the quad' meetings, and regular meetings and phone calls with the Secretary of State, I also held three-way meetings with Peter Robinson and Martin McGuinness. These 'institutional meetings' were held sequentially in Dublin or Belfast, and were intended to prepare the agenda for the North-South Ministerial Council (NSMC) which took place every six months in either Armagh or Dublin.

The NSMC is essentially a joint meeting of the Irish Cabinet and the Northern Executive, and deals with a range of issues on an all-island basis, including agriculture, tourism, trade and more recently, health and education. It has great potential to be of benefit to the whole island. North-South synergies can be harnessed to create more jobs, develop the border regions and deliver a social and economic dividend from the peace. Nonetheless, Robinson was at times reluctant to allow new issues onto the NSMC agenda, which led me to have frequent direct discussions with him.

In the course of these talks, we also discussed the decade of commemoration for the events from the Home Rule Bill and Ulster Covenant of 1912 through to the Civil War of 1922 - 23. We were both keen to ensure that the island's complex history was marked respectfully, recognising all of the traditions on the island, and in a way which would promote understanding and reconciliation rather than re-fuel any lingering divisions.

The very first such event, which was organised by the Irish Government, was a lecture in Iveagh House to commemorate unionism. I invited Peter Robinson to give the inaugural Iveagh House Lecture in memory of Edward Carson, who had lived just around the corner from the St Stephen's Green headquarters of the Department of Foreign Affairs and Trade.

I followed this with an invitation to both Peter and Martin McGuinness to join me in Dublin for the launch of Google's digitalisation of the Irish First World War records. Before that I was the first Irish Minister to lay a wreath at the Cenotaph near Belfast City Hall on Remembrance Sunday in November 2012.

I have always felt that the Dublin Government and southern Republicans need to better understand and to reach out to Northern unionism and loyalism. Dr Martin McAleese played a crucial role over many years in maintaining dialogue with loyalist groups and individuals, and I was conscious of the need to keep such channels open between Dublin and the active loyalist community. Therefore, on numerous occasions, I visited several areas of East Belfast and elsewhere and met with community activists who had contact with loyalist organisations. During my very first meeting with Secretary of State Hillary Clinton, I asked her to facilitate the granting of visas to individuals with loyalist backgrounds for study visits to the US.

I knew too that Sinn Féin was coming under pressure from dissident elements in the nationalist community, especially during the summer marching season when communities at interface areas face much provocation. I saw this at first hand when I visited St Malachy's Church and Parish Centre in the Ardoyne. Fr Aidan Donegan, the parish priest, demonstrated the way the Church grounds had to be fortified from attack and showed me CCTV footage of disgraceful and disrespectful behaviour by drunken louts outside the Church.

Despite the political competition between Sinn Féin and Labour in the Dáil and in constituencies, I made it clear to both Gerry Adams and Martin McGuinness that as Minister for Foreign Affairs and Trade, my door would always be open to them as leaders, and that I would not allow Dáil politics to compromise the work that needed to be done on Northern Ireland. I met both of them frequently, sometimes alone, sometimes with a Sinn Féin delegation. At one such meeting in mid-May 2013, Adams told me of a development which he said had the potential to seriously damage the Peace Process.

On 19 May, John Downey, a republican living in Donegal, was arrested at Gatwick Airport, and charged with the Hyde Park bombing of 1982, which had killed four soldiers and several horses. Adams told me that Downey was one of the 'persuaders' in the republican movement who had helped bring the movement to an ending of violence, and that since then he had played an important role in maintaining the peace. He had been given a letter from the Northern Ireland office stating that he was no longer wanted by the police in Northern Ireland or anywhere else in the UK. He had travelled to Britain several times over the years, and had never encountered any difficulties with police or immigration. His arrest came completely out of the blue, and gave Sinn Féin cause to worry that the British security services might be taking a new approach to former IRA suspects, and that some 200 former IRA activists who had secured similar letters might now be open to arrest. It was all very unsettling in the Sinn Féin movement.

My first concern was for Downey himself. He was apparently not in good health and was being held in a high security prison. I asked our Embassy in London to visit him and to arrange for medical treatment. I discussed the case directly with the Secretary of State, Theresa Villiers, but she, understandably, could not intervene in what was now a police and judicial matter. I asked her repeatedly to see if his high security status could be relaxed, but there was, it seemed, no budging on that matter. Downey's lawyer, Gareth Peirce, was seeking to have him released on bail, and to help her, I wrote a letter stating that I believed assurances from the leadership of Sinn Féin that if released on bail Downey would remain in London to await his trial. Though the affair dragged on for several months, in the end the Court accepted the letter that he was not wanted by the police and the case against him was dropped.

Although most of my work in Northern Ireland was with Sinn Féin and the DUP leaders, I was conscious that there were other voices on the political spectrum. The Social and Democratic Labour Party is a 'sister party' of Labour, and I enjoyed a very good relationship with Mark Durkan, Margaret Ritchie and Alasdair McDonnell as leaders. The SDLP encouraged me to engage seriously with Northern Ireland, and warned me that for all their differences, Sinn Féin and the DUP were using their power to carve up patronage between them. I spoke regularly with Mike Nesbitt of the UUP, and he and his colleague Danny Kennedy came to Dublin for talks with me. I had always had a great respect for the non-sectarian politics of the Alliance Party, and I addressed their conference and maintained contact with David Ford while their public representatives were often under siege from extremists.

Street disturbances followed some summer parades, and a controversy over the number of days for which the Union Flag should fly over City Hall, increased tensions further in Northern Ireland in the early part of 2013. I was worried that political drift, combined with increased trouble on the streets, could undermine all the progress that had been made. I was worried too that the re-appearance on TV screens of burning cars in Belfast would damage my Department's efforts to restore Ireland's reputation, knowing that not everybody draws the distinction we do, between Belfast and Dublin. They just see violence in Ireland. I decided that the body politic in Britain and Ireland needed some kind of wake-up call in relation to Northern Ireland.

I was invited to address the annual meeting of the British-Irish Association in Cambridge in early September and chose it as my opportunity to make a major speech about the North. The speech was well received and widely welcomed. Professor Ronan Fanning, writing in the *Sunday Independent*, described it as 'bold and innovative', and congratulated me for being, in his words:

'So courageous in the context of Irish, as opposed to Northern Irish, politics. For as he knows full well, the Irish electorate is so understandably self-stressed with the degradation of austerity that it is in no mood to be reminded of the importance of Northern Ireland. In this regard he was unequivocal – 'Let there be no doubt. The peace, prosperity and political stability of Northern Ireland are matters of the highest national interest to the Republic'.'

In the speech, I sought support for multi-party talks which were then being convened under the chairmanship of Richard Haass. He and Dr Megan O'Sullivan were selected by the Northern Ireland Executive itself to lead talks to resolve issues relating to the use of flags in Northern Ireland, the problems associated with parading, and the legacy of the past. It was not intended by the Northern Ireland parties that the two Governments should become directly involved, but I intended to stay close to the talks. I had previously met Richard Haass in his capacity as President of the US Council on Foreign Relations. He had once worked as an advisor to the Bush administration. I now met him again, in New York, and we agreed to remain in contact during his work in Belfast.

We spoke regularly in Dublin and by phone. He was determined to complete his mission by the end of the year. As we approached Christmas, there was still no agreement and Haass and I were in almost daily contact. On Christmas Eve he told me he was returning to the United States for Christmas but would return on

27 December, with a view to completing his work by the thirty-first.

'But it's Christmas, Richard!'

'That's just one day,' he replied, and although I tried to explain that in Ireland we knock a week, or sometimes two, out of it, he had set a deadline and he intended to stick to it.

Both the Secretary of State and I went to Belfast for the conclusion of the talks. We were not directly involved, but we stayed in close contact with them. I met the Sinn Féin leadership, the SDLP and the Alliance Party, and spent New Year's Eve at the official residence of the Irish Government's representative on the Belfast Joint Secretariat Barbara Jones, phoning participants and studying drafts of the proposed agreement.

Haass came very close to clinching a deal. I was disappointed that it fell short, describing it as a step not yet taken, rather than a step back. On my way back to Dublin, on New Year's Day, I called to the Secretary of State, Theresa Villiers, at her official residence in Hillsborough, County Down. We talked privately about what was now needed to move things forward. The Haass talks had the foundation for the agreement which was eventually secured in early 2015. As had happened so often in the past in Northern Ireland, agreement came incrementally.

One of the pieces of advice that I had given to Haass was to engage with civil society. In my own work in Northern Ireland, I had met with representatives of many different interests including community groups, business organisations, trade unions and sporting bodies, and I felt that these bodies were often more open to reasonable compromise than the politicians, who tended to be still rooted in tribal and sectarian support bases. One of the most imaginative initiatives I came across emerged from the GAA, the Irish Football Association and the IRFU. They put together the 'game of three halves', with three equal periods of Gaelic football, soccer and rugby, and they encouraged children from across the sectarian divide to come together to play it. I don't know if the game of three halves has a future as a sport. But it certainly symbolises the politics of Northern Ireland. Them, us and neither!

CHAPTER 13
AROUND THE CLOCK

Work has always defined my life. My father died when I was just fourteen months old, and so, as the older of two boys, I was introduced early to the tough physical grind of subsistence farming. But my mother always wanted to free me from the drudgery and encouraged me to work hard in school and get the scholarships and grants that would see me through college and university. I got my first paid job at the age of twelve, in my uncle's business in Castleblakeney, and for every school or college holiday thereafter I worked, initially for him, and later in hotels, bars and restaurants in Galway, Ballinasloe and London.

I carried the same work ethic with me through my eleven years as a trade union official when I toiled long hours and travelled all over the country trying to improve pay and conditions for my members. My application to constituency casework and campaigning got elected me to the Council and the Dáil, and re-elected for three decades thereafter. I was proud of my reputation as a hard-working TD.

But in all my life, I never worked as hard as I did during the 174 weeks I served in Ireland's crisis Government. To give a sense of the non-stop activity, I reproduce here the items from my work diary for one week right in the middle of that period, in November 2012:

Saturday, 10 November

10 a.m.: Vote in Children's Referendum at Scoil Mhuire, Shankill. [Usual doorstep interview, photographs etc.]
Then travel to Northern Ireland to attend SDLP Conference.
7.30 p.m.: Address SDLP Conference Dinner in Armagh. [Honoured to be seated beside John Hume.]
10 p.m.: Depart Armagh for Belfast.
Overnight at Ireland's official residence in Belfast.

Sunday, 11 November

8 a.m.: Briefing on Northern Ireland issues by Irish officials on British Irish Secretariat.
10.15 a.m.: Belfast City Hall to meet First Minister Peter Robinson and the Lord Mayor of Belfast before Remembrance Day ceremonies.
11 a.m.: Wreath-laying ceremony at the Cenotaph.
12 noon: Brief discussion with Secretary of State for Northern Ireland.
12.30 p.m.: Travel to Culturlann MacAdam O'Fiach on Falls Road for meetings with West Belfast community and Irish language groups.
2 p.m.: Visit Peace Wall at Duncairn Gardens and meet East Belfast community activists.
4 p.m.: Visit Titanic Centre for meeting with Martin McGuinness.
6 p.m.: Attend finals of All-Ireland Schools Choir Competition, which is televised from Titanic Centre. Present prizes with Deputy First Minister. Short speech for TV audience.

7.45 p.m.: Chat and photos with schools and TV and Radio interviews about results of Children's Referendum. [Delaying scheduled departure for Dublin.] [Arrive home at 11.30 p.m.]

Monday, 12 November

9.30 a.m.: Attend my constituency Advice Centre in Patrick Street, Dun Laoghaire.

Talk with Chief Executive of Dun Laoghaire Harbour Company about their plans for a Diaspora Centre.

2 p.m.: Meeting of Labour Party Ministers and Ministers of State to discuss upcoming budget and consider difficult decisions ahead.

4 p.m.: Meet advisors to go through agenda and papers for tomorrow's Cabinet meeting and consider the issues on which we differ with Fine Gael.

5.30 p.m.: Meet with Secretary General David Cooney to discuss Department of Foreign Affairs and Trade business.
[Take Carol out for dinner to celebrate her birthday!]

Tuesday November 13th

6.30 a.m.: Up and about to prepare for an interview on Morning Ireland. *[Read papers and inform myself on all the possible questions I could be asked.]*

8 a.m.: RTÉ for Morning Ireland *interview.*

9 a.m.: Arrive at Government Buildings. [Media doorstep on the way in accompanied by Cathy Madden.]

9.30 a.m.: Pre-Cabinet meeting with Labour Ministers.

10.15 a.m.: Pre-Cabinet meeting with the Taoiseach.

11 a.m.: Cabinet meeting.

1 p.m.: Post-Cabinet briefing for Cathy Madden and my advisors.

2 p.m.: Briefing by Department officials for Dáil questions tomorrow.

[I had to be briefed on all the possible supplementaries for approximately twenty parliamentary questions which I and the Ministers of State would have to answer orally in the Dáil chamber.]

3 p.m.: *Briefing by officials from the European Division before my appearance at the Oireachtas Joint Committee on European Union Affairs (JCEUA).*

3.30 p.m.: *Attend the JCEUA to make opening statement and answer questions on European Union issues for about ninety minutes.*

5 p.m.: *Meeting with former US congressman, Bruce Morrison [who works with Irish American lobbies] regarding immigration reform and plight of the undocumented Irish in the USA.*

6 p.m.: *The Labour Party Management Committee meeting [fortnightly meeting of Party officers and senior staff to coordinate the Party's national political and organisational business].*

8 p.m.: *Dun Laoghaire Constituency Council of the Labour Party. [Monthly meeting at which I report to the local members of the Labour Party and at which I hear their views on local, party and national issues.].*

[Arrive home at about 11 p.m.]

Wednesday November 14th

8.15 a.m. *Briefing with Department officials [leaving home at 7.30 a.m.].*

8.30 a.m.: *Meet Hillary Clinton's Special Representatives for global partnerships.*

10 a.m.: *Meet Brendan Howlin to discuss EMC and Budget matters.*

11 a.m.: *Meet Party press office.*

11.30 a.m.: *Meet Labour Political Director David Leach [for brief on* issues which TDs and Senators may raise at the Parliamentary Labour Party meeting].

12 noon: Weekly meeting of the Parliamentary Labour Party [I give report on Party and Government matters and answer questions for over an hour].

1.30 p.m.: Depart for the Royal Marine Hotel Dun Laoghaire.

2 p.m.: Address the graduation ceremony for Dun Laoghaire College of Further Education, and present the certificates and awards.

3.30 p.m.: Depart Dun Laoghaire for Leinster House. [On the drive back study the final drafts of the replies to Dáil questions.]

4.30 p.m.: Dáil chamber to answer ministerial parliamentary questions. [Lasts for an hour and a quarter.]

6 p.m.: Meet with Fine Gael's Mary Mitchell O'Connor TD [my constituency colleague] to coordinate on constituency issues. [Throughout my entire thirty years as a public representative, in the interests of the Dun Laoghaire constituency, I cooperated with Councillors and TDs of every political persuasion.]

8.30 p.m.: Political EMC meeting. [The Taoiseach, Michael Noonan, Brendan Howlin and I have another late night meeting to try to resolve our differences on Budget 2013. At about midnight, I depart for home. In the car, I try to read the briefing book for tomorrow's Leaders' Questions but I am too tired and decide instead to get up early and give it another go in the morning.]

Thursday November 15th

7 a.m.: Between spoons of porridge, washed down with a strong mug of coffee, I try to absorb the contents of the big black briefing book. This contains briefing notes on the approximately forty or fifty issues which might be raised with me at Leaders' Questions and

the *Order of Business in the Dáil. The Taoiseach takes these
questions on Tuesday and Wednesday. I take them Thursdays. Like
someone frantically cramming for an exam, I continue reading as
I am driven in to Government Buildings.*

9 a.m.: *Meet advisors to prepare for Leaders' Questions.* [They have
been in since early morning going through issues which have
developed overnight, and already Jean O'Mahony has an
additional set of briefing notes for me.]

10.30 a.m.: *Leaders' Question.* [I face the opposition for questions
across the House. They are free to ask me about anything, and the
exchanges are televised live! On this particular morning, Fianna
Fáil's Niall Collins and Sinn Féin's Mary Lou McDonald question
me about the death of Savita Halappanavar and the Government's
plans for legislation on the X case. Independent, Thomas Pringle
asks me about the survivors of symphysiotomy, and, on the Order
of Business, I am asked about bankers' salaries, the Garda
compensation scheme, the Middle East, the Health budget, Public
Transport, the Central Bank, minimum alcohol pricing, the Courts
Bill, internet gambling, farmers and the budget, SOLAS, adoption,
legal aid, the N17, the N18, admission to schools and legislation
for parental leave.]

11.30 a.m.: *Meet with Second Secretary General, Geraldine Byrne
Nason who is waiting for me in my office,* [I am due to meet the
top officials from the European Council in 15 minutes time and I
need to be filled in on some key European issues.]

11.45 a.m.: *Meet Uwe Corsepius, Director General of the European
Council, and a former advisor to Chancellor Merkel, to discuss the
forthcoming Irish Presidency of the EU.*

12.15 p.m.: *Seminar, conducted by Corsepius and his senior officials,
for Irish Ministers who will be chairing Council formations during
the presidency.* [This continues over lunch.]

2 p.m.: EMC in the Sycamore Room. [The struggle for Irish economic recovery continues. We discuss the banks, jobs, the promissory note and the budget.]

4.30 p.m.: Leave for Áras an Uachtarain to meet privately with the recipients of the President's Award for distinguished members of the Irish diaspora.

5.30 p.m.: Award Ceremony with the President and the Taoiseach.

7 p.m.: With Carol, I go to Farmleigh House, to host a dinner for President's Award recipients and their families. [They include the family of the late Jim Stynes, former Dublin footballer; Sally Mulready, for her work in the Irish community in Britain; and Loretta Brennan Glucksman, for her work on peace reconciliation and development.]

[Arrive home at 10.30 p.m.]

Friday November 16th

Morning: Some local media interviews by telephone from my home.

11 a.m.: Meeting in the Boylan Centre with 100 members of the Dun Laoghaire Rathdown Network of Older People. [They are worried that the upcoming budget may cut their pensions and abolish the free travel scheme.]

1 p.m.: Attend and address exporters event in the Four Seasons Hotel organised by Tesco.

3 p.m.: Receive and listen respectfully to the Ambassador of India who has come to present the deep concerns of his Government over the tragic death of Indian citizen Savita Halappanavar.

5 p.m.: My Private Secretary, Mary Connery, runs me through my diary for the next couple of weeks. [She hands me three large briefing books, for the EU Foreign Affairs Council on Monday, for a meeting with President Van Rompuy on the MFF on Monday night, and for the EU General Affairs Council on Tuesday. These, together with the papers I already have for the upcoming OSCE Ministerial Council, and the sets of option papers for the budget which is only three weeks away, make up my homework for the weekend, to be studied in between my constituency commitments on Saturday and Sunday. On top of that, Mark Garrett tells me that he expects yet another opinion poll on Sunday, this time in the Sunday Times. *As I leave the office laden down with folders, Mary reminds me that I have to be in Baldonnel for 8.30 a.m. on Monday morning and that I will be picked up at around 7.45 a.m.]*

I don't know it then, but the following week turns out to be even more difficult, as my wife, Carol, is forced to cope with yet another nasty, inaccurate and unfair media attack on her. (She subsequently complained to the Press Ombudsman about articles which appeared in the *Irish Daily Mail*. The newspaper consequently published a comprehensive clarification and apology to her. Although some media rehashed and commented on the *Daily Mail* story, none of them repeated or even reported the fact that the apology was given.)

This hectic schedule had to be sustained week-in-week-out, and at times it felt like I was trying to do four full-time jobs simultaneously. I was a TD for my constituency, the Leader of the second largest party in the Dáil, the Minister for Foreign Affairs and Trade, and the Tánaiste in a coalition government – all at a time of unprecedented economic chaos and peril. I coped by focusing separately on each area of my work. As I rushed from party meeting, to EMC, to EU commitment, to the Dáil chamber, and often back to the constituency, it was like I was constantly changing channels.

Because of the crisis, the most time-consuming and certainly the most challenging job for me was Tánaiste. The Deputy Prime

Minister of a coalition government is always at a disadvantage: unlike the Prime Minister, he or she does not lead the government, does not head a full-time department dedicated solely to his/her whole-of-government role, and does not command the same politically-beneficial media attention as a PM. Yet the Tánaiste has the same workload as the Taoiseach: every memorandum to government, every piece of government legislation, every government report, every significant appointment, and every major political development, must be scrutinised by the Tánaiste, not just for how it affects his/her own department, but for how it fits in with the agreed Programme for Government and with the Party's objectives.

Dick Spring and his programme manager, Greg Sparks, had explained to Mark Garrett and myself how they managed government business in the mid-90s, and we built our system largely on their experience.

Noon on Fridays was the deadline for ministers to submit items for the following Tuesday's Cabinet agenda. By lunchtime on Friday, the senior Labour and Fine Gael advisors had examined the agenda and identified any items of particular contention. Every Friday afternoon, Mark Garrett flagged for me the likely problem issues, and he, Colm O'Reardon, Jean O'Mahony, Cathy Madden and Niamh Sweeney would give those issues their attention over the weekend.

A meeting of the senior advisors of all Ministers, both Labour and Fine Gael, was held every Monday to go through the agenda, and later on that day, usually at 4 p.m., I would meet with Mark, Colm, Jean and David Leach to go through each item on the following day's agenda. I would also give my steer on how each problematic issue might be resolved. My team would then work, often late into the night, with their Fine Gael counterparts, and bring me the outcomes, if any, before I met with the Labour Ministers at 9.30 a.m. on the Tuesday morning in advance of the Cabinet meeting. At the Labour minister's meetings, we would again go through every item of the Cabinet agenda, and identify the issues on which we could not agree. These issues and the corresponding ones from the Fine Gael side constituted the agenda for a meeting which I then held every Tuesday morning before Cabinet with the Taoiseach. These meetings took place in my office, which was located just over the Cabinet room. There were no civil servants present and no advisors, just Enda and me.

Some issues we agreed to postpone (usually with some time frame for further discussion), some we resolved between us there and then, for others we came up with some compromise that we would then need to put to the relevant Minister before the Cabinet meeting. Often, we just argued about an item and would 'leave it for another day'!

While these meetings took place in my office, the Cabinet ministers gathered in a room just off the Cabinet room itself. Irritation sometimes grew if Enda and I were taking too long. On one occasion, just after summer recess, our discussions took a very long time and colleagues began to speculate about the future of the Government. In fact, the two of us were upstairs having a post-holiday chat, most of which had nothing to do with government business. We were, after all, two fathers with children who had done the Leaving Cert that year; naturally, we chatted about what they were planning to do in college.

Because I had already forensically examined and 'Labour-proofed' every proposal coming to Cabinet, and because most of the big economic decisions were being considered at the EMC, I did not make long speeches at Cabinet meetings, nor did I contribute to the discussions on every item. Just a few months into the life of the Government and on the first day of Labour's parliamentary party away day in September 2011, the *Irish Independent* reported that I was 'quiet' at Cabinet meetings, quoting an unnamed Cabinet Minister as the source, and claiming that 'others in the party are carrying the can for him'.

Unfortunately, this was not the only report from inside the Cabinet room which undermined me within the party and with the public. Unnamed Cabinet sources complained about the existence of the EMC and what it was doing. And there was serial leaking of Cabinet discussions, and of proposals that were before Cabinet, some of which were never actually decided on. All of this put me constantly on the back foot. It became difficult to manage the media for the Labour Party when every Labour message appeared to be constantly second-guessed. I was rarely able to give a press conference or do an interview without being asked to respond to criticisms of the Party or of myself, much of which appeared to be coming from within the Party itself.

The decline in support for the Labour Party from 2011 to 2014 was linked mainly to the decisions we made in government, particularly the three difficult budgets – December 2011, December 2012 and October 2013. Opinion poll support for Labour continued at a level close to our general election result right through 2011. At budget time in December that year it fell to the mid-teens. In March/April 2012, Red C were still putting Labour on 15/16 per cent, but we had dropped to 13 per cent in the IPSOS/*Irish Times* poll on 20 April, and to 14 per cent in the Behaviour and Attitudes poll for the *Sunday Times*. After the December 2012 budget we had fallen to 11 per cent in Red C and 10 per cent in the *Irish Times* polls, and we were down to single digits by our third budget in October 2013 – 6 per cent in the *Irish Times* poll and 9 per cent in Red C.

Fine Gael was also down in the polls, but not by anything like the drop in Labour support. Labour was attracting a disproportionate share of the blame for the Government's difficult decisions. Of course, Labour was more of a target for the opposition. Fine Gael had little, if any, political competition on the right, with the PDs gone and Fianna Fáil finding it difficult to recover from its 2011 defeat. But not so the left: Sinn Féin was making considerable progress in terms of popularity, consistently over 20 per cent in opinion polls. An array of ultra-left groups was, at the same time, ranting against austerity but offering nothing by the way of solutions. All of them targeted the Labour Party.

We expected, and could handle, the criticism from opponents, but the opposition and attacks from within the Party itself were more difficult. Deputy Tommy Broughan had lost the Labour Party whip while we were still in opposition, so it was no surprise that he would do so again in government. Joan Burton cautioned me before Patrick Nulty's selection as the by-election candidate in her constituency that he would not last the course, and just six weeks after his election he voted against the budget. Róisín Shortall announced her resignation as a Junior Minister and as a member of the Parliamentary Labour Party in September 2012. Deputy Colm Keaveney, after losing the whip, insisted on remaining as Chairperson of the Party and promoted himself as the conscience of the rank and file membership of Labour before leaving to join Fianna Fáil.

All four of these used their departure, and several opportunities afterwards, to attack the Party, in some cases (but not all) with a degree of unnecessary bitterness. Some argue that once outside the Party, they have free rein to say what they like, but the truth is that the general public is not concerned with technicalities like 'losing the whip' and 'resigning membership'. Ultimately, when someone is described for years as a Labour representative, they are seen as Labour for long afterwards. And when they are heard to criticise the Party or its leader, that is seen as Labour being criticised by one of its own and it makes a bigger impact. The criticism of Labour, apparently from 'inside', reinforced by disloyal comments from 'unnamed sources' within the Party, is what did the greatest damage.

Membership of a political party, even for TDs, is voluntary. Every time a candidate is selected to contest an election for Labour, they are required, in front of the members of the Party in their constituency, to publicly sign a pledge that they will vote with the Party in the Dáil, Senate, European Parliament, Council or whatever body to which they are elected. Sometimes it can be hard to always honour that pledge. Willie Penrose had to resign his office as a minister in the Cabinet and the party whip over the closure of Mullingar army barracks. Anne Ferris lost the whip to support an opposition Private Member's Bill that sought to permit abortion in circumstances of fatal foetal abnormality. And more recently, Michael McNamara suffered the same fate when he voted against the Government's plans for Aer Lingus. But none of these three used their difficulties to attack the Party, and in all cases went to great lengths to show their respect for their Party colleagues. Indeed, all three rejoined the parliamentary party after a period of absence, during which their wise counsel and political judgement were sorely missed.

The Party's TDs and senators showed great courage throughout the difficult years in government. So too did the Party's councillors and our loyal party members. In government at a time of unprecedented crisis, Labour had to implement unpopular policies to save our country. And we had to endure harsh criticism for doing so. I knew that our public representatives were getting it in the neck in their constituencies, and that it was becoming increasingly difficult for members to defend the Party's decisions within their communities and in their places of employment or recreation. But defend the decisions they did, with great courage and loyalty.

Following the tragic death of Fine Gael Minister of State, Shane McEntee, a by-election arose in the Meath East constituency in March 2013. The Labour TD there, Dominic Hannigan, volunteered to run the campaign. I attended a well-attended selection convention in Ashbourne at which Councillor Eoin Holmes was selected as our candidate. Eoin is a talented film-maker, television producer and businessman, and he campaigned hard in the weeks before polling day. He had his young family with him at the selection convention, and introduced me to his children. To the visible alarm of her mother and father, their daughter said 'Gilmore? We have a goose called Gilmore!' I was curious and asked her why Gilmore. 'It's very cross,' was her matter-of-fact answer. Here now, unintentionally offered was Cathy Madden's advice that I should smile a bit more!

By-elections are very different to general elections. Voters generally feel free to experiment a bit with their vote, and support tends to consolidate around one or two candidates, in this case, a former Fianna Fáil TD Thomas Byrne and Shane McEntee's daughter, Helen, who won the seat for Fine Gael. Eoin Holmes finished a disappointing fifth. The result, and the reaction to the Party during the canvass, alarmed the parliamentary party.

I had planned on taking a few days break around Easter, but due to the down beat mood in the Party, I decided to cancel my plans and spend the time talking individually to the Party's TDs, senators and members of our executive board. One by one, I met with each of them, and asked them for their thoughts on what needed to be done to restore the Party's fortunes.

The message was clear: we were doing a good job in government but needed to communicate it better. The last two budgets had taken a toll on the Party's reputation, and we needed some visible Labour wins at the next budget. The local elections were looming and we needed to prepare organisationally and politically for those. At the same time, we needed to set out some long term vision as the basis of a manifesto for the next general election.

Those who mentioned my leadership of the Party did so to reassure me of their continuing support for me as Leader. A few colleagues told me they had been sounded out by some figures in the Party about my leadership, and some suggested I should move out of Foreign Affairs. I clearly could not do so during the EU Presidency, but I privately intended to make the move at the next major Cabinet reshuffle.

The economy was beginning to recover and it was clear to me that the deficit target of 5.1 per cent could be met at the next budget with an adjustment of considerably less than the proposed €3.1 billion. I began to talk publicly about this, and began pushing for an agreement on the introduction of free GP care for children under six as the first step in the introduction of our new model of health care.

We won the budget battle to keep the adjustment down to €2.5 billion; we got agreement on free GP care for under sixes, and Ireland exited the bailout programme in December without a 'precautionary programme' which was normally sought by the IMF. Our Party Conference in Killarney on the last weekend in November was a success, and as we rounded Christmas and the New Year, Labour support was beginning to pick up again in the polls. Red C had us at 12 per cent; Behaviour and Attitudes at 11 per cent and Millward Brown at 12 per cent. The trend in all the polls was upwards. Having taken the hard decisions to get Ireland out of the bailout, and having said goodbye to the Troika, and with the economy recovering, perhaps at last Labour could look forward to better days in 2014 and beyond. There was plenty to be optimistic about as the New Year dawned.

On Thursday 9 January 2014, I was on my way to visit the annual Young Scientist Exhibition when I heard about a breaking story that Irish Water had spent €90 million hiring consultants. I pulled into a side street to think about it and prepare my answers for the inevitable press doorstep that would greet me at the RDS.

This was the worst possible start for the new water utility, which had been set up to lead investment in the country's water infrastructure and to take the cost of water provision off the State's balance sheet. Over the decades, there had been massive under-investment in water, such that in some parts of the country water was badly polluted and in others, such as Dublin, water shortages were looming. New money was needed to upgrade reservoirs, replace leaking pipes and improve water quality. The State itself did not have sufficient money to carry out this essential investment, unless we were prepared to take it from the already strained budgets for schools, hospitals and transport. When Britain had to confront a similar challenge, it decided to privatise water, and this was a route that the Irish Labour Party was not prepared to countenance. We were determined that water would remain in public ownership, and our only way to achieve that was to set up a State-owned utility – an ESB for water, as it were – which could borrow independently of the State. To do this however, the new utility would need to have an income stream, and therefore would have to charge for water. We knew that would be a difficult ask for people, so in the Programme for Government we had agreed to '… introduce a fair funding model to deliver clean and reliable water. We will first establish a new State owned water utility company to take over responsibility from the separate local authorities for Ireland's water infrastructure and to drive new investment. The objective is to install water meters in every household in Ireland and move to a charging system that is based on use above the free allowance.'

Now, before the details of water charges had even been considered, Irish Water was under fire for hiring consultants, which in the public mind equated to wasting taxpayers' money. Moreover, it was way behind with the metering. At best, only 40 per cent of households would have meters by the end of 2014, we were informed.

Conscious of the fact that the first full year of the property tax would also be in 2014, I felt that to add water charges too, as per Fianna Fáil's agreement with the Troika, would be a step too far. I said at the EMC that I wanted water charges to be held back until at least 70 per cent of houses were metered and until the Government had agreed measures to ensure that charges would be affordable for households on low incomes, families with children and those with illnesses requiring extra water. We agreed that the actual charging would be deferred until the beginning of 2015, but that the first bills would date from October 2014. This would give Irish Water time to develop a reasonable and hopefully acceptable water charging regime.

In the Dáil the opposition goaded the Taoiseach with questions and accusations: how much would the average household have to pay? When would they first become liable? October: 'so aren't you just hiding the figure until after the local elections?' Will you publish the average charge before the local election? Kenny relented and committed to doing so. He sought an agreement at the EMC for the average figure. I resisted, and it was decided that we should first establish what was the minimum figure required to keep water off the national balance sheet.

To enable Irish Water to borrow independently of the State, it needed to generate 51 per cent of its income from charges, and the result of the EMC study showed that the minimum average household charge would be €240 per annum. Unfortunately, making the most of the information vacuum, opponents of water charges were by now claiming that the charge would as high as €700, or even €1,000! Householders were becoming alarmed and Fine Gael argued that we should settle the figure. Michael Noonan said to me: 'A fiver a week is a lot more manageable than a thousand a year.' I continued to resist. A fiver was still a lot from a pensioner's weekly budget, and an extra burden on hard-pressed families who were still struggling from the recession.

The Taoiseach was conscious, as was I, that this was the first big financial decision the Government would have to make, after the departure of the Troika, and would be seen abroad as a measure of our continued determination to prudently manage the public finances. Recovery was still fragile, so this was not just an issue of perception. But Kenny's biggest worry was that he had said in the Dáil that he would release the figure before the local elections and he feared a failure to deliver. He put the issue on the agenda for a Cabinet meeting without my agreement – the first time he ever did that. This resulted in a full scale argument across the Cabinet table, between the Taoiseach and myself. He did not push it to a vote, knowing that because the Cabinet operated by agreement rather than vote, to do so would have meant an end to the Government. The discussion was parked for another day.

In the meantime, I was getting reports from the Labour local elections canvass that it would be better to have certainty about the figure. So I turned my mind to mitigating the €240. The Programme for Government spoke of the charges applying only after each household had been granted a minimum allowance of free water. What should that allowance be? We agreed a free allowance for every household. Shouldn't it be greater for larger families? So we agreed additional allowances of free water for children up to the age of 18. And shouldn't people with medical conditions which required extra water also get special allowances? Agreed. Now what about pensioners and others on low incomes? We have free schemes for electricity, television and telephones. Shouldn't there be a free scheme for water? We came up with a 'Water Conservation Grant' of €100. But not every household would be metered by the time the charges come in? Those not metered would be given an estimated bill, and when they were eventually metered they could claim back any excess they had paid!

Overall, it was not a bad deal, and a far cry from the full cost-recovery charge to which Fianna Fáil had agreed, which would have resulted in average charges of around €500. If we could just get the message out there. While canvassing in the Blackrock electoral area in my own constituency, I met one voter who was particularly angry about water charges. She was the mother of six young children and when I went through the various allowances we had secured, she was reassured. Similarly, I managed to illustrate to a pensioner couple whom I met in Waterford that, provided they were careful with their water usage, they would have little, if any charge. Unfortunately, though, it was too late at a national level. We were now only five weeks from the local elections – many voters had given up listening to the details, and the media was more interested in controversy than in facts. Water charges, no matter how logically explained and rationally justified, were the final straw for people already worn down by years of austerity. They were also Labour's biggest political handicap in the local elections. But not the only one. Medical cards came a close second.

The savings to be achieved in the Health budget included a review of medical cards. It was estimated that about 5 per cent of all the medical cards issued were for people who were now dead, or who, for one reason or another, no longer needed a medical card. In January, the HSE began issuing letters to *some* medical card holders, which caused widespread alarm among *all* medical card holders, the vast majority of whom were never in any danger of losing their cards. The alarm was amplified when some cases were highlighted in which the HSE had withdrawn cards from people with serious medical conditions. Despite the fact that more people now had medical cards that at any time in the history of the State, Labour canvassers were getting hostile receptions in places, especially at houses where the HSE letters had arrived that week.

On top of that came the Garda Síochána controversies, which first came to my attention at the Labour selection convention for the Dublin constituency in the European Parliament elections in Liberty Hall on Sunday 9 February. When I arrived, I was ushered to a corner at the top of the stairs for a media interview. Did I think 'the Gardaí should be bugging the offices of the Garda Ombudsman Commission?' asked a reporter, referring to a story in that morning's *Sunday Times*, which I had not yet read.

That story became part of a number of allegations made about the Gardaí, including those made by Sergeant Maurice McCabe, all of which led to a series of investigations, and to questions for Justice Minister, Alan Shatter, and Garda Commissioner, Martin Callinan. In reply to questions at the Dáil Public Accounts Committee, Commissioner Callinan used the word 'disgusting' to describe some of the allegations, and subsequently refused to resile from it. Alan Shatter then got into difficulties with comments he made during a television appearance. Before long, there was a media and public storm over confidence in the Gardaí, the Garda Commissioner and the Minister for Justice. Both the Taoiseach and I were repeatedly asked if we had confidence in the Minister and in the Commissioner. I answered, as did other Ministers, that it would be helpful if the Commissioner withdrew the offending remark, but he didn't, and the controversy continued.

I saw in this controversy, however, an opportunity to progress a Labour policy objective which Fine Gael had not accepted in the Programme for Government. As Labour Justice spokespersons in opposition, Brendan Howlin and Pat Rabbitte had advanced the case for an independent Garda Authority. The structure and governance of the Gardaí had remained intact since the turbulent days of the Civil War. Labour argued that twenty-first century Ireland needed a reformed police service, governed by an independent authority drawn from civil society. I now pursued the case for it again, and eventually achieved success when the Taoiseach came on board with the idea.

The establishment of an independent Garda Authority is the biggest reform of the Garda Síochána since the foundation of the State, and is one of Labour's most significant achievements in this Government. Yet it has gone almost unnoticed because public and media attention continued to focus on Minister Shatter and Commissioner Callinan, and the manner of their eventual departures.

On Friday 21 March the Taoiseach telephoned me from the European Council meeting in Brussels. He was due to meet the press following the Council meeting and was worried that if he went as far as I had on the Callinan issue, the Commissioner might have to resign. We agreed a formula of words which we would both use. We spoke again on Saturday morning as I was due to meet the press at an event in Belfast. On both occasions, I emphasised the need to proceed with Garda reform and the establishment of a

Garda Authority. In our discussion on Saturday, I felt that the Taoiseach had warmed to the idea, and seemed keen to get on with it. We said we would talk again about it at our regular pre-Cabinet meeting on Tuesday.

When I arrived in Government Buildings at 9 a.m. on Tuesday morning, 25 March, my Private Secretary, Robert O'Driscoll, told me that the Taoiseach wanted to see me urgently, and he stressed that I needed to talk to him before the Labour Ministers meeting. I walked the long corridor to the Taoiseach's office. When I got there I found him to be untypically agitated.

The Attorney General, who had to miss this Cabinet meeting due to a family commitment, had briefed him the previous Sunday afternoon about matters on which she had been due to report to the Cabinet. In the course of that briefing she had informed him that she had become aware of recordings which the Gardaí had made of telephone conversations to and from certain Garda stations, and in some cases between Garda stations. She explained that the public would become aware of the existence of these recordings, because of a court case that would be heard later that week. The Taoiseach, went on to tell me that he had met with the Minister for Justice and the Secretary General of that Department, Brian Purcell, on Monday evening; that Mr. Purcell had travelled out to Commissioner Callinan's home to discuss the issue; that the Commissioner had decided to retire and that a letter advising of his decision was on its way, as we spoke.

I was shocked. Firstly at the Gardaí tape recording of conversations, then at the possibility that people acting out of civic responsibility who had rung a Garda station with information or a complaint, could be on tape and that these tapes might have to be produced. Could criminals seek to have cases re-opened on the basis of such tapes? Might some walk free? What about supposedly privileged conversations between detainees and their lawyers? Such were the questions of civil liberties, justice and confidence in the Garda Síochána that occurred to me. Furthermore, I was deeply concerned that the Taoiseach had been aware of the problem since Sunday evening but was only telling me about it two days later, and that in the meantime the Commissioner had chosen to retire from his office.

I spent a long time discussing the crisis with the Taoiseach, but we both knew we had to act promptly. News of the Commissioner's retirement was bound to leak out quickly. We agreed not to proceed with the usual parallel meetings of the Labour and Fine Gael Ministers that morning, and instead to go directly to the Cabinet Room to bring the Cabinet up to date. However, we were also concerned about the prospect of a leak directly from the Cabinet meeting. (The Taoiseach told me about one occasion when details of a Cabinet discussion were being summarised on a radio station while the meeting was still in progress. A texting minister!)

For this meeting, the Taoiseach and I put our mobile phones in the middle of the Cabinet table and all other Ministers followed suit. We had to decide on the appointment of an Acting Commissioner and prepare a Government statement. A small group of ministers from both parties went to rework the draft statement which had been produced by the Government secretariat. The sticking point was the proposed establishment of an Independent Garda Authority, but the Taoiseach and I reached agreement on that in a side meeting. The retirement of the Commissioner was big news. There were statements from all sides in the Dáil and wall-to-wall media coverage.

Late in the afternoon, Mark Garrett entered my office with news that he had just heard from an RTÉ source that there was a letter from Commissioner Callinan which had not apparently been brought to the attention of the Cabinet. I knew of no such letter and asked Mark to get a copy from his counterparts in the Taoiseach's office right away. Commissioner Callinan's letter, addressed on 10 March to the Secretary General of the Department of Justice, and clearly requesting that the contents be brought to the attention of the Minister, related to the taping of telephone conversations at Garda stations. I was greatly alarmed. If the Commissioner had reported to the Minister in these terms fifteen days ago, why was he now retiring? Why had Alan Shatter not informed Cabinet of the existence and contents of this letter today? Did the Taoiseach know anything about the letter? These questions added to my anger with the Taoiseach for failing to keep me informed about the tapes issue and the Commissioner's decision to retire. If it turned out that I and the Labour Party had been blind-sided by Fine Gael on all of this it would certainly mean the end of the Government.

I requested to speak with the Taoiseach, Minister Shatter and the Attorney General, separately. The Taoiseach was having an unusually long day in the Dáil chamber. I knew he was mourning the recent passing of the very popular Fine Gael TD, Nicky McFadden, to whom tributes were being paid in the Dáil that day. I expected he would not be available to talk until later in the day. Meanwhile, the Attorney General called to my office on her return from Galway, and I was reassured by the fact that her account of the events of the previous few days tallied in every respect with that of the Taoiseach. Standing at the fireplace in my office, Alan Shatter told me that he had not seen the letter until it was delivered to him at the very end of that day's Cabinet meeting, and that he had not read it until after the meeting. I did in fact recall a large envelope being delivered to Minister Shatter just before the end of the Cabinet meeting, but as I left Leinster House that evening, I was still uncertain. I had yet to speak to the Taoiseach and as I travelled home, I began to assemble the kind of statement I might make the following morning, if the Taoiseach was unable to assure me that nothing untoward had been attempted.

I was sitting at the kitchen table when the Taoiseach called me on my mobile phone. He told me that he had not seen the letter either and concurred that it was strange and unacceptable that a letter of such importance had not been passed on to the Minister. I told him that I was taking the most serious view about how the details had unfolded, and he assured me that he was fully aware of the seriousness of the situation for the coalition. In all my dealings with him, he had never been untruthful with me, so I accepted at face value what he was saying.

A few weeks later, I was sitting in the church at Arbour Hill, awaiting the start of the annual 1916 commemoration service. A protocol officer tapped me on the shoulder and pointed out that as the Taoiseach had not yet arrived, he wondered would I step out to greet the President, who was on his way. Outside the church, I met Alan Shatter and we were joined a few moments later by the Taoiseach himself. There was no hint of anything off course. When the ceremony was over, I returned to Leinster House for an appointment, and then travelled to Castleknock for a campaign event for the Dublin West by-election. Just before the event started, I noticed a text message from the Taoiseach: 'Eamon can you take a call?' I assumed it was about a difference of opinion on an unrelated matter which had arisen that morning between our respective Chiefs of Staff, the two Marks, and decided to leave it for the moment. At the campaign event, I was asked by the press if the Guerin Report on Alan Shatter's handling of the allegations made by Sergeant Maurice McCabe had been delivered yet. I said it had not. In fact, it had.

On my return to Leinster House, I went immediately to the

weekly meeting of the Parliamentary Labour Party, only to be called out of it to take an urgent call from the Taoiseach. He informed me that he had received the Guerin Report that morning, that he had given it to Alan Shatter, and that Minister Shatter had since decided to resign. Though, in fairness to the Taoiseach, he had tried to contact me, it appeared that I was being kept in the dark once again and this did not help my cause within the Party.

Relations with Fine Gael had been worsening for some time. The abortion issue and the Meath East by-election set off a series of, initially, small clashes, which by mid-2014 had grown into a considerable gulf. Fine Gael had lost members due to the X case legislation and they were inclined to blame Labour. In the aftermath of the Meath East by-election, I decided that Labour needed to assert its differences from Fine Gael more vocally. We began, for example, to assert our particular budget proposals more in public. In addition, a rather juvenile prank during the election campaign itself soured relations further. On the eve of the election, the Labour campaign circulated a leaflet, caricaturing the Taoiseach. I knew nothing about it and assured the Taoiseach so, and I believe he accepted my own bona fide about that. But others in Fine Gael suspected that some who were close to me had a hand in it.

In late September 2013, I was at the United Nations General Assembly in New York when I was told that Dell was to create 100 new jobs at Cherrywood in my constituency. I was delighted, and asked my staff to put out a press release welcoming it. After a few hours, I enquired about the statement only to be told that the jobs had already been announced by Richard Bruton. I got the full picture later that day, that Richard Bruton, Michael Noonan and the Taoiseach himself had travelled out to Cherrywood to announce the jobs in my constituency. I exploded. The Taoiseach's people told Mark Garrett that it was not planned that way.

Apparently, the jobs announcement was initially intended for Limerick, and Michael Noonan had arranged a photo with Dell executives for his Department Office in Merrion Street. Somebody suggested that the Taoiseach might like to be in the picture. Then Richard got wind of it, and as the Jobs Minister, he too wanted in on it. Then somebody on the PR side thought it might be even better to do it on site in Cherrywood, where Dell is based. It never crossed anybody's mind that Cherrywood was in the Tánaiste's constituency!

I wasn't buying this, if for no other reason than it ought to have occurred to someone in Fine Gael that there should be a Labour TD included. To make matters worse, one of the weekend newspaper colour writers wrote about how I had missed a jobs announcement in my constituency, and concluded something like, 'Gilmore is always abroad'! All kinds of assurances were given by our partners in government that in future all jobs announcements would be done on a 50/50 basis and some separately by the Tánaiste. Such a mix up would never happen again, we were assured. But it did!

As we approached the December date for Ireland's exit from the bailout, my press people began to talk with their Fine Gael counterparts to coordinate communications on this very good news story. There seemed very little come-back on it until a few days before the deadline when my people were informed that the Taoiseach was to make a national televised broadcast on RTÉ! Such national broadcasts automatically entitle the opposition parties to an equivalent amount of airtime, but not so for the second party in government (in this case, also the second largest party in the Dáil).

Mark Garrett and Cathy Madden challenged their Fine Gael counterparts, who claimed that RTÉ had offered the broadcast. Mark and Cathy went to see RTÉ management, who said that Fine

Gael personnel had requested the broadcast on behalf of the Government. Not only that, but apparently when RTÉ enquired of Fine Gael if the Labour Party was agreeable to the arrangement, the Fine Gael people had assured them that we were!

Some on the Fine Gael side of the Government were now turning tribal. Every piece of good news was to be seized and exploited for Fine Gael's sole advantage. This was going to do enormous damage to the cohesion of the Government. By working together, in the country's interests, both parties had succeeded in getting Ireland out of the bailout and on the road to recovery. Now, if that successful joint venture is to be super ceded by partisan politics, there will be no winners!

14 THE LAST WEEKENDS

Mid-term elections are always difficult for government parties. Even in good times voters use them to give governments a kicking. But as Labour struggled through the 2014 local and European election campaigns, it became clear that despite the improving economy, we were taking more than our fair share of the hit from the unpopular decisions of Government, and from a series of badly handled crises in departments led by Fine Gael ministers. A short-lived lift in the polls around New Year was followed by a period of declining ratings as we headed towards polling day on 23 May.

Our candidates and members soldiered on bravely through the campaign. I travelled around the country once more to knock on doors and support local canvassing. It was an uphill battle all the way for everyone involved. On polling day, I sat down and composed personalised text messages to each of the Labour candidates, congratulating them on rising to the challenge. Most of them replied appreciatively.

The election results were worse than we had feared. All through Saturday, the day of the count, I received the bad news from all over the country with a sinking heart. Even my closest political friend,

Councillor Denis O'Callaghan – who five years previously, with Councillor Carrie Smyth, had topped the poll for Labour in my local six-seater – was struggling to retain his seat. And there was nothing I could do. Thankfully, they both eventually did make it, in one of our better results in that election, but Denis had a particularly long and anxious wait out in Citywest before he got over the line. A principled man who had done so much for his community and for the county over the previous twenty-three years should not, I felt, have to struggle so hard to get re-elected.

Our constituency colleague, and my friend, Councillor Jane Dillon Byrne was not so fortunate. The longest serving Labour councillor in the country, she lost her seat by a mere eighteen votes. (In Jane's case, however, the problem was not just the kicking Labour was getting, but also her support for the new library and cultural centre in Dun Laoghaire … about which many who voted against her now enthuse!)

Mark Garrett suggested that I give an interview to *RTÉ News*. Inevitably, I was asked about my future as Leader. In politics, to even deal with the question is to hand over advantage, so I batted it away as best I could. But I was already thinking about it.

That afternoon, I had telephoned Councillor Denis Leonard, whom I had persuaded to contest the Westmeath by-election for Labour. I thought he had done quite well given the short campaign and the fact that first preferences for the Government side were likely to go to the late Nicky McFadden's sister, Gabrielle. Denis was distraught and I tried to re-assure him about his performance. 'Eamon, I am not bothered about the by-election. I am going to lose my Council seat!' Irish public life can ill afford to lose talented and conscientious councillors like Denis Leonard.

I did not sleep well that night and got up around 5 a.m. I went online to examine in detail the results so far. By that time most local authorities had reports on the count on their websites, so it was possible to follow the pattern of transfers and to estimate where the final seats would go. It did not look good. All over the country we were losing good councillors like Martin Coughlan from Macroom; Gillian Wharton from Tralee; Virginia O'Dowd from Nenagh. I couldn't see us winning even one seat in Cork City. I waited until after 8 a.m. to ring David Leach and get him to go through the results county by county. He was a bit more optimistic (and as it subsequently turned out, more accurate) than I was. But it was still a very bad result. For the Party. And for me.

I called a meeting of Mark Garrett, Colm O'Reardon and David Leach for 11 a.m. at my house and we reviewed the results and the consequences. I raised the issue of my continued leadership. They all strongly advised that I should continue on. When they had left, I made two phone calls, one to Brendan Howlin, the other to Pat Rabbitte.

Leading a political party is a lonely job. Friendships with colleagues grow cold as ministerial and other appointments are made and relationships change. Brendan once told me that leading the Labour Party was like walking the tight rope in a circus: 'They all look up at you in admiration and wonder when you are going to fall!' After seven years, there are very few parliamentary colleagues with whom you can, in confidence, discuss your own future.

In the days leading up to the local elections, I had broached the subject hypothetically with both of them separately. 'Where will I stand if we get a really bad result?' I had asked. They both assured me of their support if I wanted to continue on. Of course I realised that was not an answer to the question I had asked!

Now I needed to talk to them again, this time about the reality, and I arranged to meet them together. Brendan suggested 3 p.m. at the home of his close friends Pat Magner and Anne Byrne in Monkstown, as they were away that Sunday afternoon.

I realised that I was being undermined as Leader for some time, and that this represented an ideal opportunity for my opponents in the Party to go even further. I knew that in count centres around the country, defeated candidates and their supporters were understandably looking for someone to blame. In football, it's the team manager. In politics, it's the party leader. I recognised that I carried an added responsibility: in 2011, I had recommended that the Party enter government in a risky mission to save our country. Now, right across that country, good Labour councillors and courageous candidates were paying a high price for that risk. As Leader, I could not absolve myself from my role in that. I was leaning toward resignation as I arrived in Monkstown.

By the rules of the Labour Party, the only way that the Leader can be removed from office is for a 'motion of no confidence' to be passed by a two-thirds majority of members of the Central Council (made up of a delegate from each constituency, the members of the Executive Board and representatives of the parliamentary party, the councillors and Party sections such as Labour Youth). I knew it would be impossible for a no-confidence motion to secure such a majority, and therefore if it came to it, I could survive. But to lead the Labour Party, one needs to do more than technically survive such a motion. One needs a broad level of support in the parliamentary party and in the constituencies. There is no way of measuring that mathematically. It comes down to political judgement.

When we met, Brendan and Pat again assured me of their own continued support. If I wanted to stay on as Leader, they would both stand by me. Being the kind of good friends they are, though, they quickly added that if I was thinking of resigning, I should do it sooner rather than later.

We already knew that one member of the Central Council had submitted a 'motion of no confidence in the leader' for the meeting which was scheduled for 14 June, but that was a constant critic and I knew I could win the motion. Pat and Brendan both sensed, however, that matters would not wait until mid-June, that a heave could come as early as the next meeting of the parliamentary party the following Wednesday.

In the middle of our discussion, Brendan got a phone call from Jack Wall, Chairperson of the parliamentary party, who had always been very loyal and supportive. Apparently, some members of the parliamentary party, whom he did not identify, had been in touch with him to ask if he would put the leadership issue on the agenda for Wednesday's meeting. They were not submitting a motion, as such, but were asking him to use his discretion as Chair to put it on the agenda. He was, in turn, asking Brendan for advice. Perhaps Jack did tell Brendan who was involved, but Brendan never told me. He did, however, offer me his reading: that I was losing the middle ground. Pat concurred.

I went home and discussed the situation with Carol. She wanted me to stay on and fight off any challenge. But I knew where that would end. I might win the first round, but that wouldn't be the last of it. There was now more than one person working against me within the Party.

I looked at it from a Party perspective: it was now a year and nine months to the next general election. The Party needed to use that time to recover and to rebuild. It could not do so if it was consumed by a continuing brawl over the leadership. I did not want to be in the middle of that. Politics for me had always been about getting things done, about sharing ideas, negotiating agreements, and solving problems for the sake of communities and country. It has never been about holding on to some particular office no matter what.

I decided I would resign as leader the next day.

There was one problem. Mark Garrett's wife, Jennifer, was due to give birth to their second baby the next day. I could hardly call him with my decision on the morning of such a great occasion, perhaps even while he was in the delivery room! I rang Mark and asked him to call out, apologising for doing so 'tonight of all nights'.

We sat in the sitting room and I told him of my decision. He replied that it was the wrong decision, but he knew me well enough not to argue. Always the professional, he moved onto suggesting how it should be managed. I stopped him: 'Mark, you have more important things to think about tomorrow!' We went silent for a minute, and then we both began to shed silent, sad tears. Sitting across from each other, now slightly embarrassed by the emotion, were two men, who had shared the toughest battles of political life.

We had worked together for almost seven years in total. We'd had great victories in the local and European elections in 2009, the presidential election and the general election of 2011. We had seen Labour rise to become, for the first time ever, the second largest party in the State. The past three-and-a-half years in government had been very tough, but having helped get Ireland out of the bailout programme and back on its feet, we'd had every intention of working together to rebuild the Party and confound the critics at the next general election in 2016. Now we wouldn't even have the opportunity to try. Whatever else we'd expected, neither of us had expected it to end like this.

When Mark left, I rang Colm, and he tried to talk me out of the resignation. I then called the Party's legal advisor, Richard

Humphreys SC, congratulated him on his own re-election to Dun Laoghaire Rathdown County Council, and arranged to meet him the following morning. I asked him to bring his copy of the Party rules. Richard and I met for breakfast at 8 a.m. in the Tara Towers Hotel in Booterstown. I asked him to tell me the procedure for resigning and, in particular, I needed to know if I could have my resignation take effect from the moment of the election of my successor. I did not want my resignation to unnecessarily disrupt the work of government, and I was conscious that the election of a new Labour Leader would take a few weeks. He confirmed that I could resign and state the effective date.

I was in my office in Iveagh House shortly after 9 a.m. and met with Colm O'Reardon and David Leach, both of whom made a last-ditch effort to change my mind. We quickly moved on, however, to how we would manage the resignation. Labour Ministers and Ministers of State would have to be told, so we decided to convene them to meet with me at 3 p.m., following which, I would hold a press conference to make the public announcement. Colm undertook to draft a statement and David went off to make the practical arrangements.

I asked to see the Party's General Secretary, Ita McAuliffe, and at about 10.30 a.m. I submitted my letter of resignation to her, but asked her not to act on it until I had an opportunity to speak personally with family and staff. Ita was shocked and greatly upset by my decision.

I called my son, Oisín, in Holland. I had not been able to reach him the previous night, but now discovered that he had heard the news already from his brother, Seán. I then started to talk individually to each of my team: Jean O'Mahony, Niamh Sweeney, Derek McDowell, Sharon Gibbons, Doreen Foley, Karen Griffin,

Aideen Blackwood and Jeni Gartland, all of whom would now lose their jobs with my resignation. I also called Angela Loscher, who had worked with me from 1993 until her retirement the year before. All of these conversations were sad and emotional. At some stage during that difficult task, Cathy Madden and Derek McDowell shoved in the door to tell me that news was breaking that eight members of the parliamentary party were tabling a 'motion of no confidence' in me for Wednesday's meeting of the parliamentary party. Seven of the eight would later speak with me individually and apologise for their role in this unnecessary heave, but at that very moment I felt hurt and angry that I had not been given the few hours I needed to do things properly, and to share the news with my staff whose outstanding and loyal service deserved first consideration.

After the press conference, which according to the media was 'dignified', I returned to my office, where my Private Secretary Robert O'Driscoll was waiting for me: 'Tánaiste, I know this is not the best time to ask you this, but the Department needs you to clear a statement on the presidential election in Ukraine!'

Within days of my resignation, there was media speculation that I might be appointed as Ireland's next EU Commissioner. I was flattered by some of the commentary.

Meanwhile, the leadership contest between Joan Burton and Alex White continued up to Friday 4 July – my final day as Leader. Officially, I could remain on as Tánaiste and Minister for Foreign Affairs and Trade until the following week, when the Dáil would approve the re-shuffled Cabinet. But as the date approached, it occurred to me that if Joan was elected as the new Leader, she should immediately take over as Tánaiste as that appointment would not require Dáil approval. I asked the Taoiseach to facilitate this and met with Joan on the Thursday to inform her. I also assured her – her win now widely anticipated – that I was available to help in any possible way in her role as Leader.

At the end of our meeting, I asked her about her intentions regarding my own position. I had no expectations that she would include me in her ministerial team and was somewhat surprised when she said she had not yet made any decision. This led me to wonder if I might be re-appointed as Minister, possibly in the same department, as I had seen similar situations occur recently in Germany, Denmark and Luxembourg: a Party Leader resigning as Deputy Prime Minister but remaining on as a Foreign Minister. In any event, I believed that if I were to be sacked as Minister, as the outgoing Leader, I would at least be afforded the courtesy of some advance notice so that I could make some practical arrangements.

I expected the reshuffle to take place when the Dáil reconvened on Tuesday, but the new Tánaiste's talks with the Taoiseach continued until Friday morning, 14 July. Shortly after eight that morning, I got a telephone call at home from Joan's new Chief of Staff, Ed Brophy. Could I meet the Tánaiste at 9 a.m? I explained to Ed what morning traffic is like on the N11, and undertook to contact him when I got to Government Buildings. But I knew what the call meant. Ministers getting fired are always the first to be called!

Joan's assistant, Karen O'Connell, escorted me down the corridor to the familiar Sycamore Room. Inside the room was Joan Burton, her papers spread across the big inlaid table. She beckoned me to sit and told me that the nomination of the new EU Commissioner was a matter entirely for the Taoiseach, and not for the Government, and that he was not going to appoint me and there was nothing she could do about that. I had never seen the Taoiseach exercise such a prerogative before, nor even attempt to. She went on to state that she would not be nominating me to the Cabinet, and asked me to write my resignation as Minister for Foreign Affairs and Trade immediately. The entire exchange took two, maybe three minutes.

In the corridor on my way out, I met Martin Fraser, Secretary General to the Government. 'What's the score?' he enquired.

'I have just been court-martialled and I am to be shot at dawn!' We both laughed.

I went to Brendan Howlin's vacant office on the ministerial corridor and hand-wrote my resignation. Robert O'Driscoll undertook to take it to the Taoiseach and to copy it to the Tánaiste. Jean O'Mahony and Cathy Madden took me to the Merrion for a coffee.

I returned to the Dáil chamber, took up a seat in the midst of my Labour colleagues and listened to the Taoiseach announce the Ministers. He paid me a tribute in his speech which drew a warm round of applause from right around the chamber: a nice gesture from fellow-TDs of all parties, many of whom had been my strongest critics.

I left the chamber by the main entrance. Waiting for me at the top of the stairs were Sharon Gibbons, Aideen Blackwood and Jeni Gartland, who worked in my constituency office. I had not yet been allocated an office as a backbench TD so we had nowhere to go. We headed for the self-service restaurant, bought a pot of tea and cakes and waited the forty minutes for the bells to ring. When the final vote was over, Emmet Stagg the Party Whip turned to me and said kindly, 'Eamon, there's no need for you to come in here next week.'

Carol picked me up, and as we travelled out home to Shankill I felt the awakening of a new sense of freedom.

'What will we do tomorrow?'

15 REFLECTING ON RECOVERY

Ireland's crisis government took this country from the verge of bankruptcy, and in less than four years, turned it around to become the fastest growing economy in Europe.

We did so, without cutting core social welfare payments, without increasing income tax and without reducing the wages of the lower paid.

Instead, we concentrated on creating jobs. Unemployment was at its highest level ever when Labour and Fine Gael formed a government on 9 March 2011. Today, the country is heading for full employment.

But these were not the only achievements of the crisis Government in which I served as Tánaiste. We also restored the country's reputation in Europe and the world; legislated for the X case to protect the lives of mothers in pregnancy and held the referendum on marriage equality which enabled Ireland to become the first nation in the world to approve same-sex marriage by popular vote.

We established a strategic investment fund to invest in our future; we reformed social welfare to provide more opportunities for unemployed people (JobBridge and the Youth Guarantee) and reformed Fás.

We reformed the structure of local government and gave local government revenue-raising powers; we reformed the bankruptcy laws and introduced free GP care for children under 6 and for over 70s as the first step on the road to a fairer health service.

We established an independent Garda Authority; we protected overseas aid and we dramatically expanded what is now the ABC programme – which tackles child poverty in disadvantaged areas.

We introduced climate change legislation for the first time ever and included the rights of children in the constitution. We restored the Freedom of Information Act and introduced lobbying reform; we introduced a national literacy programme in primary schools and replaced thousands of pre-fabs with proper school buildings.

We set a requirement for political parties to stand women as candidates in general elections (a minimum of 30 per cent at the next election and 40 per cent at the one after that); and legislated for collective bargaining and restored JLCs.

No government since independence took up office at a time of such deep economic crisis in Ireland. No previous Irish government ever restored the economic fortunes of the country in such a short space of time. Indeed, it is hard to think of any government, anywhere, which so transformed the economy of its country. Neither is there any other previous Irish government with such a record of reform in just one term.

And yet, this government, as it approaches the end of its five years in office, is deeply unpopular. The Labour Party, in particular, has taken the brunt of public criticism for the unpopular decisions, but has got little credit for the economic recovery, or even for the reforms.

One morning in early 2014, after a particularly bad opinion poll,

Mark Garrett, in an effort I think to console me, said 'Eamon, you cannot be popular when you are doing unpopular things'. Many of the decisions which our government had to make, to get the country to recover, were indeed unpopular. Nobody likes new taxes. Every cut in public expenditure hurts somebody. New taxes and spending cuts impact immediately but the recovery takes longer to be felt.

The difficult decisions we took in Government were necessary for recovery. And they have worked.

Those who once felt that there was a less painful route to recovery have been disabused of that, by Greece's recent experience. Whatever chance Syriza may have had in successfully facing down the ECB, the EU and IMF in 2015, there was no such prospect at all in 2011, when those institutions were scared of the crisis widening to the larger economies of Spain and Italy.

We chose to renegotiate the bailout programme from within, through quiet diplomacy, which was more effective in terms of the outcome, but less effective in terms of public perception. People could not see the radical shift from Frankfurt's way towards Labour's way. But we did succeed in renegotiating the terms of the bailout programme to reduce the interest rate, to end the promissory note, to relax many of the conditions and to pursue a strategy of jobs-led growth. In the end we helped to change Frankfurt's own way. The ECB and the EU now pursues very different policies on banking to those which we encountered at the beginning of 2011.

But we made mistakes. My own biggest mistake was over water charges. It was one of the last issues to be settled, in the negotiations on the Programme for Government. I had been Labour's Environment spokesperson for many years and I know that Ireland is teetering on the edge of a water crisis. The pipes are old and leaking; pollution risks are high; investment in water supply has not kept pace with housing development and the greater Dublin area could face a water shortage if something suddenly goes wrong. In opposition, I had spoken of the need for a national water authority, so I agreed with the establishment of Irish Water. I insisted that it be a state owned public utility, as that would ensure that our water resources are kept in public ownership. I agreed too that Irish Water should be enabled to borrow off the State's balance sheet for the huge sums which would be required for investment in the water supply, and I accepted that that would eventually result in charging for water. But I wanted that to be done on a metered basis, which would encourage conservation, and I also wanted measures introduced to ease or even eliminate the financial burden on low income households, on large families and on those with medical conditions. We achieved all that, but the timing and handling were wrong.

At the beginning of 2014, I wanted to postpone charging for water. Irish Water told us that, at best, only 40 per cent of households would be metered by the end of 2014. That was not enough for a charging regime based on metering. Moreover, this new charge would be coming right on top of the first full year of property tax, and both would be taking effect as we approached the Local and European elections. There had been very little explanation for the public of the rationale for water charges.

I should have held out on the issue. But perhaps if I did, the Government's opponents would have convinced voters that the Government was secretly planning a charge of over €700 rather than €250, and we would have suffered anyway. I should have held out, not for electoral reasons, but because the water charges had not been adequately planned and thought out and because the metering was way behind.

We failed too, to effectively communicate what we were doing, not just in relation to water, but concerning the recovery itself. At the beginning, we were constrained from telling people just how bad things were. Imagine the panic if the Government admitted that the country could run out of cash by the end of the summer; that the euro might collapse; that unemployment might go over half a million people! Imagine too the damage all that would do to our prospects of attracting investment. In the early days of the government, we had to talk up our prospects, which probably masked the atrocious scale of the mess we inherited. Throughout the life of the Government, we concentrated on solving the crisis, rather than publishing what we were doing and why.

We also found ourselves with no organ of the media supporting the Government, in the way that *The Daily Telegraph* will always support a Tory Government or the way that the *Sunday Independent* publicly supported Fianna Fáil. A small number of commentators occasionally commended the actions of the Government, but that was too often lost in the tsunami of criticism. Left leaning commentators, it seemed to me, felt themselves obliged to criticise the Labour Party even more severely than their right wing co-writers. There are very few, if any other, examples in a developed democracy of such lack of overall media balance.

Political opponents allege that Labour broke all its election promises. No we did not! Any fair examination of Labour's election manifesto and comparison with our performance in government shows that we delivered on our principal commitments; to get Ireland out of the bailout, to bring about economic recovery, to create jobs and bring about reforms. We did not deliver in full or on all the commitments we made. How could we? It is impossible to deliver 100% of an election programme with 19% of the vote, and hard to get one's own way all of the time, while comprising just one-third of the government.

Critics claim that the Tesco ads, in particular, were a step too far. Perhaps. But at the time they were placed, Fine Gael were galloping to an overall majority and to a single party government. If they had succeeded, would it have been better for the Labour Party? Maybe. But would it have been better for the country? Would such a government have been stable, and been able to maintain social stability through 3 difficult budgets? Would it have survived? Would it have negotiated a deal with the public service unions or would it have gone ahead with compulsory redundancies in the public sector, and ran into serious industrial strife? How would it have cut public spending by a 3:1 ratio without reducing social welfare payments and pensions? Would it have restored the minimum wage? Or reinstated the JLCs? Or legislated for trade union rights and collective bargaining? Would it have legislated on abortion or held the marriage equality referendum?

No doubt, a Fine Gael supporter could draw up a corresponding list of questions about a Labour-led government. Perhaps, in its hour of crisis, Ireland was best served by the balance which was achieved by combining the left of centre with the right of centre.

Labour took an enormous political risk in embarking on such a government, at a time when it would have to do unpopular and counter-intuitive things. I knew we were taking such a risk and I said so at the conference in the O'Reilly Hall when Labour voted to enter government.

But Labour has already paid a high price for it. It did so at the local and European elections last year. I have no regrets about the political price, which I too had to pay. It was worth it, to see our country recover, to see jobs being created again, and to look forward, not just to a benign budget this year, but to better days ahead for the people.

Because of Ireland's recovery, we can all dare to hope again. But we cannot take it for granted. There is no guarantee of continued prosperity. A major conflict somewhere, a slowdown in a large economy, another financial meltdown or political instability at home could haul us back to recession. As citizens, we all share responsibility for the future.

EPILOGUE

Sally Glen Road

It's June 2015, just a few days after I announced that I would not be standing in the next general election, and I'm driving home from a meeting in Dun Laoghaire. My journey, as usual, takes me over Glenageary Hill, and as I come off the roundabout the traffic lights turn red, so I stop and look down the length of Sally Glen Road.

In a sense, this road spans my thirty years as a public representative. In May and June 1985, I introduced myself to the local people while canvassing the streets around here, as a young Workers' Party candidate in the local elections. Sally Glen Road was not yet built, but it was very much an issue on the doorsteps in the election.

For more than twenty years, the Council had been planning to run a dual carriageway all the way from Glenageary Hill, along Church Road, through Wyattville, through the N11 to link up eventually with an envisaged South-Eastern motorway (whose eventual name of M50 wasn't even a twinkle in a planner's eye at that stage). In 1985, the grassy reservation for the planned dual carriageway – known officially as the 'Church Road extension' –

was set out along the middle of Glenageary Avenue and Thomastown Road, a stretch which was regarded by many residents of these roads as a kind of unofficial linear park. They wanted the plan to be scrapped.

Others, in adjoining estates, thought the new road would relieve traffic congestion and ease the 'rat-running' through their neighbourhoods. Some thought the Council should get on with it and suggested it would also reduce the potential for anti-social behaviour on the poorly-lit reservation. Others thought its construction would divide the parish, physically and socially: Sallynoggin from Glenageary, the Sally from the Glen.

In the middle of that election campaign, a public meeting was organised in the Old Folks Centre, beside Sallynoggin Catholic Church. All the candidates were invited and asked if they would commit to opposing the road. At the meeting, there were different levels of opposition to the road: some were adamant that they would never allow it to be built and would, if necessary, lie in front of the JCBs to stop it. They were loudly applauded and cheered. A more pragmatic, and I judged, minority view, which was politely applauded but not cheered, seemed to acknowledge that the road would be built eventually, but that the Council should change some details and meet the residents' wishes halfway.

Following my election to the Council, I worked with fellow councillors of all parties and political persuasions to find a pragmatic solution. To the irritation of the road's engineers, I suggested that the project be re-designed as a single carriageway road, to incorporate cycle lanes and footpaths. It was. And in the course of time, we got boundary walls to muffle the traffic noise; trees and plants were introduced to screen the concrete harshness of the wall and road; and traffic lights and speed limits were added to improve safety.

Today, I can see the exact spot where I stood on a wet autumn morning back then with representatives of the Resident's Association, when the Council appeared to be welching on its commitments. I can also see the place beyond that wall where one of my most loyal supporters told me that he would never vote for me again because I had not opposed the road outright.

Just beside me is the still undeveloped site of the Deerhunter pub. I used to hold a constituency clinic in the Deerhunter for many years – 12.30 p.m. every Monday. And the kindly barman used to serve me a ham sandwich and a small pot of tea before I rushed off to my next clinic at 2 p.m. in Ballybrack.

At the opposite end of Sally Glen Road is The Graduate, where in a few weeks' time, I remind myself, the members of the Labour Party will gather to select a new candidate for the next general election.

In between are the playing pitches which I helped to get developed and allocated to Cuala GAA Club, and on the opposite side, is Sally Glen Park, which I witnessed mature over the years as a community green and as a playground for Dalkey School Project.

At The Graduate roundabout, the roads branch towards Dalkey and Killiney, Ballybrack and Loughlinstown, Cabinteely and Cornelscourt. The roundabout at the Deerhunter end opens out to Sallynoggin and Deansgrange, Monkstown and Blackrock, Dun Laoghaire and Glasthule. Sally Glen Road is like the spine of my constituency. How many thousands of times have I driven up and down this road, my mind pre-occupied with the stories and worries I heard at constituency clinics; preparing the cases I might make to the Council, the Health Board or the VEC on behalf of troubled constituents; rehearsing carefully the words I might say at a community meeting on some unpopular issue like the settlement of travellers or the delivery of drugs services, or more recently thinking about as many ways as possible to save the country from bankruptcy.

This fine morning the lights turned green and I began another drive down Sally Glen Road. I looked up and saw something new. There, in the distance, at the end of Sally Glen Road, I saw the Sugar Loaf Mountain, with its distinctive, neatly defined peak, and its even slopes drawing down to either side of the carriageway, forming an almost perfect triangle with the far end of Sally Glen Road.

I had never noticed that before.

INDEX